CRIME PREVENTION AND TREATMENT POLICIES

This book shows how to use biopsychosocial assessment for crime prevention and to achieve more individualized treatment for those who commit crimes. Author Anthony Walsh, a prominent figure in biosocial criminology for more than four decades, examines the treatment policy recommendations of major criminological theories and how they might be improved by integrating relevant biopsychosocial insights. Walsh contends that sound crime prevention and treatment policies must be based on empirical evidence derived from theories about the causes of crime if they are to reduce incarceration rates. The biopsychosocial perspective improves on traditional theories by examining all putative causes of crime from the micro to the macro—from neurons to neighborhoods—and should thus improve prevention and treatment efforts.

The understanding of the genetic, neurobiological, and physiological components of antisocial behavior has improved exponentially over the past three decades. The relevant biological measures (e.g., genotyping, hormone assays, autonomic system arousal levels, resting heart rates) are routinely examined in university labs for research purposes. This book shows how measures of these components can be fruitfully integrated into the risk-need-responsivity model of offender treatment.

Offering a fresh perspective, this book is essential for both scholars and practitioners wishing to explore treatment modalities that consider the biological aspects of criminality.

Anthony Walsh is a professor emeritus of criminology at Boise State University. He has taught biosocial criminology, statistics, and philosophy of law there for 34 years. He received his Ph.D. in criminology from Bowling Green State University in 1983. He worked as a marine, merchant seaman, police officer, and probation officer before entering academia at the age of 44. He is widely published, with 55 books and over 150 articles and book chapters on a variety of topics including biosocial aspects of crime and natural theology. He has received the Boise State Foundation Scholar Award for Research and lifetime achievement awards from both the Biosocial Criminology Association and the Biopsychosocial Division of the American Society of Criminology for his research in biosocial criminology. His work has been featured on the *Phil Donahue Show*, *Nova*, and *Nippon* (Japanese) TV.

Routledge Frontiers of Criminal Justice

The Quest for Reparations for Indian Residential School Abuse
Confronting the Legacy of the Independent Assessment Process
Konstantin Petoukhov

The Role of Food in Resettlement and Rehabilitation
Good Food and Good Lives
Edited by Julie Parsons and Kevin Wong

Overseeing Rights in Prison
The Irish Experience of Human Rights Protection in Prisons
Sophie van der Valk

Crime Prevention and Treatment Policies
A Biopsychosocial Approach
Anthony Walsh

Education in Youth Detention Homes
An Ethnographic Study of Schooling Against the Odds
David Wästerfors

For more information about this series, please visit: www.routledge.com/Routledge-Frontiers-of-Criminal-Justice/book-series/RFCJ

CRIME PREVENTION AND TREATMENT POLICIES

A Biopsychosocial Approach

Anthony Walsh

Routledge
Taylor & Francis Group
NEW YORK AND LONDON

Designed cover image: Getty Images

First published 2026
by Routledge
605 Third Avenue, New York, NY 10158

and by Routledge
4 Park Square, Milton Park, Abingdon, Oxon, OX14 4RN

Routledge is an imprint of the Taylor & Francis Group, an informa business

ISBN: 9781041078029 (hbk)
ISBN: 9781041078012 (pbk)
ISBN: 9781003642268 (ebk)

DOI: 10.4324/9781003642268

Typeset in Sabon
by Newgen Publishing UK

CONTENTS

PREFACE

The 19th-century American novelist Nathaniel Hawthorne (2003, p. 1) opens his book *The Scarlet Letter* with these words of wisdom and woe:

> The founders of a new colony, whatever Utopia of human virtue and happiness they might originally project, have invariably recognized it among their earliest practical necessities to allot a portion of the virgin soil as a cemetery, and another portion as the site of a prison.

Hawthorne reminds us of two things we cannot avoid—death and human iniquity—and that we must make provisions for both. Death is inevitable; all we can do is resign ourselves to it and allot more soil to cemeteries. Human malfeasance is inevitable also, but we should never resign ourselves to it or believe that the only solution is building more prisons. However, we will always need prisons, for as James Q. Wilson once remarked: "Wicked people exist. Nothing avails except to set them apart from innocent people" (1975, p. 391).

However, people can change their errant ways and do so all the time although, as all correctional scholars and practitioners know, reoffending is a lot more probable than rehabilitation. The objective of correctional treatment policy is to reduce recidivism, which current low-ball estimates put at about 65% within three years after release from prison and 75% within five years. Optimistic treatment scholars maintain that a recidivism reduction in the 10%–20% range is not an unrealistic expectation with the right treatment, but what is the "right" treatment? Efforts to determine the right treatment at present work within the risk-need-responsivity

(RNR) framework. The risk principle predicts the probability of reoffending, the need principle addresses what should be done to prevent it, and the responsivity principle refers to how well offenders respond to treatment and how treatment should be provided. The RNR model is the premier treatment model in corrections today, but recidivism is still unacceptably high.

This book discusses the biopsychosocial approach to criminal behavior and what it has to offer to efforts aimed at crime prevention and the treatment of offenders. Prevention and treatment involve policy decisions about how to implement effective programs. Policy is a selected course of action designed to solve a particular problem chosen from among alternative courses of action. Correctional policies, like all policies, should be based on empirical evidence from research based on theories about the putative causes of the problem. All theories of crime imply that changing the conditions they hold responsible for causing crime should reduce it.

Two policy levels address the crime problem: prevention and treatment. Crime prevention policies are proactive and are aimed at preventing or reducing the occurrence of crime, and most generally involve federal and state government policy. Treatment policies are reactive to the problem (treating individuals who have already committed crimes in an attempt to prevent further offending) and are made and implemented largely locally by local prison agencies or probation/parole departments. President Johnson's 1964 war on poverty was implemented with the assumption that reducing poverty would reduce crime by attacking what many criminologists considered its root cause. After consuming about $23 trillion from 1964 to 2018, poverty remained intractable and crime rose to record levels during the latter period of the 20th century.

Before the policy recommendations of the various criminological theories can be meaningfully addressed from a biopsychosocial perspective, we must address the perspective. The biopsychosocial perspective examines all putative causes of crime from the micro to the macro; from neurons to neighborhoods. The bio part of this perspective encompasses five areas: evolutionary biology, physiology, molecular genetics, behavioral genetics, and neurobiology, and the psychosocial part includes all the familiar criminological theories. Few modern criminologists doubt that genetic, neurobiological, and physiological variation among individuals influences their behavior, but these influences are always felt and expressed in an environmental context. Gene-environment interaction (G*x*E) and correlation (rGE) emphasize the duality of nature and nurture and the inseparability of genes and environments. Thus, there are chapters on behavioral genetics, molecular genetics, neurobiology, and emotion after the first chapter on policy.

Following this are five chapters addressing traditional criminological theories, their policy recommendations, and how they might be improved by incorporating biopsychosocial insights relevant to the theory discussed. These theories are human ecology/social disorganization theory, the various versions of anomie theory, subcultural theories, social learning theories, and social and self-control theories. The programs derived from these theories include the Chicago Area Project, Moving to Opportunity, Mobilization for Youth, the Provo Experiment, the Teaching Family Model, the Nurse-Family Partnership Program, and a variety of smaller programs designed to reduce offending by improving attitudes, behavior, and self-control.

These chapters are followed by three chapters on the causes and treatment of conditions that are strongly associated with crime and delinquency: attention deficit-hyperactivity disorder (ADHD), schizophrenia, and substance abuse. Although ADHD and schizophrenia affect only a small number of individuals (ADHD is more prevalent than schizophrenia) the rates of offending among these groups are greatly disproportionate to their numbers. Alcohol and drug addiction are much more common than ADHD and schizophrenia and therefore are responsible for much more criminal offending. Unlike treatment for general criminality, treating these conditions by pharmacological means is relatively uncontested for its efficacy.

The following chapter addresses neurogenesis and the impact of teratogens such as alcohol, drugs, tobacco, and lead on the developing brain. The cliché that we are what we eat may be oversold, but the better the diet the better the brain functions. To the extent to which this is true, we expect that diet should affect behavior, including antisocial behavior. High-quality food containing vital vitamins, minerals, antioxidants, and polyunsaturated fatty acids nourishes the brain and makes it run smoothly, while foods high in refined sugars, saturated fats, and carbohydrates make it sluggish. The best food we will ever ingest is breastmilk, and several studies have shown that extended breastfeeding has beneficial developmental effects. We then look at the metabolic role of the human gut microbiome and studies that have shown that dietary supplementation positively affects prison inmate's behavior.

The next chapter examines current correctional assessment and treatment programming. Working within the RNR model, correctional counselors use instruments such as the Level of Service/Case Management Inventory that measures skills, attitudes, beliefs, strengths, weaknesses, needs, and deficiencies of offenders that may help or hinder rehabilitative efforts. Offenders in anger management and sex offender programs are treated with traditional methods such as cognitive behavioral therapy and sometimes with less traditional pharmacological methods such as selective serotonin reuptake inhibitors and androgen antagonists and agonists. It is consistently found that psychosocial counseling methods augmented by pharmacological agents provide more positive results than psychosocial counseling alone.

The final chapter looks more specifically at biopsychosocial prevention and treatment. Because many theories in criminology place significant stress on the effects of fatherless homes, we begin with the crime prevention benefits of biological fathers in the home. Data from the periodic National Incidence Study of Child Abuse and Neglect have shown that children living with a single parent or the mother's live-in partner had over 10 times the rate of abuse and almost 8 times the rate of neglect in comparison with children living with both married biological parents.

Traditional offender treatment programs show only small to modest effects. The results of these programs are typically analyzed for the total sample or subsamples based on demographic variables such as race or sex. Such procedures may mask evidence of strong effects for some participants, weak or no effects, or perhaps even negative effects, for others. The use of individual genetic and neurobiological profiles of offenders should alleviate this problem. Modern personalized medicine uses genetic profiles and machine learning to guide the prevention, diagnosis, and treatment of disease, thus it is not far-fetched to maintain that similar personalized offender profiling will likewise lead to a better understanding of what treatment protocols might work. Some studies have used genetic, neurological, and physiological profiles (hormonal levels, heart rate, and autonomic nervous system arousal) to assign offenders to homogeneous groups. Such studies show markedly better results in treatment completion and treatment effects.

An important next step is to develop risk assessment instruments similar to the Level of Service/Case Management Inventory that integrate biological risk factors. Measuring biological factors is more expensive than paper-and-pencil measures, but much less so than the current unacceptable level of treatment failure and offender recidivism. However, these measures are not all that expensive. Computerized neuropsychological assessments that correlate fairly strongly with imaging results such as the Go/No-Go task, the Cambridge Neuropsychological Test Automated Battery, and the Stroop task may be used to measure the ability to control immediate impulses. Physiological measures such as resting heart rate can be obtained with instruments costing less than $100, and hormonal (testosterone/cortisol ratios) and genetic profiles are routinely assessed in university labs at little cost. It is only necessary to test for risk or susceptibility genes, primarily of the serotonergic and dopaminergic systems. Of course, the overall assessment instrument containing the biological risk factors and the psychosocial risk and needs factors will take decades of research and fine-tuning before we can determine its efficacy just as it took decades to hone the instruments associated with the RNR model.

Once such an instrument is developed, treatment can proceed using cognitive behavioral therapy (CBT), the premier counseling method used in corrections. CBT aims at restructuring thought patterns, modifying feelings and behavior patterns, and promoting new learning, and thus it involves brain synaptic changes. CBT is a powerful means of behavioral change for people who are motivated to change. Meta-analyses have shown no statistically significant differences between CBT and pharmaceutical treatment with serotonin and norepinephrine reuptake inhibitors in efficacy. Thus, what reuptake inhibitors do in the brain, so does CBT.

It has also been found that CBT + medication is superior to either CBT or medication alone. Medications such as selective serotonin reuptake inhibitors (SSRIs), stimulants, agonists, antagonists, and so forth stabilize a person's biology so that non-medication treatment by CBT can stabilize peoples' minds and lives.

ACKNOWLEDGMENTS

I first want to acknowledge acquisitions editor Ellen Boyne for her faith in this project. Ellen and I have worked together on five previous books; she is a super-efficient and congenial person to work with. I also want to acknowledge production editor, Hayley Kennard and the rest of the Routledge team. Thanks to the five anonymous scholars who reviewed this work and provided excellent suggestions that have improved this book. I am most thankful to the Lord God for providing me with the time and ability to complete this work. I also acknowledge my most pleasant and gorgeous wife, Grace (AKA, Grace the Face). She takes so good care of me that I can devote more time to my writing than I would otherwise have. She is indeed the center of my universe. Szeretlek, gyönyörű hercegnőm, Facie.

PART I

Introduction to Crime Prevention and Treatment Policy

1

WHAT IS CRIME PREVENTION POLICY?

Policy and Ideology

This book discusses what the biopsychosocial (sometimes "biosocial") approach to criminal behavior offers to efforts aimed at crime prevention and the treatment of offenders. Prevention and treatment involve policy decisions relating to how to implement effective programs. Policy is simply a selected course of action designed to solve a particular problem chosen from among alternative courses of action. We thus begin with a discussion of policy, how it is arrived at, and the problems involved with the process. One problem associated with criminal justice policy is that it is bedeviled by ideology. Ideology has a firm grip on criminal justice and criminology (Walsh & Wright, 2015; Williams & Robinson, 2004; Wright & Cullen, 2012), and the schools of thought policymakers and policy implementers have been educated in often determine the policy road they are willing to travel. We are traveling the biopsychosocial road because, as Michael Vaughn (2016, p. 708) points out: "One of the major attributes of biosocial research is that it can spur forward a renewed commitment to prevention science in criminology, which in turn can have important implications for public policy."

We will be examining certain criminological theories and the policy recommendations they point to. Connecting problems with solutions is a tricky business when human beings are the target, but perhaps nowhere more so than in the area of crime. No single strategy can be expected to produce dramatic results, and billions of dollars later we may discover that it made matters worse. All theories of crime imply that changing the

DOI: 10.4324/9781003642268-2

conditions they hold responsible for causing crime should reduce it. Most criminologists are concerned with seeking knowledge for its own sake rather than with policy implications. For their part, policymakers are less concerned with the hypothesized causes of a problem than with what can be done about it. However, theories and policies are intertwined and can inform one another. A good theory should have good policy implications, and the results obtained from implementing those policies provide grounds for judging the practical efficacy of the theory upon which they are based. As Hans Zetterberg (1962, p. 189) remarked long ago: "The phrase 'nothing is as practical as a good theory' is a twist of an older truth: Nothing improves theory more than its confrontation with practice."

Because the biopsychosocial approach to crime and policy includes everything from neurons to neighborhoods, it should provide superior evidence to base crime policy on rather than programs based on purely environmental theories, but its policies have to overcome strong ideological barriers. As Guy and Chomczyński (2018, p. 96) maintain:

> Driven by advances in molecular biology and neuroscience, biosocial approaches are increasingly being used in research designs to better explain the proximate influences of criminal and other forms of antisocial behavior, and by implication assess their usefulness in crime prevention or criminal justice policy.

However, they also point out:

> Although biosocial criminology has the potential to contribute to existing evidence-based intervention treatment modalities and early prevention efforts, there are ardent efforts to impede this line of research. In short, social science is prepared to sacrifice research findings that have implications for crime prevention.
>
> *(2018, p. 100)*

The problem with the biopsychosocial approach is that contemporary criminology is populated by scholars with virtually no education in biology. Cooper, Walsh, and Ellis's (2010) survey of American criminologists found that the modal number of biology classes they had taken was 0 and the median was 1. The survey also found that 68% self-identified as left of center politically (liberal or radical). Walsh and Ellis (2004) found the same thing in an earlier survey of American criminologists. The lack of engagement with biology, as well as the leftward political orientation in criminology, would seem to indicate that because the biopsychosocial approach engages with genes and brains, many may fear that the approach implies genetic or neuro-determinism, that it is a right-wing perspective, and that eugenics rides on its coattails (Bedoya & Portnoy, 2023). The notion of biological determinism is dead, and let us not forget that eugenics was enthusiastically embraced by the left as integral to its program of social perfection (Abu El-Haj, 2007). As one eugenicist put it: "Unless the socialist is a eugenicist as well, the socialist state will perish from racial degradation" (Paul, 1984, p. 568). It was the religious right that most strongly opposed eugenics for much the same reason that it opposes abortion today (Lucassen, 2010).

The Policymaking Process

The policymaking process is an exercise in informed problem-solving in which a problem is identified, data collected, the problem analyzed, and possible solutions are discussed. Cochran and Malone assert that policymaking takes the form of a series of "what" questions:

> What is the plan for dealing with the problem? What are the goals and priorities? What options are available to achieve those goals? What are the costs and benefits of each of the options? What externalities, positive or negative, are associated with each alternative?
>
> *(1999, p. 46)*

These questions must be informed by expert knowledge from evidence-based actuarial studies, not by knowledge based on anecdotes or personal experience that may lead to unintended consequences that exacerbate the problem. As Brian Head (2015, p. 472) notes: "Within public policy discussions, it is axiomatic that reliable information and expert knowledge are integral to sound processes for formulating and implementing policy." Policy choices are often value choices, and only those policies that are ideologically palatable to the majority of those within the policymaking loop, that enjoy broad public support, and that are not overly financially burdensome are most likely to be implemented.

Good policymaking involves a series of steps taken by people charged with overseeing some areas of public interest such as national defense, health, housing, education, law enforcement, corrections, and so on. These steps involve the following six considerations:

1 Agenda setting. This step identifies a problem of concern.
2 Policy formulation. Some solution to the problem is proposed.
3 Policy decision. A proposed solution is chosen over others proposed.
4 Implementation. The chosen policy is put into action.

5 Evaluation. Monitoring of the policy results to determine if it proved effective.
6 Policy decision. Based on the evaluation, should the policy be continued or terminated?

Policies with the most potential for significantly reducing crime must be evidence-based and have strong empirical support. They also require huge chunks of taxpayer money, and the urgency of the crime problem notwithstanding, policymakers are politicians or people who are answerable to politicians. We might also note that politicians are loathe to entertain policies seen as "soft on crime." Tackling the crime prevention problem thus involves political and financial considerations, the urgency of other problems (schools, health, highways, environmental protection, border security, national defense, etc.) competing for scarce resources, and a host of other considerations deemed more important by various segments of the voting public.

Two policy levels address the crime problem: prevention and treatment. Treatment policies that are reactive to the problem (treating individuals who have already committed crimes in an attempt to prevent further offending) are made and implemented largely locally by local prison agencies or probation/parole departments. Crime prevention policies are proactive and aimed at preventing or reducing the occurrence of crime in society. Crime prevention policies involve federal, state, and city government policy and are the policies that require the lion's share of public money. They are also the most difficult to implement—translating a policy's intentions into desired changes—because there is a vast distance between policymakers and those who must implement them. Money allocated for such policies must pass through many sieves as the relevant local agency administrators decide how to allocate it. Agency heads must look at not only the prescriptive goals of a policy but also the nature of the social problem (the causes of crime and target populations in this case) that a policy is intended to address.

One big problem of most crime prevention policies is that they tackle putative distal symptoms of crime and not necessarily the causes. For instance, President Lydon Johnson's "unconditional war on poverty" policy was implemented with noble goals but bore meager fruit. While not a crime prevention policy per se, the assumption was that reducing poverty would have a significant impact on the crime problem by attacking what many criminologists at that time considered its "root cause," and many still do. Very few criminologists back then (or today) entertained the notion that poverty may be a symptom of more fundamental causes, and it was those causes that needed to be addressed. Programs derived from Johnson's policy currently involve 126 different federal and state programs that consumed $23 *trillion* in taxpayer dollars from 1964 to 2018 (Tanner, 2019). Despite this cascade of programs and rivers of dollars, the problem of poverty remains intractable and the anti-poverty programs have had no effect in terms of reducing crime. On the contrary, crime rose to record levels during the latter period of the 20th century (Walsh & Ellis, 2006) while the poverty rate dropped a mere 4.5%, primarily for the elderly (Bitler & Karoly, 2015); not much for 50 years of effort and $23 trillion.

Another high-profile example of failed crime prevention policy is the Volstead Act of 1919 which was in effect from 1920 to 1933 and prohibited the manufacture and sale of alcohol in the United States. Although based on a true premise (that is, alcohol is a major factor in facilitating crime, particularly violent crime), it cost the government millions in lost revenue and ushered in a wild period of crime as gangs fought over control of the illegal alcohol market. The current war on drugs has had the same negative consequences and fills our prisons to overflowing. Policies attempting to control human behavior often have effects unanticipated by policymakers or the theoretical ideas they may have relied on when formulating their policies. All three examples given above, while formulated and implemented with the best intentions, failed because of one important factor: a flawed understanding of human nature. One cannot assume that simply giving people money will change habitual lifestyles or characters, or that legally banning substances will prevent people who crave them from obtaining them illegally.

It is thus obvious that policies attempting to control human behavior often have effects unanticipated by policymakers or by the theories and assumptions on which those policies were based. For example, Bitler & Karoly (2015) note:

> House Budget Committee's appraisal of the War on Poverty, which emphasized the existence of a multiplicity of programs that create a "poverty trap," leading to hundreds of billions of dollars in spending with unclear benefit given that the official poverty rate has remained little changed.
>
> *(p. 640)*

When the war on poverty was declared, the poor were likely to be the elderly living on fixed incomes, but now the poor are more likely to be unmarried women with children (Haveman et al., 2014), so perhaps this is this issue that needs tackling.

The Problem of Fatherless Households

The family is the nursery of human nature because it takes an infant's biological potential and begins actualizing it. Human infants must be fed, protected, nurtured, and taught about their social worlds for much longer than newborns of any other species, making the family an institution necessary for survival and well-being in the strictest sense. The long period of infant dependency requires selection for strong bonds between mother and infant, which in turn demands selective pressure for male-female bonding: "The co-evolution of the family and the brain, building on the maternal/offspring attachments of our mammalian ancestors, involved profound adaptations in the hominid biology" (Papero et al, 2018, p. 22). The primary function of the family is to raise children to be good citizens in an atmosphere of love. The term *nuclear* is apt to describe the modern family because the triad of man, woman, and child is the nucleus around which the web of kinship revolves. The man-woman-child triad is the minimal core of the "expected environment" of human rearing derived from evolutionary theory and a biological adaptation *par excellence* (Kramer, 2021). To the extent to which this is true, we can expect negative outcomes when children lack such a family.

It is often said that the value of something is best defined by its absence, and the absence of a father in a household has many negative consequences. The U.S. Department of Health and Human Services noted that "children from two-parent families live longer and enjoy overall better health than children from single-parent families or whose parents divorced in childhood" (Wood, Goesling, & Avellar, 2007, p. 48). A Swedish study of 986,342 children found that children living in a single-parent household had a greatly elevated risk of many psychiatric issues, suicide or attempted suicide, crime, and drug and alcohol addiction (Weitoft et al., 2003).

African American activists, Bill Cosby and Alvin Poussaint note: "A house without a father is a challenge. A neighborhood without fathers is a catastrophe" (2007, p. 3). These are the neighborhoods of concentrated disadvantage in which crime abounds and generates further disadvantage. Figure 1.1 shows that there is a large number of children currently living in fatherless homes in the United States. Across all Races/ethnicities, in 1968, 85% of children lived in two-parent families versus 70% in 2020 (Hemez & Washington, 2021). The Centers for Disease Control and Prevention (2022) tells us that in 2019, just over 40% of children born in America were born out of wedlock, but to focus on this problem, according to James Q. Wilson, "is to risk being called a racist, unless you quickly add that families are not important to children, in which case you may be called either a progressive or a fool" (2000, p. 107). Edward Kruk paints a grim picture of the pathological consequences of growing up in fatherless homes:

> Eighty-five percent of youth in prison have an absent father, 71% of high school dropouts are fatherless, 90% of homeless and runaway children have an absent father, and fatherless children and youth exhibit

higher levels of depression and suicide, delinquency, promiscuity and teen pregnancy, behavioral problems and illicit and licit substance abuse, diminished self-concepts, and are more likely to be victims of exploitation and abuse.

(2012, p. 49)

Because most sociologically based theories of crime consider poverty a major cause (and not infrequently, *the* cause), we should examine what the data have to say about one major cause of poverty. Based on Census data, Wilson (2020) reported median household income and poverty rates by race/ethnicity, and Martin et al. (2021) reported rates of out-of-wedlock births by race/ethnicity. These data are presented in Table 1.1 with the rank ordering of crime rates for each race/ethnicity added. As seen, Blacks have the lowest median household income and the highest poverty and crime rates, and there are perfect inverse rank-order correlations between median income and poverty rate with crime rate. This could be taken as

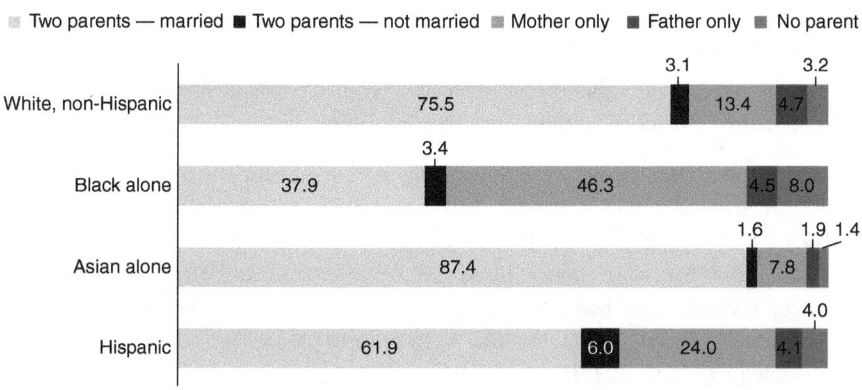

FIGURE 1.1 Living arrangements of children under 18 by race/ethnicity (in percentages).

Source: Hemez and Washington (2021). U.S. Census Bureau.

TABLE 1.1 2020–21 Group averages on income, illegitimacy, poverty, and crime

Group	*Median income*	*Out-of-wedlock birth rate*	*Poverty rate*	*Crime rate rank*
Asian	$98,174	11.7	7.3	4
White	$76,057	28.2	7.3	3
Hispanic	$56,113	52.1	15.7	2
Black	$46,073	70.0	18.7	1

supporting the claim that poverty causes crime. However, it is also noted that crime rates also have a perfect *positive* rank-order correlation with the rate of out-of-wedlock births, and median household income levels have a perfect *inverse* rank-order correlation with out-of-wedlock births.

Ellwood and Crane noted over 30 years ago that the prevalence of single-parent families is so high in the Black community that: "[A] majority of black children are now virtually assured of growing up in poverty, in large part because of their family status" (1990, p. 81). The U.S. Census Bureau's (McKinnon & Humes, 2003) breakdown of family types by race and income showed that White single-parent households were more than twice as likely as Black two-parent households to have an annual income of less than $25,000 (46% versus 20.8%) in 1999 dollars ($46,869 in 2024 dollars). To state it in reverse: *a Black two-parent family is less than half as likely to be poor as a White single-parent family*. This constitutes powerful evidence that family structure and not the racism that is usually invoked as the cause of Black poverty. To be consistent with a racism argument, one would have to claim that the Asian advantage on the measures in Table 1.1 is the result of pro-Asian bias in American society, but I wager that no one is likely to accept that claim.

Government Policies Addressing the Problem

To the extent that poverty is driven by single parenthood, attacking that problem should affect poverty. But how do we address such a problem without appearing to be puritanical moralizers attempting to police the private behavior of others? However, while sexual behavior begins in private, its sequelae have far-reaching public and private consequences, as we have seen. In a hearing on welfare reform before the United States Congress (1995, p. 22), it was stated:

> A recent study found that higher welfare benefits increased the number of women who left the labor force and enrolled in welfare. A 50 percent increase in monthly AFDC and Food Stamp benefit levels led to a 75 percent increase in both the number of women enrolling in AFDC and in the number of years spent on AFDC. In other words, an increase in benefits values causes a dramatic extension in welfare caseloads.

African American Economist Walter Williams (2011, p. 8) added to the tale by noting: "Using National 1979 Longitudinal Survey of Youth data, Anne Hill and June O'Neill found that a 50 percent increase in the monthly value of welfare benefits led to a 43 percent increase in the number of out-of-wedlock births." Alarmed by this, and by evidence that being raised in single-parent homes promotes childhood poverty, poor health, low educational attainment, substance abuse, and delinquency, the 104th United States Congress passed the Personal Responsibility and Work Opportunity Reconciliation Act (PRWORA) in 1996. Upon signing the act, President Bill Clinton stated that it

> gives us a chance we haven't had before to break the cycle of dependency that has existed for millions and millions of our fellow citizens, exiling them from the world of work. It gives structure, meaning and dignity to most of our lives.

The PRWORA was designed to reduce welfare benefits and to promote personal responsibility. These goals were to be accomplished by reducing the number of out-of-wedlock births and by providing the motivation and means to enter the workforce. It ended the Aid to Families with Dependent Children (AFDC) program, which was an entitlement program, and replaced it with the Temporary Assistance for Needy Families Block Grant Program (TANF) which, unlike AFDC program, was means-tested and temporary (not to exceed five years), and required welfare recipients who could do so to work or be engaged in seeking it. The PRWORA tried to discourage nonmarital births by awarding $25 million under the provision of the Out-of-Wedlock Birth Reduction Bonus (the so-called "illegitimacy bonus") to the five states that achieved the biggest decline in out-of-wedlock births (as defined by the ratio of nonmarital to total births for the most recent two-year period compared to the prior two years). The 23 states that tried for the bonus using various methods, 5 reduced or restricted welfare benefits, and 18 reduced benefits or denied increments for additional nonmarital births.

The Out-of-Wedlock Birth Reduction Bonus program did not work as well as hoped (few programs ever do), but there were significant drops in nonmarital births. For instance, it was found that in New Jersey from 1993 to 1996, women whose benefits were capped had "roughly 4,000 fewer births, almost 1,500 more abortions, and some 7,000 more family planning visits among welfare recipients than would have occurred in absence of the cap" (Boonstra, 2000, p. 8). In another study, "the cap was associated with reductions in nonmarital childbearing among women of all races and ages—including a 9% decrease among teens and a 12% decrease among older women" (Boonstra, 2000, p. 8). Although these percentages are small, they translate into many thousands of children not being born and raised in abject poverty and its related problems. On the other hand, we see from Figure 1.1 that out-of-wedlock birth still presents a major social problem. This does not imply that children born out of wedlock are necessarily doomed to a life of woe and crime; many will grow up to be solid citizens with the right guidance. As we will see later, some programs help to accomplish this.

The PRWORA had other effects besides reducing out-of-wedlock births. Several studies have reported a heightened sense of personal responsibility and self-worth among those who left welfare and went to work, and a reduction in child poverty. For instance, Blank and Schoeni (2003) report that poverty among Black children reached a historical low of 30% in 2001, with the greatest income increases in evidence in single-parent families, and show that the states producing the greatest increase in the income of single-parent families (averaging around 30%) were those that adopted the strongest carrot-and-stick incentives. Lichter, Graefe, and Brown (2003, p. 60) note the positive effects of PRWORA:

> If measured by employment take-up rates among single mothers and by reductions in welfare case-loads, the success of "work first" welfare programs is unprecedented. Caseloads have been cut by more than 50 percent after peaking in 1994, while poverty rates among female-headed families with children were the lowest on record in 2000.

Finally, economists June O'Neill and Ann Hill report that: "By the end of the second year after leaving welfare their [single mother's] incomes were 50 to 70% above poverty" (2003, p. 2). The lesson is clear; the best cure for poverty is inculcating personal responsibility and a job.

As with any policy, the PRWORA is not without its critics. It has been accused of racism and sexism because Black women were disproportionately targeted as more likely to give birth nonmaritally, violating women's rights to procreation choices and privacy, enforcing heterosexual marriage, and even "involuntary servitude" (e.g., Bailey, 1995; Brush, 2003). While some criticisms are valid, the above seem more emotional and ideological than reasoned and ignore the positive effect of PRWORA. The PRWORA encouraged personal responsibility, discouraged self-indulgence at the expense of others, encouraged (not "enforced") marriage, and discouraged behavior that eventually leads to offspring engaging in behavior that costs society billions of dollars in criminal justice costs. These critics should listen to Black activists Cosby and Poussaint who know the situation in the Black community better than most. Magnet (2008, np) quotes them on the problems children born out of wedlock and their mothers face:

> One of black America's most disabling problems, Cosby and Poussaint think, is this wounded anger—of children toward parents, women toward men, men toward their mothers and women in general. Some

> try self-sedation, whether by "wallowing in sedated victimhood," by music "loud enough to wake the dead," by "a lover or some crack or, if nothing else, a bag of burgers."

Liebertz and Bunch (2018, p. 481) describe some of the major impacts of the PRWORA ignored by its critics:

> The critics' worst fears failed to materialize in the earliest years of TANF's implementation, and many analysts declared PRWORA to be a great success. The number of welfare recipients had been decreasing prior to the legislation, and continued at an even greater rate afterward. From 1993 to 1997, the national welfare rolls declined by 31%. By 1999, the number had jumped to 50%. The new welfare system did not appear to cause a spike in poverty either, as the Urban Institute and others had cautioned. Although nearly a third of female headed households with children were impoverished in 2000, that percentage was one of the lowest levels in recent history.

PRWORA was not intended to be a crime prevention policy per se, or even a policy specifically designed to reduce nonmarital births. It was meant to induce a sense of personal responsibility in welfare recipients by getting them into the labor force and to get those who were on drugs off them (a requirement of TANF was that recipients had to be tested for drug usage). However, we see from Figure 1.1 that out-of-wedlock birth still presents a major social problem, although there was a 61% decline in teen birth rates between 1991 and 2014 (Lindo & Packham, 2017). How much, if anything, we can attribute this to PRWORA is an open question, but Kearney and Levine (2012) claim that 2.7% of the decline in teen birth rates can be attributed to it.

Overall, PRWORA is a success because it saved taxpayer money while increasing the income of the targeted population. Not only that, the small decline in out-of-wedlock births attributed to it meant thousands of children not being born into poverty, with all its attendant problems. No matter how a policy may ultimately be beneficial for women and children, some despise it for the reasons given above. In a Congressional Ways and Means Committee report, Dick Morris (2012, np) provides an example of how ideology and personal concerns go a long way in determining the direction of public policy. He notes that President Obama scuttled welfare reform by doing an end-run around the law by defining "work" as such things as attending hula dancing and Weight Watchers classes, and:

> Now that the Obama Administration has abolished those standards, we can expect "work" in the TANF (welfare) program to mean anything

> but work. The loosened requirements on what constitutes work are of a piece with Obama's strategy of expanding his political base by widening the dependency on government handouts. ...We are rapidly becoming a nation that doesn't work, doesn't pay income taxes, and gets entitlement checks.

In 2002, Congress eliminated the Illegitimacy Bonus from PRWORA and replaced it with the Supporting Healthy Marriage Project (SHMP), which maintained that the best anti-poverty programs support healthy two-parent families. This project was a large-scale, multisite, multiyear, voluntary marriage education program for low-income married couples who were given small financial incentives to participate. A SHMP evaluation found small but statistically significant, generally positive impacts for low-income married-parent couples (Hsueh et al., 2012). Kirkham and Ford (2009) found that projects supported by SHMP-type programs in 11 high-activity states were associated with declines in the percentage of divorced couples and reduced childhood poverty in those states. Hawkins, Amato, and Kinghorn (2013, p. 501) conclude:

> Cumulative per capita funding for HMIs [healthy marriage initiatives] between 2005 and 2010 was positively associated with small changes in the percentage of married adults in the population and children living with two parents, and it was negatively associated with the percentage of children living with one parent, nonmarital births, and children living in poverty.

But as Lichter, Graefe, and Brown (2003, p. 62) point out: "whether marriage affords long-term economic benefits ultimately depends on whether disadvantaged women are able to get married, stay married, and marry well (i.e., marry economically attractive men)." In the marriage market, securing a desired marriage mate depends on what one has to offer in return, and disadvantaged women with children born out of wedlock cannot be expected to obtain an "economically attractive" man. Indeed, looking at marriage patterns among unwed mothers before and after PRWORA, Graefe and Lichter (2008, p. 479) found that:

> Compared with other women, nonmarital birth mothers also were less likely than other women to marry "economically attractive" men in the post-welfare reform period. The success of marriage promotion initiatives may depend heavily on whether women themselves are "marriageable" and whether potential spouses have the ability to support a stable family life.

Men with poor employment records, substance abuse, and criminal records make unattractive marriage prospects. Having such a man in the home is more harmful to both a female's economic well-being and to the probability that children will be victimized by abuse and neglect than having no man in the home (Rodney & Mupier, 1999), especially if the man is not the children's biological father (Daly & Wilson, 1996). As Jaffee and her colleagues (2003, p. 120) noted in terms of antisocial behavior:

> When highly antisocial fathers reside with the family, children experience a double whammy of risk for antisocial behavior. They are at genetic risk because antisocial behavior is highly heritable. In addition, the same parents who transmit genes also provide the child's rearing environment.

Moreover, "Marriage alone will not offset the long-term deleterious effects associated with unwed childbearing" (Lichter, Graefe, & Brown, 2003, p. 60).

PART II

The Biopsychosocial Perspective

2

THE BIOPSYCHOSOCIAL PERSPECTIVE AND BEHAVIORAL GENETICS

The Biopsychosocial Perspective

Before we address the policy recommendations of the various criminological theories from a biopsychosocial perspective, it is necessary to outline what the perspective entails. This perspective in criminology is also known as biosocial, although psychological processes were already contained in it, "psycho" was added when it became a division of the American Society of Criminology. The "bio" part of this perspective encompasses five areas that complement each other: evolutionary biology, physiology, molecular genetics, behavioral genetics, and neurobiology (Barnes & Boutwell, 2015). The "psychosocial" part encompasses all the well-known theories and concepts in the psychosocial sciences. We need to add the bio to the other perspectives since, according to Matthews and Turkheimer (2021, p. 2297), no single discipline is sufficient to explain the complexities of human behavior:

> Why are some of us brilliant, criminal, depressed, schizophrenic, or aggressive? If researchers interested in these questions agree about anything, it's that providing satisfactory answers to these questions is an arduous, if not impossible, task that must draw on countless resources from different disciplines, kinds of evidence, methodologies, techniques, technologies, explanatory approaches, etc. Explaining human behavior is a Herculean endeavor.

Once we add the bio to the psychosocial, we can engage Nobel laureate ethologist Nikolas Tinbergen's (1963) famous four questions that maintain

DOI: 10.4324/9781003642268-4

that if we are to understand the behavior of any animal, including humans, we must look at all levels of explanation from its distal evolutionary history to the most proximate causal mechanism. While no one carries out a research agenda animated by all levels of analysis, all levels must be mutually consistent with no contradictions moving from one level to another. Tinbergen's first question asks: What is the current adaptive function of this behavior, and how does it contribute to the concerns of all living organisms—survival and reproductive success? The second is: What is the phylogenic history of the behavior, and how did it come to have its current form? The third question is ontogenetic: How do genes and environments interact in individual developmental history to produce this behavior? The fourth is causation: What are the mechanisms that trigger this behavior?

We can thus see why Matthews and Turkheimer say that explaining human behavior is a Herculean endeavor. No one can be expected to be an expert in all the disciplines biopsychosocial research imports, but we should know them at a level needed to understand the relevance of a piece of research in these disciplines to criminology. After all, we are all presumably sufficiently acquainted with statistics to use and interpret them without being Ph.D. statisticians. I suggest that we should be acquainted with quantitative and molecular genetics and neuroscience at the same level that we are acquainted with statistics to do biopsychosocial criminology.

Integrating the bio, particularly genetics, with the psychosocial must overcome ideological barriers as well, for as Richard Dawkins (2016, p. 12) has written, genes have a "sinister, juggernaut-like reputation" among social scientists because they imply genetic determinism. Jamieson and Radick (2017) maintain that this belief can be traced back to the limited understanding of genetics obtained in Biology 101 and Mendel's pea experiments. In Bio 101 we placed alleles in Punnett squares and learned that if a pea plant had a particular allelic profile, its immutable destiny was fixed and unalterable. If social scientists think genes work this way free of environmental input to form the contours of human personality and behavior, their nervousness is understandable. But they need not be nervous, for as Plomin writes: "It is ironic that, after a century of environmentalism, genetic research provided the strongest evidence for the importance of the environment; previous environmental research was confounded because it ignored genetics" (2023, p. 77).

Although all human traits are undergirded by genes, their expression depends crucially on environmental input. There is no tidy algorithm by which we can know which genes produce certain kinds of brains, personalities, or behaviors. Genes code for the manufacture of proteins that *influence* how our personalities develop and what behaviors we are inclined to perform, but genes do not *cause* them independent of environmental influences. By various neurohormonal routes, genes *facilitate* our behavioral responses to environmental instigation only in a probabilistic fashion. It is axiomatic that genes have to be expressed in the brain before they can influence behavior, and 70% of our genes are expressed in the brain where they produce and regulate the complex neurochemistry underlying behavior (Chiao & Ambady, 2007).

Behavioral Genetics and the Concept of Heritability

Paige Harden notes that "perhaps no concept in the social sciences has been the subject of as much confusion as heritability" (2021, p. 40). She also maintains that this confusion must be rectified because: "Genetic differences between people are a nonignorable source of heterogeneity in psychological and behavioral traits, including cognition, achievement, personality, psychopathology, social relationships, health behaviors, fertility, and beyond" (p. 45). Heritability (h^2) is central to behavioral genetics. It is a quantification ranging between 0 and 1 indicating the extent to which variance in a trait or behavior is attributable to genes in a particular population. It is a *population* parameter that apportions variance averaged over all subjects into genetic and environmental sources. Its values will differ widely across different populations and environments. It should be noted that behavioral genetic analysis is about *variation* in traits or behaviors in a particular population at a specific time. It tells us nothing about causation or which genes are involved in influencing a particular trait or behavior, it only tells us the extent to which people in a population differ with respect to a particular trait or behavior. That is, it tells us that genes cause variation in a trait or behavior, not a cause of the trait or behavior.

A meta-analysis of 2,748 twin studies published over 50 years containing more than 14.5 million twin pairs from 39 countries showed that all human traits (n = 17,804) are heritable (Polderman et al., 2015). Even before that study, there was ample evidence to posit that $h^2 \neq 0$ is the first law of behavioral genetics (Turkheimer, 2000). Heritability coefficients of around 0.30–40 have been calculated for such things as divorce, which may cause some social scientists to wince. Of course, there are no "divorce" genes; what h^2 captures is a variety of genes for personality traits that together make divorce more likely than not, such as possessing alleles for psychological traits that make a person more difficult to get along with, who is unwilling to compromise, is prone to aggression and substance abuse, and who finds it difficult to remain faithful (Spikic & Mortelmans, 2021). Likewise, the heritability of liberalism-conservatism is between

0.30 and the mid-0.50s depending on how strongly political attitudes are held (Dawes & Weinschenk, 2020; Wajzer & Dragan, 2023). Again, geneticists do not expect to find conservative or liberal genes rummaging around among our chromosomes. Our ideological views are arrived at via meandering routes, with our temperaments guiding the cultural information we deem salient and shaping environmental experiences in ways that increase the likelihood of developing the attitudes that color our worldviews.

Criminality is like divorce and ideology. It is a complex phenotype consisting of several component traits called endophenotypes (endo = "within" the phenotype). Endophenotypes are essential parts of the complex chain leading from genotype to phenotype. However, each may have only minor effects on the phenotype, and only if combined with other relevant endophenotypes and the right circumstances. Reducing the criminality phenotype to its constituent endophenotypes such as impulsiveness, low empathy, or low fear makes it easier to identify their genetic basis because intermediate endophenotypes "sit closer to the genotype in the development scheme" (Gottesman & Hanson, 2005, p. 268).

Behavioral geneticists examine genetic influence on a trait via adoption and twin studies. Adoption studies are "natural experiments" that randomize genes to investigate the effect of common environments and randomize environments to determine the effects of common genes. The extent to which genetically unrelated individuals reared together display phenotypic trait similarities, similarities must be entirely a function of shared environment, and phenotypic trait similarities between genetically related individuals reared apart must be entirely a function of their shared genes. The correlation between identical twin pairs reared apart is a straightforward indication of heritability since there is no shared environment, and the correlation between unrelated individuals reared in the same home is a clear-cut measure of shared environment effects since they share no genes.

Twin studies rely on comparisons of interclass correlations for a trait between identical (monozygotic; MZ) twin pairs and same-sex fraternal (dizygotic; DZ) twin pairs to obtain genetic and environmental sources. MZ twins share 100% of their genes, and DZ twins, on average, share 50%. If genes are a source of trait variance, the more genes individual pairs share the more similar they should be on their phenotypic traits. Behavioral genetic studies are not perfect, but they provide unparalleled precision in social science research. Turkheimer (2000, p. 162) notes that gene-free environmental research could only achieve the same level of precision it was to "have 'identical environmental twins' whose experiences were exactly the same, moment by moment, and another variety who shared exactly but randomly 50% of their experiences." No such environmental twins exist, of course. But we don't need them because behavior genetics informs us of the environmental contribution to human traits and behaviors as surely as if there were because 1.0 – h^2 is the proportion of phenotypic variance attributable to the environment.

Heritability is the variance in a trait attributable to *actualized* genetic potential in a population; we cannot infer from it what the unactualized potential may be (Ferguson, 2010). Determining heritability requires that every genotype be exposed to identical environments because variation can only be attributed to factors that vary. To illustrate this, Lewontin (1970) proposed a thought experiment in which he took a random sample of genetically mixed corn seeds and planted them in identically nourishing environments. In this case, phenotypic trait variance (color, height, breeding efficiency, etc.) would be *entirely* attributable to genetics ($h^2 = 1.0$). Because the environment was held constant it cannot be a source of variance. Likewise, in a random sample of genetically homogeneous seeds planted in diverse environments, genes are held constant, and thus phenotypic trait variance would be 100% attributable to the environment ($h^2 = 0.0$). If $h^2 = 1.0$, it does not mean that the environment is irrelevant for the trait in question because genes need an environment to give them life; it only means that the environment did not contribute to the *variance* in the trait. Similarly, if $h^2 = 0.0$, it does not mean that genes did not contribute to the trait in question, it means that genes accounted for none of the *variance* in the trait, but without genes the environment produces nothing. Genes provide the potential; the environment determines the extent to which that potential is actualized—think of the fates of identical rose seeds planted in an English garden, an Alberta forest, or a Nevada desert.

Environments Matter

No one doubts that sociocultural environments matter tremendously in understanding a person's behavior. This is illustrated by heritability estimates that vary greatly according to the environments in which genotypes find themselves. Heritability estimates are higher in advantaged than disadvantaged environments because advantaged environments bring out the best in the genetic material—like roses planted in an English garden. Advantaged environments offer a greater range of opportunities for individuals to seek out environments consistent with their genetic proclivities, leading to more genetically influenced behaviors, and thus to higher heritability values (Selita & Kovas, 2019). Disadvantaged environments (poverty, single-parent homes, disorganized neighborhoods, etc.) minimize options and produce behavioral similarities regardless of genotypic differences (Beam et al., 2022). Such adverse environments are, however, likely to trigger the expression of alleles associated with antisocial traits. Being raised in adverse environments is analogous to planting roses in a Nevada desert and expecting them to thrive. Prosocial traits, such as intelligence, altruism, and honesty, are like roses; they need careful cultivation. Antisocial traits are like weeds; they shoot up through the cracks unaided. In disadvantaged families, parents are often unable to cultivate their children's prosocial potential, so antisocial behavior grows like rank weeds between the cracks.

Indicative of different effects in different environments is Turkheimer et al.'s (2003) finding of h^2 values for IQ of 0.72 in advantaged and 0.10 in disadvantaged environments. Another study of adolescent aggressive behavior found h^2 to be 0.70 for youths with low levels of familial conflict, 0.53 for youths with moderate familial conflict, and 0.28 for youths with high levels of familial conflict (Bartels & Hudziak, 2007). A Swedish study of 1,133 twin pairs aged 16–17 found that the heritability of antisocial behavior was 0.37 in advantaged environments and not reliably greater than zero in adverse environments for boys. Shared environment was most important for boys (0.69) in disadvantaged environments, but negligible (0.13) for boys in advantaged environments. Heritability for girls was 0.69 in advantaged and 0.61 in disadvantaged environments (Tuvblad, Grann, & Lichtenstein, 2006). Although the mean level for genetically influenced risk factors for criminal behavior is low in advantaged environments, individuals who cross the criminal threshold in those environments typically have a greater genetic liability to do so because advantaged environments are crime-constraining. The heritability of criminality is low in disadvantaged environments because strong environmental influences mask genetic contributions, even though there are doubtless more individuals with a stronger genetic load for criminal behavior in those environments than in advantaged environments.

Gene-Environment Interaction and Gene-Environment Correlation

Gene-environment interaction (G*x*E) and correlation (rGE) emphasize the duality of nature and nurture and the inseparability of genes and environments. Manuck and Caffery (2014, p. 41) note that G*x*E studies have proliferated in psychological research, and that:

> Among the aims of such studies are testing developmental hypotheses and models of the etiology of behavioral disorders, defining boundaries

of genetic and environmental influences, and identifying individuals most susceptible to risk exposures or most amenable to preventive and therapeutic interventions.

The commonsense notion underlying G*x*E is that people are differentially sensitive to identical environmental influences and will respond in different ways: "The heat that melts the butter hardens the egg" (Nettler, 1984, p. 295). In other words, an individual's genes will affect his or her sensitivity to environmental risk factors. An impulsive child with low fear is genetically more vulnerable to opportunities for antisocial behavior than a prudent and more fearful child in an identical environment.

The concept of rGE is that people seek environments compatible with their genetic dispositions. There are three kinds of rGE: passive, evocative, and active. Passive rGE is the correlation between a child's genotype and its environment and is called "passive" because neither a child's genes nor its behavior is responsible for the correlation. Parents create a home environment influenced by their heritable characteristics which correlate with the genetic architecture shared between parents and their offspring (Sesardic, 2003). For example, children who receive parental genes conducive to high intelligence will likely find themselves in a rich and stimulating environment where intellectual activities are modeled and reinforced and can reach their intellectual potential. The reverse is also unfortunately doubtless true.

Evocative rGE involves children's genotypes coming into play and refers to how others in their environment react to them based on their behavior. Meta-analyses have shown that the behavior of others toward a child is more a function of the child's evocative behavior than of the interaction style of those who react to it (Avinun & Knafo, 2014). Children's behavior increases or decreases the probability of evoking positive or negative responses. Regardless of a responder's characteristics, a disrespectful and misbehaving child will evoke a less positive response than a well-behaved and respectful child. Some children may evoke such punitive reactions from others that will exacerbate their already antisocial tendencies and drive them to seek out similarly disposed peers, which further reinforces their antisocial tendencies. Evocative rGE thus greatly magnifies differences among phenotypes.

Active rGE refers to environments sought by individuals compatible with their genotypes. Our genes determine what features of the social world will be salient and rewarding to us, and we seek them within the range of cultural freedoms and constraints. In active rGE, genes guide the selection of environments which then loop back to shape and reinforce further expression of genetic dispositions. As Beam et al. (2022, p. 322) aver, "nonrandom exposure to environments based on genetically influenced characteristics is part of what it means to be a person embedded within continuously changing social environments." Active rGE gains more explanatory power as individuals mature and acquire the ability to take greater control of their lives. This coheres with consistent findings that adult MZ twins reared apart construct their own lives about as similarly as MZ twins reared together (Carey, 2003), and that MZ twins reared apart construct their environments considerably more similarly than DZ raised together (Bouchard & McGue, 2003). This continual series of gene-environment correlations across the life course is why cognitive and trait heritability increases with age (Segal, 2022).

Because genes affect differential *exposure* to environmental risks via active rGE and differential *susceptibility* to them via G*x*E, both processes operate simultaneously and are difficult to untangle. People self-select into different environments based on their genetic preferences when they are able, and because they select a particular environment, they will be more susceptible to its influence (G*x*E) than those there by chance. In addition to furthering our understanding of the role of genes in understanding behavior, the concepts of G*x*E and rGE have yielded enormous benefits to our understanding of the environment's role in shaping behavior; as Baker, Bezdjian, and Raine (2006, p. 44) put it: "the more we know about the genetics of behavior, the more important the environment appears to be." However, G*x*E and rGE demonstrate a flaw in strict environmental criminology in that it cannot separate its putative causes from the effects of self-selection. Without behavioral genetic study designs, criminology cannot disentangle social causes from self-selection effects (Moffitt & Beckley, 2015).

Shared and Non-Shared Environment

Variance in environmental effects on traits and behavior are apportioned into shared (c^2) and non-shared (e^2) components. Shared effects are experiences that may make people similar; non-shared effects are experiences that may make them different. The shared environment is everything siblings have in common, such as neighborhood and socioeconomic status (SES) of rearing, and non-shared environments are environments unique to each, such as differential treatment experiences and different friends. Most environmental influences for most traits are non-shared, with shared childhood effects on cognitive and personality traits disappearing almost completely in adulthood. This means that the environmental shaping of personalities is more specific to individuals (e^2) rather than shared with siblings (c^2). Plomin (2011, p. 589) remarks that this consistent finding comes as a shock to gene-free socialization researchers because for them:

> It was reasonable to assume that the key influences on children's development are those that are shared by children growing up in the

same family: their parents' personality and family experiences, the quality of their parents' marital relationship, their parents' educational background and socioeconomic status, the neighbourhood in which they are raised and their parents' attitude to school or to discipline.

A meta-analysis of 103 twin and adoption studies (28,709 sibling pairs) revealed that 58% of the variance in antisocial behavior was accounted for by genes. The shared environment accounted for about 15%, and the remaining 27% was accounted for by non-shared environment and measurement error (Burt, 2009). The low variance accounted for by c^2 is counterintuitive for Burt and Simons (2014, p. 224) who write:

> Indeed, the conclusion from many of these heritability studies that little—if any—of the variance in criminal behavior is due to shared environments, often interpreted to include parenting and community factors, contradicts a wealth of research conducted during the past century as well as the major theories of crime.

However, the low effects of shared environments mean only that shared effects on personality and cognitive traits that made siblings somewhat similar when they shared a home largely failed to survive the period of common rearing. This is not to say that shared parents or communities do not affect the *mean* level of these features. The weak effects of shared environments mean that they have little *similar* effects on siblings' phenotypical traits; it does not mean they have had *no* effect. Familial factors such as poverty, abuse and neglect, divorce, etc. can have large effects on the mean of any number of phenotypic traits without affecting trait *variance*. The stability of genetic variance means that heritability can remain stable even as the mean level of a variable rises, falls, or stays the same.

Burt and Simons see heritability as presential us with a "false nature-nurture dichotomy" (2015, p. 10) and state: "Genes and environments do not have identifiably separate influences on variation in complex phenotypes" (2015, p. 105). They are right; there is no nature *versus* nurture dichotomy, only nature *via* nurture. Behavioral geneticists and biopsychosocial criminologists know that in individuals, genes and environments are tightly woven and firmly glued fibrils in all behavioral and psychological threads and always operate in tandem. However, heritability tells us in which environments genes are more likely to realize their potential. They also know that at the individual level, "environmental and genetic threads in the fabric of behavior are so tightly interwoven that they are indistinguishable, but at the population level, they are distinguishable" (Wright et al., 2015, p. 116).

Other Criticisms of Behavioral Genetics

Burt and Simons (2014) offer several other criticisms they note were first made in the 1970s, as if repeating something enough times makes it gospel, as former British Prime Minister Margret Thatcher once said. The major criticism is that behavioral genetics models violate the equal environment assumption (EEA) because they upwardly bias heritability estimates if violated. The EEA is that every organism must be exposed to equal environments to tease out genetic effects, as with Lewontin's corn seed thought experiment. Behavioral geneticists are aware of the criticism and acknowledge that neither the adoption nor twin designs equalize environments completely. However, using many different methods, researchers have shown that violating this assumption upwardly biases h^2 by only about 1% and 2% (Conley et al., 2013; Cronk et al., 2002). Moreover, critics aver that MZ twins share more of their social environment than DZ twins, and maintain that this shared and non-shared genes that make MZ twins more alike than DZ twins. This criticism also assumes that only twins reared together will develop similar behavioral, cognitive, and personality phenotypes and that MZ twins reared apart would not. But as we have seen, the correlations on traits among MZ twins reared apart are consistently much greater apart than DZ raised together (Bouchard & McGue, 2003; Carey, 2003).

A similar argument is the selective adoption placement argument, which avers that the similarity between MZ twins reared apart is explained by the tendency of adoption agencies to place adopted MZ in similar homes for SES. There is indeed a small correlation (about .30) between the SES of the adoptive homes of MZ twins adopted out separately. However, as Lykken (1995) points out, the SES correlation between DZ twins and other siblings reared together is 1.0, and MZ twins reared apart score significantly more similarly than DZ twins reared together on almost all behavioral, personality, and cognitive measures.

Another criticism, albeit not addressed by Burt and Simons, is that random mating is required for heritability studies, but human mating is never random; it is assortative. Assortative mating is the tendency of individuals with similar traits and characteristics to mate at a rate significantly greater than would be expected by chance. Assortative mating has the effect of producing DZ twins more genetically similar than it would be with random mating, but it does not affect MZ genetic similarity because they share 100% of their genes regardless of whether they are the products of random or assortative mating. This deflates heritability estimates and inflates shared environment estimates because DZ twin correlations are inflated by assortative mating while MZ correlations are unaffected, leading to heritability estimates about 5% less than would be obtained under conditions of random mating and upwardly biases shared and non-shared environment estimates (Barns et al., 2014).

In addressing the EEA criticism, studies compare twin pairs with misidentified zygosity. If it is environmental rather than genetic similarity that leads to personality and behavioral similarity, MZ twins wrongly identified as DZ would test more like DZ twins than MZ twins, and DZ twins wrongly identified as MZ would test more like MZ than DZ twins. However, it is always found that twins score consistent with their true zygosity rather than based on social expectations derived from their wrongly perceived zygosity (Connolly & Beaver, 2014; Gunderson et al., 2006). Using 500 simulated data sets, Barns et al. (2014) found that violating the EEA assumption inflated h^2 between 1% and 5%, but violations of the random mating assumption bias h^2 downward, so the two biases cancel out.

Studies have also attempted to determine if twins with greater physical similarity were behaviorally more similar than twins less physically similar. The assumption is that the more twins look alike the more they would be treated alike. None of the studies found any relationship between treatment similarity and similarity of scores on the various behavioral, personality, or cognitive measures. It is also found that MZ twins whose parents *emphasize* their sameness do not score any closer to each other on various behavioral, personality, or cognitive measures than twins whose parents strive to *minimize* their sameness (Hannagan & Hatemi, 2008).

Although MZ twins are usually treated more alike than DZ twins when parental behavior is divided into parent-initiated and twin-initiated, it is observed that parent-initiated behavior is similar for MZ and DZ twins, but significantly different when responding to twin-initiated behavior (Lytton, 2013). Parental responses to MZ twin-initiated behavior are significantly more similar than parental responses to DZ twin-initiated behavior, leading to the conclusion that parents *treat* MZ twins more similarly than DZ twins because MZ twins *behave* more similarly than DZ twins. That is, parenting reflects genetic differences in children's characteristics (their personalities and behaviors) as well as parent's own (Avinun & Knafo, 2014). Parents react to differences in their offspring's behavior; they do not create them (evocative rGE).

Another factor with the potential for downward biasing of h^2 is *in-utero* twin-to-twin blood transfusion. Blood is transfused from a donor twin to a recipient twin through fetal placental anastomosis, which only occurs in MZ twins, 10–20% of whom share their chorionic membrane (monochorionic), and results in twins born less similar than they would otherwise be (Waszak et al., 2017). Because this occurs only in MZ twins, it has the effect of underestimating genetic effects. Because DZ twins are different zygotes and are dichorionic, they are thus not susceptible to transfusion syndrome. A significant number of MZ twins are thus exposed to an intrauterine environmental factor that may make them less similar than their shared genes would have otherwise made them, but DZ twins are never exposed to this phenomenon.

3

MOLECULAR GENETICS AND ANTISOCIAL BEHAVIOR

A Molecular Genetics Primer

Behavioral genetics is important for identifying the interplay of genes and environments in human traits and behaviors, but heritability estimates capture a wide variety of genes, and quantitative genetics has no way of identifying what those genes might be. Molecular genetics is the discipline that seeks to identify the specific genes involved in the traits or behaviors of interest to behavioral geneticists at the molecular level. Molecular geneticists are most interested in the minutia of genes: their molecular structure, sequence, and activity, particularly as they relate to disease conditions rather than behavior per se. However, the increasing availability of genome-wide data has allowed biopsychosocial criminologists to access it to build more advanced explanatory models aimed at identifying genetic variants that moderate environmental factors and vice versa.

Robert Plomin (2023) informs us that quantitative (behavioral) and molecular genetics have been synthesized in a process that began in the 1980s with the development of polymerase chain reaction (PCR) technology. PCR is a laboratory technique by which any nucleic acid DNA sequence derived from minute bodily fluids or hair samples is amplified exponentially by adding short DNA fragments known as primers with a defined sequence complementary to the target DNA. The mixture is then first heated to break the hydrogen bond in the DNA helix (denaturation) and immediately followed by cooling it allowing the hydrogen bond to reform (annealing). This is a cyclic process that, over hours, generates multiple identical copies and provides multi-allelic DNA profiles. The next

DOI: 10.4324/9781003642268-5

step involves gel electrophoresis and exposing the gel to ultraviolet light with fluorescent dyes that bind to the DNA. The electrical charge separates the molecules similarly to a sieve separating particles by size and showing sequence-specific barcode-like patterns. Sample DNA is easy to obtain from buccal swabs costing as little as $10 each to obtain and analyze.

Molecular genetic research has progressed at warp speed, as can be discerned from the shifting estimates of how many genes there are in the human genome over the last 50 years. This number has been on a downward spiral from its estimate in the 1980s of about 100,000; after the completion of the Human Genome Project in 2003 it was 20,000–25,000. Nurk et al. (2022) sequenced the complete human female genome and identified 19,969 protein-coding genes and 43,525 non-coding regulatory DNA/RNA sequences, and Rhie et al. (2023) published the complete sequence of a human Y chromosome and identified 41 additional protein-coding genes. The number of protein-coding genes is thus beginning to settle at around 20,000, although in common with the Human Genome Project, both these studies only sequenced a single person's genome. Efforts are underway to combine multiple (at least 300) genomes in the Human Pangenome Project (Marco-Sola et al., 2023) for a more complete picture.

Molecular genetics is interested in identifying protein-coding genes, but this does not mean that non-protein-coding components of the genome are not just as important. These components were once labeled "junk DNA" because it does not code for proteins. "Junk" sequences were seen as genetic fossils that once functioned but now do not. The end of junk talk began with a consortium of 442 scientists from 32 different institutions worldwide engaged in a decade-long project called the Encyclopedia of DNA Elements (ENCODE). After the equivalent of about 300 years of computer time, ENCODE found that 80% of the human genome serves some function in regulating when, how, and where a gene is activated, with the promise of new technology finding function for the remainder. ENCODE's Ewan Birney remarked: "By carefully piecing together a simply staggering variety of data, we've shown that the human genome is simply alive with switches, turning our genes on and off and controlling when and where proteins are produced." It was also noted that: "The ENCODE project has revealed a landscape that is absolutely teeming with important genetic elements—a landscape that used to be dismissed as 'junk DNA'" (Hall & Birney, 2012, p. 82).

Geneticist Nessa Carey asks us to imagine an automobile factory in which only 2% of the employees were involved in building cars and 98% (the non-coding part of the genome) sitting around doing nothing. She says that no one imagines that only 2% of employees are sufficient to run the car factory, so why would anyone think only 2% of the genome is sufficient to run the protein factory? Cars are the endpoint of the factory as proteins are the endpoint of the genome; neither could be produced without the "junk." Carey says that while two people can build a car, just as 2% of the genome can build proteins, they cannot sustain the whole process alone:

> and certainly can't turn it into a powerful and financially successful brand. Similarly, there's no point having 98 people mopping the floors and staffing the showrooms if there's nothing to sell. The whole organization only works when all the components are in place. And so it is with our genomes.
>
> *(2015, p. 3)*

Transposons, or "jumping genes," are part of the genome that used to be called junk. They make up about 25% of the human genome and are short sections of DNA that "jump" around and insert themselves into new DNA sites and they used to be considered worse than junk. They were thought of as parasites because they jump around randomly, but new research finds that they are critical regulators of the first stages of embryonic development when cells are dividing vigorously. As Branco and Chuong (2020, p. 1) note: "Transposons are an abundant source of transcriptional modulatory elements, such as gene promoters and enhancers, splicing and termination sites, and regulatory non-coding RNAs." A key transposon is an enhancer of the SOX9 gene critical for male sex development from the inherent female form of all mammals. A chromosomal XY male will develop as a female if that transposon fails, although such a person cannot reproduce (Gonen et al., 2018).

It is not easy to appreciate the mind-boggling complexity of the genome that reads, interprets, replicates, and edits itself forward and backward. The enormous information content of DNA led Francis Collins, head of the Human Genome Project at the time of the completion of the first draft in 2000, to call it the "language of God" (2006). Most of that information contributes to making every human alike and some of it makes each person unique. It also contributes to making some of us genetically part of some other people because genetic material is differentially distributed among different human populations that evolved in different regions of the planet. Despite these differences, any two randomly chosen human beings differ only in about 0.01% of their genetic material. This does not sound like much, but 0.01% of 3 billion-plus base pairs yields at least 3 million base pair differences. Although most of these base-pair differences have little or no effect on phenotypic differences, Bonham, Warshauer-Baker, and Collins (2005, p. 12) state that "about 200,000 common variants are responsible for the genetic components of the differences in health, behavior, and other human traits."

Small differences at the molecular level can thus lead to meaningful differences at the phenotypic level. Think about the effect of small genetic differences among the 500 recognized primate species. Despite the remarkable array of morphological, physiological, and behavioral differences among them they share an average of about 98–99% of their protein-coding genes with all other primate species (Kuderna et al., 2023). This is not surprising since all animals share the evolutionarily necessary metabolic, survival, and reproductive functions; evolution is a conservative process and does not invent an entirely new genome when species branch off from the ancestral line. Many observed differences among primate species reflect small differences in a gene sequence affecting the quantity of the gene product, and how these proteins function in the brain to regulate neurotransmitter functioning (Babbitt et al., 2010).

Genetic Polymorphisms

Genetic polymorphisms are the most common type of genetic variation among people. A gene is polymorphic if more than one allele type occupies the same chromosomal locus of a coding region in a population. Polymorphisms are variations in a gene sequence that lead to the diversity of human morphological, psychological, and behavioral traits. The least common allele must have a frequency of at least 1% in the population to be classified as a polymorphism. Polymorphisms arrive via mutations but persist over generations because neither form possesses an overall advantage or disadvantage over the other in terms of natural selection concerns. Most polymorphisms are silent and do not change the structure and function of protein molecules produced by their genes. Others substitute a single amino acid for another in the protein without changing its functional capability but change gene expression leading to the formation of variant proteins that alter a person's response to substances such as alcohol or drugs. Single-nucleotide polymorphisms (SNPs) are the most prevalent polymorphisms, and more than 14 million different SNPs have been found in the human genome (Jin et al., 2018).

As the term indicates, a difference in just one nucleotide is all that differentiates one allele from another in a SNP. For instance, the enzyme catechol-O-methyltransferase (COMT) consists of 27,222 nucleotides that produce the Val158Met polymorphism of the COMT genes, and only one out of that number differentiates the gene. Beaver (2009, p. 58) notes: "The amino acid produced by the tri-nucleotide sequence ATG in Person 1 would be methionine, while the amino acid produced by the codon GTG would be valine." Adenine (A) produces methionine and guanine (G) produces valine. Valine (Val) and methionine (Met) influence the function of brain-derived neurotrophic factor (BDNF), a protein that plays an important role in neuronal survival, support, proliferation, and plasticity. As Dincheva, Glatt, and Lee (2012, p. 2) remark: "The BDNF Val66Met polymorphism has been the focus of several genetic association studies of cognitive function and a host of neuropsychiatric disorders." The Val variant, especially in Val-Val homozygotes, catabolizes dopamine about four times faster than the Met variant, which may lead Val-Val homozygotes to addictive pleasure-seeking. The Val-Val variant has been related to a variety of outcomes associated with antisocial behavior such as ADHD, addiction, and various personality disorders.

Using functional magnetic resonance imaging (fMRI) scans of 105 healthy males, Yacubian et al. (2007) monitored activity in the prefrontal cortex (a rational regulator of thoughts and emotions) and ventral striatum (a reward-related area) areas of the brain. It was found that Val-Val subjects showed high levels of activity in the ventral striatum in anticipation of rewards, Met-Met subjects showed blunted activity in anticipation of the same rewards, and Val-Met heterozygotes showed intermediate activity. On the other hand, Tosato et al. (2011) found that Met/Met homozygous Italian schizophrenic patients displayed more aggressive behavior compared to Val-Val homozygous patients. They posited that the Met/Met genotype may have an effect on aggressive behavior in schizophrenia because norepinephrine (NE) is less effectively inactivated. Schizophrenia is a condition of excessive dopamine activity (Holttinen, Pirkola, & Kaltiala, 2023) and dopamine is a precursor of NE (Costa & Schoenbaum, 2022) so this may be why norepinephrine is less effectively inactivated in people with schizophrenia.

Other polymorphisms are repetitive DNA tracts called *microsatellites* or short tandem repeats, which repeat an amino acid sequence 2–6 times, and *minisatellites*, or VNTRs (variable number of tandem repeats) with between 9 and 100 repeats. Microsatellites occur in thousands in the human genome and differ in the number of repeats of contiguous nucleotide bases. For example, the dopamine receptor gene (DRD4) is 48 base-pair VNTR polymorphism repeated from 2 to 11 times. The 7-repeat (7R) allele of the DRD4 genes encodes a receptor with lower affinity for dopamine than the 4R (the most common) variant, and "is associated with various psychiatric disorders including ADHD, dependences, pathological gambling, alcoholism, [and] drug dependence" (Ptáček, Kuželová, & Stefano, 2011, p. 216). The dopaminergic system is frequently implicated in behavioral problems because it plays an important role in neural processes encoding motivational and reward salience networks (Bromberg-Martin, Matsumoto, & Hikosaka, 2010). As Gard, Dotterer, and Hyde (2019,

p. 47) note: "Researchers have typically focused on genetic polymorphisms that are involved in dopaminergic and serotonergic neurotransmission, due to their roles in emotion, reward, and learning-processes that are often impaired in AB [antisocial behavior]."

Although the 7-repeat of the DRD4 is considered a "risk" allele, it can confer valuable benefits in some environments. The DRD4-7R allele is a young mutation that arose about 40,000 years ago and has been positively selected for (Kitiyama et al., 2016). Positive selection indicates that some traits such as impulsivity, aggression, and novelty seeking associated with this allele may have been adaptive at certain periods in human evolution. The emergence of the 7R coincided roughly with the first signs of complex horticultural/agricultural societies, and when humans were exploring and expanding widely around the planet (Eisenberg et al., 2008). Charles Darwin suggested the major adaptive function served by the restlessness characterized by traits common in 7R carriers: "Restless men who will not follow any steady occupation—and this relic of barbarism is a great check to civilisation—emigrate to newly-settled countries, where they prove useful pioneers" (1871, p. 172). Consistent with this observation is a study of 2,320 individuals from 39 ethnic groups around the world reporting a correlation of 0.85 between the prevalence of the 7R allele in a population and geographic distance from the parent population (Ding et al., 2002). The Han Chinese and Yemeni Jews who have remained in the same geographic region for the last 30,000 years have practically zero 7R alleles, while six populations of South American Indians have an average of 63%, which is about 3.3 times greater than the global average (Ding et al., 2002).

The 7R allele was not necessarily causative of its carriers migrating from parent populations to explore the outside world. Migration itself likely exerted pressures for the selection of the allele since restless and bold individuals would have functioned better in novel environments (Matthews & Butler, 2011). The 7R allele is well represented among groups with a reputation for boldness, restlessness, and fierceness:

> It is probably no accident that two of the best known ethnographies of the twentieth century are titled "The Harmless People," about the !Kung who have few or no 7R alleles, and the "Fierce People," about the Yanomamo with a high frequency of 7R.
>
> *(Harpending & Cochran, 2002, p. 12)*

Hunting for Genes Linked to Antisocial Behavior

Criminality is a phenotype that has no single "culprit" gene by which we may identify it because all human traits and behaviors are massively polygenic. When geneticists seek to identify the combined influence of many genes on the development of phenotypic traits, behaviors, or diseases they study the whole genome, or genomics. As the World Health Organization (2020, np) differentiates genomics from genetics:

> The main difference between genomics and genetics is that genetics scrutinizes the functioning and composition of the single gene whereas genomics addresses all genes and their interrelationships to identify their combined influence on the growth and development of the organism.

Genetics and genomics may not sound like a big distinction, but we might say that genetics is more reductionist and genomics is more holistic. It is rather like behavioral genetics in that it looks at how multiple genes interact with the environment; only it searches for them at the molecular level. The genomics goal is to find specific genes underlying the traits, behaviors, and disease syndromes that heritability studies reveal. Genomics uses SNP data to match heritability values, but thus far the variance captured is minimal. If SNP data account for 10% of the variance in a trait is consistently found to be 50% in heritability studies, we know that at the molecular level, we are underestimating genetic effects and need to consider more SNPs (Felson, 2014). Forero, Pereira-Morales, and Gonzalez (2017, p. 6) note that the genetic contribution to human personality ranges between 30% and 50%, "of which between 15% and 37% is explained by variation in common single-nucleotide polymorphisms."

Plomin and Von Stumm (2022, p. 50) confidently assume:

> The missing heritability gap will be narrowed with bigger and better genome-wide association studies and with whole-genome sequencing that assesses all DNA differences in the genome rather than several hundred thousand SNPs assessed in current studies. The only way is up for the predictive power of polygenic scores.

Most geneticists also believe that we will eventually discover the missing heritability and that it is a matter of obtaining sample sizes with sufficient statistical power to identify the SNP variants using genome-wide data (Yang et al., 2015). This is a difficult endeavor since human traits are associated with many thousands of SNPs each with minute effect sizes. Further complicating the effort is that each variant may affect different traits. This is known as pleiotropy or "genetic overlap"; that is, the proportion of variance that two separate traits share because of shared alleles.

In the hunt for the missing heritability, genomic-relatedness-matrix restricted maximum likelihood (GREML) is the statistical method used. GREML studies typically use samples of well over 100,000 subjects to obtain sufficient statistical power because of the small effect sizes of each SNP.

Significance levels with such large samples must greatly exceed the standard levels and are typically set at < .0000005, but even then, they capture only the largest effect sizes. Chabris et al. (2015, p. 309) state that: "GREML studies have now confirmed that for many phenotypes, including height, intelligence, and schizophrenia, the combined additive effects of common SNPs do account for a large fraction of the variance," and that much of the heritability was not missing "but merely hiding in the form of small but additive effect sizes." However, SNP heritability for personality and behavior may never equal h^2 because h^2 includes very rare variants that are hard to detect, nonadditive genetic effects (dominance and epistasis), and multiple G*x*E and rGE processes. For instance, Okbay et al. (2022) examined an immense sample of over 3 million people and almost 6 million SNPs. They constructed a Genome-Wide Polygenic Score (GPS) and found that it only accounted for 16% of the variance in educational attainment.

GPSs are typically generated from genome-wide association studies (GWAS); GPSs are promising quantitative predictors of heritable traits premised on the fact that heritable human traits are the result of the aggregated influence of a large number of common and rare SNPs. A single SNP may account for no more than 0.001% of the variance in a trait, but aggregating the weighted effects of millions of SNPs into a GPS allows researchers to identify individuals by their genetic propensity for the traits of interest. The value of GPS is explained by Plomin and Von Stumm who maintain that unlike correlated purely environmental measures in which causal directions are rarely clear, using GPS data the causal direction is entirely unambiguous:

> Polygenic score predictions are correlations, and correlations do not necessarily imply causation. However, polygenic scores have a unique causal status among predictors in one important sense: correlations between polygenic scores and traits can only be interpreted in one direction causally. That is, there can be no backward causation in the sense that the brain, behaviour or the environment cannot change inherited DNA variation. The unchanging nature of inherited DNA variation from the moment of conception also makes polygenic score predictions unique in that they are just as predictive of adult traits early in life as they are in adulthood.
>
> *(2022, p. 50)*

The Differential Susceptibility Hypothesis

Complicating the search for the causal effects of genes is that a putative risk allele in one environment is a protective allele in another. For instance, a strong reward drive in a supportive environment may result in positive risk-taking and personal success, while the same reward drive in a non-supportive environment may result in negative risk-taking and personal failure. In other words, some individuals are more negatively impacted by negative environments than others, but more positively by positive environments. This learning-related genetic variation is known as the "differential susceptibility hypothesis (DSH)" or the "orchid–dandelion hypothesis." The DSH stresses that some people are like hardy dandelions that can grow in a variety of conditions, while others are like delicate orchids that cannot tolerate environmental hardship but will thrive in the right conditions. Fox and Beevers (2016, p. 1657) inform us as to why this pattern undermines the search for genetic main effects:

> The essence of the differential susceptibility hypothesis (DSH) is that with similar group sizes of more and less susceptible individuals there will be no main genetic effect. Instead, there will be a crossover interaction with susceptible individuals doing worse in adverse environments but better in supportive environments than less susceptible individuals. This pattern does of course undermine large-scale genome-wide association studies (GWAS) that look only for main genetic effects.

This model may replace the diathesis-stress model that posits negative outcomes resulting from genetic risk factors interacting with environmental stressors. The DSH model suggests that "plasticity factors" should replace "risk factors" on the genetic diathesis side of the equation (Ellis et al., 2011). Bakermans-Kranenburg and Van Ijzendoorn (2007) have suggested that variation in sensitivity to environmental susceptibility is underpinned by allelic variation in DA and serotonin brain circuitry because these systems govern sensitivity to reward and punishment. The serotonin transporter (5-HTT) gene recycles serotonin from the synaptic cleft back to the presynaptic neuron, thus terminating its effects and enabling reuse. Variants in the 5-HTT gene promoter, 5-HTTLPR ("serotonin transporter linked polymorphous region"), provide different levels of serotonin expression. The 5-HTTLPR comes in short (s) and long (L) versions. The s variant reduces gene expression, resulting in less efficient transporter function, allowing serotonin to remain in the synaptic gap longer, resulting in a net reduction in circulating serotonin.

Carriers of the s allele, particularly s/s homozygotes, are not only more susceptible to negative environmental experiences, but also more responsive to positive experiences (Hankin et al., 2011). That is, carriers of the s allele suffer more from negative experiences than L carriers but benefit more from positive experiences (Belsky, Zhang, &

Sayler, 2022). In a sample of twins, Bakermans-Kranenburg and Van Ijzendoorn (2007) showed that children carrying the DRD4-7R raised by insensitive mothers displayed more externalizing behaviors compared with children carrying other variants, but children with the DRD4-7R raised by sensitive mothers showed low levels of externalizing behavior. This may explain the anomaly wherein a significant G*x*E risk effect is found in the absence of a main effect, which implies a reversal of the association between a negative outcome and life experience. That is, the risk of a negative outcome increases with increases in negative experience for those homogeneous or heterogeneous for the s allele but decreases among those homogeneous for the L allele such that the effects of the two genotypes cancel each other out (Bakermans-Kranenburg & Van Ijzendoorn, 2015).

Support for the DSH is found at the cultural level. About 75% of East Asians carry at least one s allele compared with about 44% of Europeans (Chiao & Blizinsky, 2010), but fewer East Asians than people of European descent are diagnosed with depression and anxiety disorders, for which the s allele is a strong marker (Mrazek et al., 2013). Why is a risk allele in one culture a protective allele in another? It has been hypothesized that historically high levels of pathogen-borne diseases have imposed selective pressures on cultural practices resulting in a behavioral "immune system" (Murray, Trudeau, & Schaller, 2011). Fincher et al. (2008) looked at over 100,000 individuals from 68 countries and found that individualism-collectivism scores are strongly associated ($r = -0.69$) with a historically high prevalence of pathogens in their cultures.

Cultural values that serve an anti-pathogen function may also serve an anti-psychopathology function in that a high prevalence of the s allele drives the selection for collectivist personalities: "Collectivist cultural values serve an adaptive function by reducing the probability of environmental stress, a known catalyst for negative affect, thus leading to genetic selection of the s allele within collectivist cultures" (Chiao & Blizinsky, 2010, p. 3). Chiao and Blizinsky found a correlation of 0.70 between the prevalence of the s allele and collectivism over 29 countries and concluded:

> Emphasizing social norms that increase social harmony and encourage giving social support to others, collectivism serves an "anti-psychopathology" function by creating an ecological niche that lowers the prevalence of chronic life stress, protecting genetically susceptible individuals from environmental pathogens known to trigger negative emotions and psychopathology.
>
> *(2010, p. 6)*

Epigenetics and Nurturing

The genome is no longer viewed as a "blueprint" with one-to-one mapping from gene to phenotype. A better metaphor for the genome is a recipe because the phenotype is "baked" from the genetic recipe according to the skill of its bakers and the ingredients they may add or subtract. Nature generates emergent properties and complex features from the genome recipe without revising the DNA cookbook. The circumstances the infant or fetus encounters may affect its genome by altering gene transcription, which leads us to epigenetics. Epigenetics is, "any process that alters gene activity without changing the DNA sequence" (Weinhold, 2006, p. 163). Epigenetic modifications affect the ability of the DNA code to be read by rendering it accessible or inaccessible (O'Donnell & Meaney, 2020). Many genes of interest to criminologists are regulated by signals from environmental events, "which may be internal or external to the organism; e.g., a change in the availability of glucose, an electrical impulse, or a social interaction" (Meaney, 2010, p. 50).

The genome has been analogized to an orchestra with polymorphisms capable of a variety of music, and epigenetics as the conductor governing the performance:

> The epigenetic "conductor" controls when and what "instruments" (genes) are to be activated and when they are to be silenced, and when they are activated, the gusto with which they may be played and what other instruments will accompany, augment, and modify the "music" they make.
>
> *(Walsh, 2009, p. 51)*

This regulation of genetic activity is accomplished by two main processes: DNA methylation and histone acetylation. Methylation may be permanent (retained during cell replication and may be passed to offspring) while acetylation is transient. Methylation is a process by which the enzyme DNA methyltransferase attaches a methyl group of atoms to a cytosine base to form 5-methyl cytosine. When a signal is received to manufacture a protein, the enzyme RNA polymerase (RNAP) that transcribes template DNA into RNA, runs along the DNA strand reading the code for that protein. The methyl group is a barrier that prevents the code from being read—no transcription order, no protein (see Figure 4.1). Methylation is identified by examining genes and determining the total amounts of 5-methyl cytosine they contain (Khodadadi et al., 2021).

The opposite effect is acetylation or histone modification. Acetylation involves histone acetyltransferases (HATs) transferring an acetyl group of atoms that bind to the amino acid lysine tail of the histone, thus reducing lysine's attraction to DNA's negatively charged phosphate backbone. The reduced charge loosens the chromatin-enabling RNAP to read the gene code more readily. After transcription, another group of enzymes called histone deacetylases (HDACs) removes the acetyl atoms, reinstating the electrostatic attraction and repressing chromatin activity. Epigenetics engages individuals' non-shared environments because the effects of an experience will not be uniform across all individuals experiencing them because some are dandelions and others are orchids (McEwen & Gianaros, 2010).

Rodent studies linking methylation with maternal nurturing—measured by the level of pup licking and grooming (LG) and arch-back nursing (ABN)—have shown significant results (Weaver et al., 2004). Pups receiving high levels of LG/ABN showed better responses to stress and were more socially adept than pups receiving low levels of LG/ABN. A portion of the pups from each strain was cross-fostered (high LG/ABN mothers fostering pups born to low LG/ABN mothers and vice versa) to determine how much of the variance in pup behaviors was attributable to genes and how much to nurture. It was shown that LG/ABN led to similar epigenetic modifications in pups, regardless of whether they were the mothers' offspring or cross-fostered. These modifications resulted in stable behavioral differences in adulthood between the high- and low-nurtured pups.

Low-nurtured pups showed high methylation of the glucocorticoid receptor (GR) gene in the hippocampus. The hippocampus modulates the functioning of the hypothalamic-pituitary-adrenal (HPA) axis, the primary stress response system. Methylation of receptors renders them inoperable, while unmethylated genes produce more receptors, resulting in better feedback control of the stress response. The GR gene is heavily methylated and inactive at birth, but in highly nurtured pups, the GR gene gradually demethylates and becomes active. Poorly nurtured pups retained a high level of methylation and responded to stress with anxiety and fear, but in a world of cats and other dangers, it pays to be hypervigilant. The early environment teaches lessons about the world we will inhabit that are captured in our genomes and brains.

A high degree of HPA methylation has been observed in children raised in low-quality orphanages. Comparing children raised since birth in Russian orphanages with children raised by both biological parents, Naumova et al. (2012) found that the orphanage-raised children had greater methylation of the HPA. They noted: "the presence and level of maternal care are highly responsible for the epigenetic regulation of genes involved in the control of the hypothalamic-pituitary-adrenal system" (Naumova et al., 2012, p. 8). Wismer-Fries et al. (2005) compared Romanian children who had been in orphanages for an average of 16.6 months before being fostered to American middle-class families with a matched control group of children reared by both biological parents. The foster children showed significantly lower levels of vasopressin and oxytocin, which help to regulate the HPA and are the basis of emotional empathy, than controls. This suggests epigenetic down-regulation of neuropeptide receptors in response to months of early deprivation of attachment experiences (Schury & Kolassa, 2012). Epigenetics thus emphasizes the permeable boundaries between the biological and the social, poised as it is between reductionism in biology (the attachment of atoms to a DNA strand) and that great whole called "the environment." As Boyce and Kobor (2015, p. 16) note:

> [E]epigenetic processes.... comprise a broad, complex set of molecular points of connection between the experiences of early life and the proclivities, capacities and risks encoded within the individual human genome. The adversities inherent within environments of poverty, neglect and trauma are transduced into molecular events controlling the expression of neuroregulatory genes, which in turn guide brain development, calibrate stress reactivity, and influence lifelong risks of psychopathology and other morbidities. Similarly, positive early environments of nurturance, care and stability provide an anticipatory programming of many of the same genes, thereby diminishing mental health risks, optimizing neurodevelopmental preparation for learning, and ensuring normative socioemotional development.

4

NEUROBIOLOGY AND ANTISOCIAL BEHAVIOR

The Wonder of the Brain

What a wonder is this 3-pound lump of tofu-like tissue sitting on our shoulders. It is evolution's magnum opus and the most complicated entity in the universe about which Nobel laureate physicist Sir Roger Penrose wrote: "If you look at the entire physical cosmos, our brains are a tiny, tiny, part of it. But they're the most perfectly organized part. Compared to the complexity of a brain, a galaxy is just an inert lump" (Holt, 2012, p. 178). Within this enchanted loom reside the soup, and sparks represent our thoughts, memories, emotions, and talents we develop and add to from cradle to grace. Although this marvel of design constitutes only 2% of average body mass, about 50–60% of all genes contribute to its development, and it consumes a voracious 25% of the body's energy budget to keep it running (Balasubramanian, 2021). Genes build brains, but as complex as the genome is, the building is more complex than the builder. The brain's electrochemical circuitry captures our genetic dispositions and environmental experiences and blends them into an efficient adaptive machine. No wonder criminologist Matt Robinson (2004, p. 72) was led to write that any theory of behavior "is logically incomplete if it does not discuss the role of the brain."

Paul Maclean's Triune Brain Theory

Neuroscience is difficult because it is essentially the brain trying to understand itself, and as the maxim goes: "If the brain were so simple

DOI: 10.4324/9781003642268-6

that we could understand it, we would be so simple that we couldn't." However, there is a great deal of well-replicated useful research, the most important of which is that the brain is a marvelously plastic organ that calibrates itself to environmental input. Although it has been heavily criticized, I make use of Paul Maclean's (1990) triune brain theory because I agree with Jaak Panksepp's evaluation:

> This three-layered conceptualization helps us grasp the overall function of higher brain areas better than any other scheme yet devised. Of course, exceptions can be found to all generalizations, and it must be remembered that the brain is a massively interconnected organ whose every part can find an access pathway to any other part.
>
> *(1998, p. 70)*

Maclean divides the brain into the reptilian (the survival brain), limbic (the feeling brain), and neocortical (the thinking brain) with each new system layered on top of the other as new animal forms (e.g., from reptilian to mammalian) appear. As Myers and Dewall (2018, p. 68) explain: "The brain's increasing complexity arises from new brain systems built on top of the old, much as the Earth's landscape covers the old with the new. Digging down one discovers the fossil remnants of the past"; "new" systems are not entirely new, but rather improved expansions on pre-existing ones.

The reptilian brain is concerned only with ritualized behaviors favoring raw survival and reproductive concerns. It consists of the brain stem and the cerebellum and controls reflexes such as breathing and heart rate, sleep, and consciousness. Modern reptiles and birds have a limbic system and neocortex also, but Maclean focuses on a period in which perhaps they did not, or when they did not yet come completely online, and we are not in the same evolutionary line as reptiles and birds. Furthermore, our brains are not compartmentalized by membranes but are fully interconnected. However, these criticisms are nuances that we can leave to the neuroscientists to debate. Maclean never claimed that the three systems operate independently or are in conflict as some have claimed.

Wrapped around the reptilian system like a protective claw is the limbic ("border") system. This is where the primary emotions of pleasure, anger, and joy, and the social emotions such as love, guilt, and embarrassment, are felt. It is a complex set of structures surrounding the thalamus, which lies just above the brain stem. The thalamus is the brain's information relay station. All information from the bodily senses (except smell) is processed through it for prioritization before being sent to the cerebral cortex for interpretation. Among other limbic system structures are the bilaterally distributed amygdala, hippocampus, and anterior cingulate gyrus (ACG). The amygdalae are almond-shaped groups of nuclei that abut the hippocampus. Their primary function is the storage of memories associated with a range of emotions, particularly threat interpretation and response. The limbic represents a balancing system between the reptilian complex and the rational neocortex by lending sensitivity and emotion to the reptilian system and permitting the interplay of emotion and reason within the neocortex.

The hippocampus is specialized for storing and processing memories. Connections between the amygdala and the hippocampus help to focus what the brain has learned regarding responses to the emotional stimuli that have formerly aroused it, and regulating it by infusing it with memories of previous experiences. Ling, Umbach, and Raine (2019, p. 631) note that: "reduced amygdala volume in adulthood has been associated with increased aggressive and psychopathic characteristics from childhood to early adulthood, it is also associated with increased risk for future antisocial and psychopathic behavior." Chronic criminals tend to have disruptions in brain regions that underlie cognitive control such as the anterior cingulate, the amygdala, and areas of the prefrontal cortex (PFC) (Schiffer et al., 2014).

The cingulate gyri surround the limbic system like a wishbone providing structural connections between it and the cerebral cortex. It straddles the emotional (orbitofrontal cortex and amygdala) and memory (hippocampal memory system) domains (Rolls, 2019). Parts of the ACG serve as processing stations for stimuli arriving from other brain areas and assign appropriate controls to them. Among the functions of the ACG is "its role in fundamental cognitive processes, including motivation, decision making, learning, cost-benefit calculation, as well as conflict and error monitoring" (Apps, Rushworth, & Chang, 2016, p. 692). Sandwiched as it is between the "feeling" limbic system and the "thinking" PFC, the ACG is ideally situated for this role (Stevens, Hurley, & Taber, 2011).

The neocortex is the site of abstract reasoning, language, foresight, and judgments that allow humans to recognize urges from the limbic system and respond to them in socially acceptable ways. The most important part of the cerebral cortex is the PFC, "the most uniquely human of all brain structures" (Goldberg, 2001, p. 2). It occupies approximately one-third of the cerebral cortex and has extensive connections with structures in the limbic system. Because of its many connections with other brain areas, the PFC plays a major integrative and supervisory role and is vital to forming moral judgments, mediating affect, and social cognition (Wolf et al., 2015). The PFC can perform these tasks because it is not concerned with processing low-level stimuli but with sorting and making sense of them (Shekhar & Rahnev, 2018).

Neurons and Neurotransmission

The foundation for the brain begins three weeks after conception when a sheet of embryonic cells folds and fuses with the neural tube. The neural tube grows and cells differentiate throughout the first trimester as chemical signals direct waves of migrating cells to their allotted place (Stiles & Jernigan, 2010). The brain contains at least a trillion cells with about 100 billion neurons (nerve cells) that communicate among themselves by converting incoming information into electrochemical impulses that the brain processes and facilitates responses. Each neuron has one axon and numerous branched extensions called dendrites that serve as receivers of impulses from neighboring neurons. Axons are coated with a cholesterol myelin sheath that acts like insulation around electrical wires that amplify nerve impulses and protect against short-circuiting. When axons receive signals, they are either passed along or terminated according to the ratio of excitatory to inhibitory messages they receive. Myelinated axons (the brain's white matter) transmit nerve impulses 100 times faster than unmyelinated axons (gray matter) (Fields, 2014). Neurons pass their information along the axon by electric signals via the exchange of atomic ions in and out of the axon's permeable membrane until they reach the axon terminal (presynaptic knob), where the message is converted from electrical to chemical. Figure 4.1 illustrates the various parts of a neuron and a synapse.

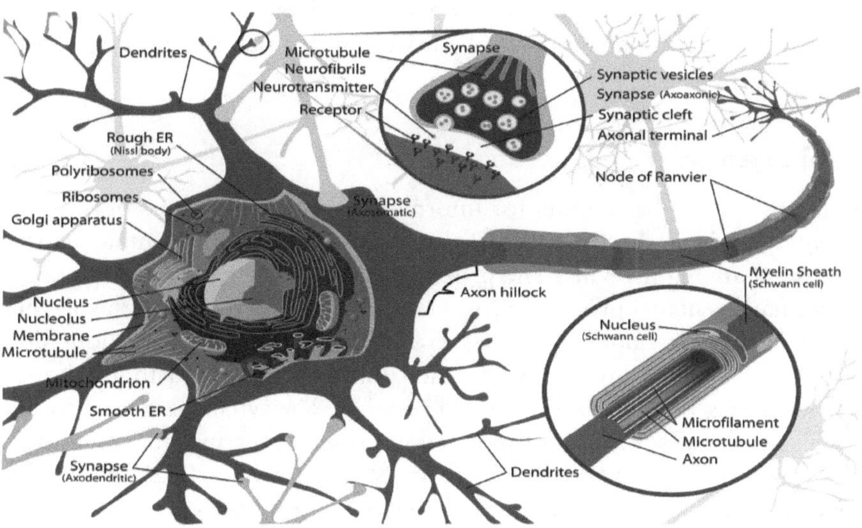

FIGURE 4.1 Various parts of a neuron and a synapse.

Source: Released into the public domain by LadyofHats. https://en.wikipedia.org/wiki/Neuron

These chemical messengers are neurotransmitters produced in the cell body and stored in tiny vesicles at the axon terminal that open up and spill out into the tiny synaptic cleft (about 3,000 times smaller than the width of a human hair) between sending and receiving axons. Neurons make an astronomical number of synaptic connections: "The human brain has 10^{15} connections and around 100 billion neurons, so roughly as many stars as there are in the Milky Way" (DeWeerdt, 2019, p. 6). Neurotransmitters remain in the synaptic gap for only 1/500 of a second; excess amounts are diffused, pumped back up into the neuron's presynaptic knob, or degraded by enzymes so that the receptor no longer recognizes it.

Neuroscientists have attempted to replicate synapsis using high-performance computers and found how complex it is. They created an artificial neural network of 1.73 billion neurons connected by 10.4 trillion synapses. The results were humbling:

> It took 40 minutes with the combined muscle of 82,944 processors in K computer [a supercomputer in Kobe, Japan] to get just one second of biological brain processing time. The simulation ate up about 1PB [that is, 10^{15} bytes] of system memory as each synapse was modeled individually.
>
> *(Scornavacchi, 2015, p. 14)*

Forty minutes, almost 83,000 processors, and one quadrillion bytes of memory to get just one second of the output our neurons produce every waking second.

Synaptogenesis

Synapses are the basic units for information processing and storage, and *synaptogenesis* is the process of forming and organizing communication pathways among neurons. The process mobilizes a variety of cellular and molecular events to promote it, but we are concerned here with the role of environmental input. Synapses are born and perish throughout life, but they proliferate at a dazzling rate during infancy and toddlerhood, followed by a phase of selection and pruning. The synaptogenesis process begins in mid-gestation with most connections occurring during infancy and peaking in toddlerhood (Rahman & McGowan, 2022). A healthy human infant may create an astounding two million synaptic connections a second at its peak (U.S. Department of Health and Human Services, 2009).

During synaptogenesis, dendrites proliferate and send out their tentacles to hook up with any available mate and glial cells wrap around axons to begin the myelination process. The lower brain regions are the first to be myelinated, but higher regions such as the PFC are not fully myelinated until early adulthood (Franklyn et al., 2022). Most synapses will not survive the competition for synaptic space and will be pruned, but others will develop more permanent relationships and strengthen. The brain creates and eliminates synapses throughout life. Creation exceeds elimination in the first two years, after which production and elimination are roughly balanced until adolescence when elimination exceeds production (Bonnycastle, Davenport, & Cousin, 2021). Although the overproduction and subsequent pruning of synapses may appear inefficient, it allows an individual organism's neural circuitry to be calibrated by its unique environmental experiences. If children's brain wiring is established by nurturing experiences they will be disposed to view the world positively, but if it is wired by maltreatment, later experiences may be diverted onto neurological tracks that signal hostility.

> We are just as capable of adapting to unhealthy environments and pathological caretakers. The resulting adaptations may help us to survive a traumatic childhood but impede healthy development later in life. ... Because the first few years of life are a period of exuberant brain development, early experience has a disproportionate impact on the development of neural systems.
>
> *(Firestone, Firestone, & Catlett, 2013, p. 14)*

Synaptic connections are selected for retention or elimination according to how functionally viable they are in the person's ontogeny in the same way that environmental challenges select from the reservoir of alleles in the species' phylogeny. The brain thus evolves in somatic time as species evolve in geological time by selective elimination or retention. Synapse retention is a use-dependent process, with only those connections that exchange information most frequently and strongly being preserved. Experiences with strong emotional content are accompanied by strong electrochemical impulses that become more sensitive and responsive to similar stimuli latency in the future (Shi et al., 2004). Like establishing a trail in the wilderness, frequently activated neurons are primed to fire at lower stimulus thresholds once synaptic tracks have been laid down. The more often a trail is trodden, the more distinct it becomes from its surroundings and the easier it is to follow; like migrants, brains like to follow well-trodden trails. This process is summed up in the pithy saying: "The neurons that fire together, wire together; those that don't, won't" (Penn, 2001, p. 339).

The Dopaminergic System

About 100 neurotransmitters have been identified, but we are concerned only with the so-called "canonical" transmitters most used in biopsychosocial criminological research—dopamine and serotonin. Dopamine (DA) underlies many functions, particularly as a motivator of pleasure and reward behavior and regulating memory, emotion, and pleasure. Neurons whose principal neurotransmitter is DA are found primarily in the ventral tegmental area (VTA), the substantia nigra (SN), and the hypothalamus. Both the VTA and the SN are involved in reward and addictive behaviors. In the hypothalamus, which links the nervous system to the endocrine system, DA functions as a neurohormone and a precursor of the hormone/neurotransmitter norepinephrine. In the frontal lobes, DA regulates the information flow from other brain areas, and thus it is also a neuromodulator (Guo et al., 2010).

There are five subtypes of DA receptors with the DRD2 and DRD4 subtypes being the most studied. The dopamine D2 receptor gene (DRD2) is highly polymorphic, with attention being primarily focused on the Taq1A (or simply A1) single nucleotide polymorphism (SNP). This SNP is the substitution of thymine (in the A1 allele) for cytosine (in the A2 allele). Individuals homozygous for the A2 allele (A2/A2) have receptors with the highest binding potential for DA, A1/A1 homozygotes have the lowest binding potential, and A1/A2 heterozygotes are intermediate. The A1 allele is considered a risk allele, largely because it "is a contributor to the reward deficiency syndrome, which typifies people who need high levels of excitement and stimulation to activate their reward system in the same capacity as those with normally functioning reward systems" (DeLisi et al., 2009, p. 1189). This DRD2-A1 allele has been linked to many crime-related syndromes such as antisocial personality, ADHD, conduct disorder, serious and violent delinquency, and drug addiction (DiLisi et al., 2009). D2 receptor antagonists (drugs that block dopamine receptors) have been used for decades to treat aggressive behavior and violent outbursts among psychotic and dementia patients, as well as for individuals with aggressive conduct disorders and borderline personality disorder.

The dopamine transporter gene DAT1 largely determines the magnitude and the duration of synaptic DA signaling by transporting DA back into the presynaptic knob for repackaging after it has excited downstream neurons. The DAT1 gene contains 7, 9, 10, and 11 repeat alleles, with the 9R and 10R being the most common (Guo, Roettger, & Shih, 2007). The 10R is more efficient in the reuptake process than the other major repeat (9R), which implies less DA in the synaptic cleft available for activation (Miller-Butterworth et al., 2008). Because DA activates the "good time" nucleus accumbens, its rapid clearing from the synaptic cleft leads the person to seek more experiences that activate DA to experience normal levels of pleasure. These pleasures, legal or illegal, raise DA to levels that are experienced more easily with less behavioral activity by persons with slower DA reuptake.

Several studies have looked at the relationship of the DAT1-10R on risky sensation-seeking and/or antisocial behavior. For instance, Guo, Roettger, and Shih (2007) found that males homozygous for the 10R allele had 80–100% (depending on age category) more sex partners than males homozygous for the 9R version. Another study found that the DAT1-10R allele was significantly related to number of sex partners (a variable long known to be highly predictive of criminal activity, particularly psychopathy) and to antisocial behavior among a sample of 1,925 males between the ages of 18 and 26 (Beaver, Wright, & Walsh, 2008). We cannot consider an allele as common as the 10R as defective. It is more reasonable to think of the 9R as a conservative allele that confers lessened motivation to seek pleasure excessively or compulsively (Guo, Roettger, and Shih, 2007).

Studies examine the interaction of polymorphisms because their effects are conditioned by other polymorphisms and by the environment. A study by Eisenberg et al. (2007) revealed that the risk DRD2 allele (A1) had a statistically significant main effect on impulsiveness, but the DRD4 allele (7R) did not. Additional analyses indicated that DRD2 and DRD4 risk alleles interacted to predict impulsivity. Beaver et al. (2007) examined the same polymorphisms and found that neither had consistent main effects on antisocial behavior or conduct disorder, but all five models that included the interaction of the two genes (G*x*G) produced statistically significant results. Another study by DeLisi et al. (2008) found that controlling for age, race, gender, and low self-control, both polymorphisms were independently predictive of the age of first criminal arrest, as was their interaction. However, this was only true for youths at low environmental risk for antisocial behavior, once again underlining that we cannot fully understand gene effects without considering the environment and that all known genetic and environmental risks should be included in studies of antisocial behavior.

The Serotonergic System

Serotonin (5-HT) is an inhibitory neurotransmitter that plays a major role in maintaining a balance between other excitatory and inhibitory transmitters. Many of the effects of serotonin have to do with causing the levels of other neurotransmitters to increase or decrease in different brain regions. Central nervous system neurons containing serotonin originate in the raphe nuclei in the midbrain and project to multiple areas of the brain such as the brain stem, hippocampus, cerebellum, and PFC, which underlines its diverse targets consistent with the wide variety of behavior syndromes associated with neural serotonin. DA projections are mostly limited to the PFC and areas of the limbic system. Two of criminology's most invoked causal variables—low self-control and negative emotionality—are highly influenced by serotonin functioning. Because both traits are underlain by low serotonin functioning, it is contended that aberrant serotonergic functioning "may be a heritable diathesis for a personality style involving high levels of negative affect and low levels of constraint [self-control], which generates, in turn, a vulnerability to criminal behavior" (Caspi et al., 1994, p. 188).

How well neurotransmitters function depends on what receptors they bind to and the functional efficiency of their transportation, reuptake, and degradation. The serotonin transporter (5-HTT) is responsible for recycling serotonin from the synaptic gap back to the presynaptic neuron, thus terminating its effects and enabling reuse. Variants in 5-HTT's gene promoter, 5-HTTLPR, produce different transporter expressions. As we saw in the previous chapter, the 5-HTTLPR has short (s) and long (L) versions. The short variant is less efficient, which results in serotonin remaining in the synaptic gap longer and is recycled more slowly, resulting in a net reduction in circulating serotonin.

Serotonin escaping reuptake is degraded by the enzyme monoamine oxidase A (MAOA). The MAOA gene is a variable number of tandem repeats (VNTRs) polymorphism repeating between two and five times. The two and three repeats produce low (MAOA-L) promotor activity and the four and five repeats produce high (MAOA-H) activity. Studies suggest that individuals with the low activity version are more likely to react to challenges with aggression and impulsivity. Brain imaging studies have shown that MAOA-L males show greater activity in the amygdala and lower activity in the regulatory prefrontal areas during emotional arousal, which suggests the emotional and cognitive channels that link MAOA-L to impulsive aggression (Mrazek et al., 2013). The amygdala is a major target for serotonin. A meta-analysis of functional magnetic resonance imaging (fMRI) studies showed that individuals with the short variant of 5-HTTLPR have heightened amygdala sensitivity; that is, the amygdala fires sooner, stronger, and more frequently (Munafo, Brown, & Hariri, 2008). Kolla and Bortolato (2020) note that neuroimaging studies have shown that MAOA-L individuals exhibit abnormalities in cortico-amygdaloid connectivity, diminished PFC activity during inhibitory control tasks, and heightened limbic responsiveness to emotional arousal, and that this evidence supports "the idea that MAOA in the PFC exerts a key role in evaluating the emotional salience of socio-affective cues and enacting adaptive responses" (p. 21).

The MAOA-L allele is possessed by 40% of American males and thus cannot be considered an independent risk for criminal behavior. For it to be a risk it requires environmental input (G*x*E). The landmark G*x*E study of MAOA and criminal behavior is the longitudinal cohort study of Caspi et al. (2002). The environmental risk was verified as child maltreatment, and the genetic risk was the MAOA-L allele. The criminal and maltreatment histories that males had accumulated by the age of 26 were verified via official police and social service records. No main effects for MAOA were found, but there were strong G*x*E effects. Males with low MAOA-L who were maltreated constituted only 12% of the cohort but were responsible for 44% of its violent convictions; the odds of these males having a violent crime conviction was 9.8 times greater than the odds of MAOA-H males who were not maltreated having such a record. The maltreatment-non-maltreatment groups did not differ significantly in MAOA activity, thus ruling out evocative rGE effects. That is, low MAOA activity did not contribute to child maltreatment via children's evocative behavior because the groups did not differ on the proportion carrying the risk allele.

A meta-analysis of the MAOA-maltreatment studies concluded that the interaction between MAOA and maltreatment is a statistically significant predictor of antisocial behavior across studies (Kim-Cohen et al., 2006). Another meta-analysis concluded: "Across 20 male cohorts, early adversity presaged antisocial outcomes more strongly for low-activity, relative to high-activity, MAOA genotype ($p = .0044$). Stratified analyses showed the interaction specific to maltreatment ($p = .00000082$) and robust to several sensitivity analyses" (Byrd & Manuck, 2014, p. 9). There are several nuances in this relationship. Widom and Brzustowicz (2006) found that while the high-activity MAOA allele buffered Whites from the effects of childhood abuse and neglect, it did not protect Blacks and Hispanics. The authors suggest that other environmental stressors may have negated the protective power of the genotype among non-Whites. Beaver, Barnes, and Boutwell (2014) looked at the MAOA 2-repeat allele, which confers the greatest risk for antisocial behavior. The 2-repeat allele is carried only by 0.1% of White males and 5.2% of Black males, so they limited the analysis to Black males ($n = 133$). They found a significant odds ratio of 12.89 between carriers of the 2-repeat allele for males who reported shooting or stabbing someone and carriers of all other alleles independent of environmental controls.

Gender is another demographic variable to consider. The MAOA gene is situated on the X chromosome, thus males have one copy whereas females have two. Females may be either homozygous or heterozygous for any variant. Holz et al. (2016) used fMRI to assess the MAOA-stress G*x*E in stress-processing areas of the brain for males and females. In proportion to the stress levels they were exposed to in childhood, male MAOA-L subjects displayed greater activity in the amygdala and hippocampus in reaction to fearful and angry faces and lower inhibitory control, as shown by decreased anterior cingulate cortex activity when performing a response inhibition task. MAOA-H males showed less emotional reactivity and better inhibitory control. Females, however, showed opposite effects. The Holz team found that in females homozygous for the MAOA-H variant, activity in the hippocampus and amygdala increased with the level of childhood life stress but, similarly to males, activity decreased in those who were homozygous for the MAOA-L variant. Likewise, in a longitudinal study of over 2,000 females, Byrd et al. (2019) found that the antisocial "risk" allele for maltreated females is the high-activity variant of the MAOA gene rather than the low-activity variant, as in males.

Serotonin plays an important role in brain development: "Serotonin acts as a growth factor during embryogenesis, and serotonin receptor activity forms a crucial part of the cascade of events leading to changes in brain structure" (Sodhi & Sanders-Bush, 2004, p. 111). If serotonin is not effectively metabolized it could lead to toxic levels that may result in aberrant brain development. Meyer-Lindenberg et al. (2006) examined brain structures in over 200 individuals with either the low- or high-activity variant of the MAOA gene. Using fMRI, they found that relative to MAOA-H subjects, MAOA-L subjects showed pronounced limbic volume reductions and hyper-responsiveness of the amygdala and hippocampus during emotional arousal. Male subjects showed impaired cingulate activity during cognitive tasks and a 14% increase in orbitofrontal cortex volume, which the researchers attributed to deficient synaptic pruning and thus impaired functioning.

We cannot directly measure neurotransmitters in live subjects, but it is assumed that their cerebrospinal fluid (CSF) metabolites reflect their activities in the brain. The metabolites of serotonin and DA are 5-hydroxyindoleactic acid (5-HIAA) and homovanillic acid (HVA), respectively. The ratios of these metabolites are balanced for most people, reflecting normal serotonin and DA functioning. A study of 28 violent Swedish offenders assessed the relationship between PCL-R psychopathy scores and HVA:5-HIAA ratios. It was found that increasing ratios of CFS HVA to 5-HIAA were strongly related to psychopathic personality traits ($r = .50$, $p < .01$) and psychopathic behavioral aspects ($r = .523$, $p < .004$). A high HVA:5-HIAA ratio implies high dopamine turnover and/or deficient serotonergic regulation of the dopamine system indicating deficits in serotonin-mediated control of impulses (Soderstrom et al. 2003). Thus, psychopaths tend to have a reward-dominant brain and poor behavioral controls since approach and avoidance-related behaviors are thought to be determined by the balance between DA and serotonin activity. Likewise, a study of dementia patients found that the HVA:5-HIAA ratio correlated with aggressiveness scores ($r = 0.59$; $p = 0.033$) (Engelborghs et al., 2004).

Experience-Expected and Experience-Dependent Brain Development

The brain is always a work in progress and depends on environmental input. Neuroscientists distinguish between two synaptogenesis developmental processes: experience-expected and experience-dependent (McLaughlin, Weissman, & Bitrán, 2019). Experience-expected development involves critical periods of brain development that encode the evolutionarily expected environment that cannot be left to the vicissitudes of the environment. The brain "expects" to encounter certain experiences when its circuitry is especially responsive to them and will organize our experiences so that we will respond consistently and stereotypically to them (Geary, 2005). Brain maturational processes always occur "as expected" in genetically normal individuals born into the normal range of human environments. Individuals who experience gross departures from these species-expected environments may experience many negative outcomes (Twardosz & Lutzker, 2010). The distinction between experience-dependent and -expected development is highlighted by language. The *capacity* for language is an entirely genetic hard-wired experience-expected species-wide capacity that is not learned in the traditional sense but absorbed as if by osmosis. The experience-expected nature of language explains why children acquire language effortlessly but struggle to learn evolutionarily novel things such as calculus. The language(s) a person speaks is entirely an experience-dependent cultural artifact.

In experience-expected development, all brains depend on the same experiences to develop normally, but in experience-dependent development, differences in brain development depend on the experiences people encounter. Experience-dependent mechanisms reflect the brain's plasticity as experiences are *physically* captured during an organism's life, particularly during its early life via synaptic strengthening or pruning. As Koukkou and Lehmann (2006, p. 47) explain: "experience-dependent plasticity refers to the learning and memory mechanisms that extract personal meaning out of the interaction of individuals with their environment and that lead to the genesis of the neuronal networks that represent autobiographical memory." Individuals will thus vary in the efficiency of their brain functioning as their genes interact with their environments to construct their brain's synaptic wiring patterns. Depue and Collins (1999, p. 507) emphasize that: "experience-dependent processes are central to understanding personality as a dynamic developmental construct that involves the collaboration of genetic and environmental influences across the lifespan."

Although brain plasticity is greatest in infancy and early childhood, it is maintained to a lesser degree across the lifespan as the brain is shaped and reshaped. As Perry and Pollard (1998, p. 36) point out: "Experience in adults *alters* the *organized* brain, but in infants and children it *organizes* the *developing* brain." Brains organized by stressful and traumatic events tend to relay future events along the same pathways laid out by early events because pathways laid down during a critical period of life are more resistant to elimination than pathways laid down later. As Kolb and Gibb (2011, p. 272) remark, "There is little doubt that the parent-child relationships are critical and that they play a key role in brain development. Differences in the pattern of early maternal-infant interactions can initiate long-term developmental effects that persist into adulthood." This underlines the necessity of prevention and intervention programs that prioritize at-risk children as early as possible.

The Triple Imbalance Hypothesis

The triple imbalance hypothesis (TIH) is a theory that attempts to account for reactive violence by imbalances in three interacting neurohormonal systems: the subcortical, cortical-subcortical, and cortical (Van Honk et al., 2010). The subcortical imbalance hypothesis maintains that aggression is the result of an imbalance between the steroid hormones cortisol (low) and testosterone (high). High testosterone (T) levels and low cortisol levels are implicated because T facilitates dominance striving and approach behavior while cortisol motivates withdrawal, and both high T and low cortisol reduce fear and anxiety. T (an anabolic steroid) is the end product of the hypothalamic-pituitary-gonadal (HPG) axis, and cortisol (a catabolic steroid) is the end product of the hypothalamic-pituitary-adrenal (HPA) axis. These axes have mutually inhibiting effects. Stress-induced activation of the HPA axis results in high cortisol, which reduces T, and high T levels inhibit the adrenal glands to stimulate the release of cortisol (Brownlee, Moore, & Hackney, 2005). High T:cortisol ratios are associated with significantly increased activation of the hypothalamus and the amygdala which are important components of the subcortical reactive stress circuit. As Terburg, Morgan, and van Honk (2009, p. 217) remark: "High testosterone/low cortisol ratios seem to predict approach motivation/

reward sensitivity. In these motivational stances, individuals are more likely to confront threat, which could result in aggressive behavior. A high testosterone/cortisol ratio therefore predisposes for socially aggressive behaviors."

The cortical-subcortical imbalance maintains that high T levels decrease the coupling of the cortical-subcortical regions and impede information transfer between the orbitofrontal cortex (OFC) and the amygdala. There are dense connections between the OFC and the amygdala, underlining the critical role of the OFC in guiding and monitoring fear-generated violent responses. The OFC interprets amygdala activity, but the ability of the OFC to appropriately guide emotional behavior depends on balanced input from the amygdala. Communication deficits between the systems may cause high levels of reactive aggression (Mehta & Beer, 2009). Much of the evidence from imaging studies of OFC-amygdala disconnectedness comes from studies of individuals with intermittent explosive disorder (IED). IED is impulsive, emotionally driven aggression, which is out of proportion to provocation. Coccaro et al. (2007) found that IED patients exhibited exaggerated amygdala reactivity and diminished OFC activation relative to controls when presented with images of angry faces.

The cortical imbalance focuses on left-side frontal cortex dominance and serotonergic activity. Left-side dominance predicts approach behavior and the right avoidance behavior (Schutter et al., 2008). Anger predicts increased left and decreased right frontal activity (Hewig et al., 2006). Using transcranial magnetic stimulation, researchers can manipulate cortical excitability by stimulating (reducing or increasing) left- or right-side activity of the frontal cortex. These studies led Van Honk et al. (2002, p. 86) to propose that extreme left-side imbalance indicates "a state of readiness to respond to social threat with anger and aggression rather than fear and submission." It has also been proposed that low serotonergic functioning promotes reactive aggression in individuals with high T:cortisol ratios because low serotonin is associated with impulsiveness and aggression (Dolan, Anderson, & Deakin, 2001). It is well established that T modulates serotonergic receptor activity in ways that can result in violence by influencing serotonin functioning in the OFC and enhancing amygdala reactivity to social threat cues (Mehta & Beer, 2009).

In their review and evaluation of the TIH, Angus et al. (2016) note that impairment of the functional connectivity between the OFC and the amygdala has been observed in fMRI studies in which T was administered to subjects. They also note that in EEG studies, coupling between slow-frequency delta waves (subcortical) and high-frequency beta waves (localized in the PFC) decreases with the administration of T, and that cortisol administration increases connectivity. As for cortical imbalance, they state: "Left-sided frontal electric cortical asymmetries have also been found within the psychopathic population and in imprisoned violent offenders, providing a neural correlate that could explain the approach-motivation-related lifestyle of these individuals that includes sensation seeking, risk taking, and aggression" (2016, p. 231). Convergent lines of evidence thus provide strong support for the TIH and biopsychosocial assessment and treatment for violent offenders.

5

THE SOCIAL EMOTIONS AND CONSCIENCE

Conscience: The Whisper of God

An abstract phenomenon, albeit with physical referents, resides in human beings and is known as a conscience. The conscience is an inner voice that informs us that it is wrong to do harmful things to others, and right to behave well toward them. The voice is strong in some people and weak to non-existent in others. It is an emotional voice felt in the limbic system informed by cognitive content that is engaged when what we are doing or thinking about doing does not conform to learned moral standards of right and wrong. The great theologian Thomas Aquinas once called the inward testimony of conscience the "whisper of God" guiding our behavior in conformity with righteousness. Charles Darwin asserted that conscience is based on: "the social instincts—the prime principle of man's moral constitution—with the aid of active intellectual powers and the effects of habit, naturally lead to the golden rule" (1981, p. 106). In common with biopsychosocial criminology, Darwin emphasized the social instincts—the emotions—as the physiological basis of conscience. Of course, conscience is not only about emotions; it is a combination of cognitive faculties that provide the information about what is morally and ethically right or wrong and the affective faculties that we "feel" when we behave or contemplate behaving in a moral or ethical right or wrong way.

The place of emotion as a positive guide to behavior is foreign to many criminologists who see emotions only in negative terms, such as describing a crime as one of passion. Caught in the Enlightenment image of humans as rational animals, most criminological theories assume that

DOI: 10.4324/9781003642268-7

rationality is the primary guide of human behavior and that emotions are "pathological," as Immanuel Kant called them, or "confused passions," as Gottfried Leibniz described them (Soloman, 1977, p. 41). This has led to an image of humans devoid of passion and relying only on cold rationality as a guide to behavior with emotions, in Leibnizian parlance, confusing the issue. Almost alone among the Enlightenment philosophers, David Hume believed that the human species should be labeled *Homo emovere* ("emotional man") rather than *Homo sapiens*. In Hume's thought, "we perceive a situation, experience emotions, pass judgment on the situation based on the emotion it evokes, and only then do we attempt to provide *post hoc* rational reasons for that judgment" (Walsh, 2014, p. 216). Emotional stimuli are highly relevant to human behavior, enabling us to quickly detect and react to situations deemed important for positive social relationships before we have time to reflect on them.

Hume's insight is supported by neuroscience claims that rationality plays handmaiden to emotion: "Neuroscientific studies have proven that most decision-making is based primarily on emotional and not rational processing of information" (Alsharif, Salleh, & Baharun, 2021, p. 72). Emotions arise in the limbic system, which predates the evolution of the "rational" prefrontal lobes by at least a million years (Suwa et al., 2009). As Douglas Massey (2002, p. 15) notes: "Emotionality clearly preceded rationality in evolutionary sequence, and as rationality developed it did not replace emotionality as the basis for human interaction. Rather, rational abilities were gradually added to preexisting and simultaneously developing emotional capacities." Jonathan Haidt (2001, p. 819) also notes the primacy of emotions: "It [emotion] comes first in phylogeny, it emerges first in ontogeny, it is triggered more quickly in real-time judgments, and it is more powerful and irrevocable [than rationality] when the two systems yield conflicting judgments." Neuroscience research has shown that emotion and cognition are integrated in the lateral prefrontal cortex which weighs cognitive/affective motivational input from their respective brain areas to guide our responses (Pessoa et al., 2019). Emotion and reason always operate simultaneously in a complementary fashion, with reason sometimes stronger and emotion sometimes stronger, but when they conflict, the more ancient system of responding will triumph (Etkin, Egner, & Kalisch, 2011). The thornier the decision, the more it will engage emotions.

The anterior cingulate cortex (ACC), an area that abuts the lateral prefrontal cortex, also plays a significant role in mediating cognitive influences on emotion and emotional influences on cognition: "The anterior cingulate cortex (ACC) lies in a unique position in the brain, with connections to both the 'emotional' limbic system and the 'cognitive' prefrontal cortex" (Stevens, Hurley, & Taber, 2011, p. 121). Several neuroimaging studies have shown considerable ACC activity as subjects experience emotional conflicts between approach ("Should I go for it?") and avoidance stimuli ("No, it's not right," or "No, it's too risky") (Amodio, Devine, & Harmon-Jones, 2007). It is thus not surprising that the ACC has been described as "provid[ing] for civilized discourse, conflict resolution, and fundamental human socialization" (Tancredi, 2005, p. 36). Consistent with this, it has been found in neuroimaging studies that the ACC is involved in the maturation of self-control, and subjects that have low self-control who suffer from attention deficit hyperactivity disorder (ADHD) do not show a normal response in the ACC to the counting Stroop task (a measure of reaction times between congruent and incongruent stimuli), and there is evidence of increased functioning of the ACC among individuals with greater social maturity and insight (Stevens, Hurley, & Taber, 2011).

It is hardly news that criminals have poorly developed consciences. Most do not feel guilt or shame when inflicting harm on others. They are cognitively aware that their activities violate standards of moral decency, but either they don't care or can neutralize any feelings that damper their antisocial activities. Many follow their nefarious lifestyle without experiencing the pangs of conscience because they have faulty pathways connecting their brain's rational and emotional networks. Among neuroscientists, this is the defining characteristic of chronic criminals and psychopaths (Patrick, 2022). Psychopaths know what is right and wrong as well as the rest of us, but poorly integrated rational and emotional systems lead them to discount their knowledge and to behave according to the self-centered emotional call of immediate self-gratification.

Neuroscientists can analyze the volume and structural integrity of the pathways integrating the rational and emotional systems using diffusion tensor imaging (DTI). Craig et al. (2009) used DTI with violent criminals with Hare's Psychopathy Check List Revised (PCL-R) scores ranging between 25 and 34 (30 is the cutoff point for a diagnosis of psychopathy) and controls matched for IQ. They examined the uncinate fasciculus (UF), a white matter tract connecting the anterior temporal lobes (home of the amygdala) with the frontal lobes. Significant correlations between PCL-R factor 2 scores and tract volume in both the left and right UF ($r = -0.88$) were found. Psychopaths also had a significantly reduced fractional anisotropy (FA) in the right UC. FA is a mathematical measure ranging from zero (isotropy) to 1 (anisotropy) providing information about water diffusion along myelinated axons. Isotropy is random movement in all directions, and anisotropy is directional and non-random, and thus higher FA values signal greater integrity of the connection between brain areas.

Craig et al. conclude: "Taken together, our findings suggest that abnormal connectivity in the amygdala-OFC limbic network may contribute to the neurobiological mechanisms underpinning the impulsive, antisocial behaviour and emotional detachment associated with psychopathy" (p. 950). A similar study of prison inmates with PLC-R scores ranging from 5 to 36 found PCL-R scores to be significantly inversely related in a graded fashion to right UC FA scores and that psychopaths had significantly lower UF FA than inmates with lower psychopathy scores (Wolf et al., 2015).

The Primary and Secondary Emotions

Psychologists differentiate between primary emotions such as anger, fear, disgust, and joy, which we share with all animals, and secondary, or social emotions, which we may or may not share with some other species. The terms "primary" and "secondary" should not be seen as signaling levels of importance because secondary emotions are vital to functional human relationships. Primary emotions are our immediate visceral reactions to situations, and secondary emotions are reactions to how we might feel after we experience a primary emotion. For instance, when we become angry, we may feel the secondary emotions of guilt or shame, but people with weak consciences will not. The primary emotions have been useful in human evolution. Fear, anger, and disgust focus our attention on an immediate unpleasant situation and narrow our responses toward alleviating it. Anger directed at injustice may prevent similar injustices in the future, fear and disgust motivate escape and avoidance, and joy is a feeling we have when we experience an unexpectedly pleasant outcome. In evolutionary environments, this would have meant encountering situations that impacted biological fitness, such as finding new food, water, and sexual opportunities that motivated our ancestors to seek similar rewarding situations.

Social emotions such as empathy, shame, embarrassment, and guilt are retrofitted to the primary emotions as mixtures that broaden rather than narrow our focus and are vital to developing and strengthening social bonds. They evolved as essential parts of our social intelligence because they provide cues about the kinds of relationships (cooperative vs. uncooperative) we are likely to have with other humans. Emotions such as empathy and guilt adjust our social behavior by arousing, focusing, and modifying brain activity, leading most people to habitually choose prosocial rather than antisocial responses when they experience anger or encounter a criminal opportunity. To take advantage of a criminal opportunity may be rational in the short term since it provides resources with little effort, but it is self-defeating in the long run. We find it easier to appreciate short-term rewards (activating immediate pleasure) than long-term consequences (activating prosocial concerns of the conscience). It is the alarm bells sounded by the limbic system and the autonomic nervous system (ANS) arousing the social emotions that prompt most people to attend to long-term consequences (self-control) rather than surrender to the temptations of the moment.

Because others typically react negatively toward those who violate prosocial norms, it is adaptive to have evolved social emotions such as guilt and shame to monitor and restrain antisocial impulses. Social emotions are self-conscious emotions that evoke self-reflection and evaluation of behavior that occurs consciously or subconsciously. If we do something harmful to others, it is socially functional to be motivated to take remedial action. Guilt involves anxiety, remorse, and concern about how one's actions have negatively impacted others. It motivates both avoidance and approach behavior because it is psychologically punitive motivating us to avoid the transgression in the future. It also motivates approach behavior by moving one toward reparation (apologies, promises, and restitution). Guilt is positively related to empathy since we are not likely to feel bad about offending others if we don't "feel their pain" (Silfver & Klaus, 2008). Social emotions are important for understanding criminal behavior because they are the components of conscience. The bite of conscience keeps us on the straight and narrow, and the relative lack of this bite grants permission to criminals to prey on others.

Empathy and Callous-Unemotionality

Empathy has been described as the social emotion par excellence (Pfattheicher, Sassenrath, & Keller, 2019). It is the cognitive and emotional ability to understand and identify with the feelings and distress of others: a form of compassionate relatedness. Empathy is a potent inhibitor of victimizing behavior, and empathy-related responding is an important facilitator of social cooperation. Empathy is an ancient capacity that predates the arrival of *Homo sapiens* by millions of years and evolved rapidly in mammals in the context of parental care (de Waal, 2008). It is reasonable to assume that the well-documented sex differences in empathy levels that favor females are the result of a strong evolutionary selection for it because of the human female role in prolonged and intensive infant care (Silke et al., 2018). Because most people feel distress personally when they witness the distress of others (a kind of affective resonance between self and others), they alleviate their own distress if they can alleviate the distress of others. People with a high resting heart rate (HRHR) are more affected by stress, and thus it is not surprising that HRHR people are more empathetic than people with normal or low resting heart rates (Lischke et al., 2018). Empathy channels helping behavior in social species because it is a response mode by which conspecifics can rapidly asses a situation without having to rely on time-consuming conscious reflection to determine the appropriate helping response (Roach & Pease, 2013).

Studies have found heritability estimates of empathy increase monotonically from infancy to old age (Knafo & Uzefovsky, 2013). Affective empathy has a larger genetic component than cognitive empathy because the latter involves learning. Melchers et al. (2016) found heritability estimates for affective empathy of between 0.52 and 0.57 among MZ, DZ, and sibling pairs of adults ranging from 18 to 58 years of age, but a much lower average estimate of 0.27 for cognitive empathy. Similarly, a meta-analysis of the genetics of empathy (Abramson et al., 2020) noted that genetics accounted for an average of 48.3% of the variance in emotional empathy and 26.9% in cognitive empathy. All the remaining variance in emotional empathy was accounted for by non-shared environment and measurement error, whereas shared environment accounted for 9.2% of the variance in cognitive empathy. The heritability differences between the two components of empathy may be explained by the fact that emotional empathy is more tied to innate temperamental traits and physiology, such as emotional reactivity and regulation while cognitive empathy has a much larger learned component (Abramson et al., 2020). Parent-child relationship quality (warmth, attachment security, consistent discipline practices) is robustly linked to the development of children's cognitive empathy and to its fine-tuning (Waller & Hyde, 2018).

Among the many antonyms for empathy are apathy, coldness, and indifference which researchers place under the umbrella of callous-unemotionality (CU), and childhood CU is viewed as a key precursor for adult psychopathy (Hyde & Dotterer, 2022). CU traits are consistently linked to reduced amygdala responses to socio-affective cues such as fearful expressions (Cardinale et al., 2018; Dugré et al., 2020). Typically, fearful expressions of others elicit empathy in observers, but among people with CU traits empathic responding is reduced, making them more willing to victimize others. A meta-analysis revealed statistically significant moderate-to-large negative associations between measures of CU traits and empathy ($r = -0.57$), guilt ($r = -0.40$), and pro-sociality ($r = -0.66$) (Waller et al., 2020). CU youths may be deficient in social emotions, but not in the primary emotions, as Waller et al. (2020, p. 9) note:

> whereas youth high on CU traits are "unemotional" in response to others' distress (i.e., low empathic arousal or concern), they exhibit strong and wide-ranging emotions in other contexts, including showing

anger when their goals are frustrated or joy after breaking the rules and getting away with it.

Bezdjian et al. (2011) found heritability estimates for CU traits to be 0.64 for males and 0.49 for females in a sample of 605 twins and non-shared environmental effects of 0.36 for boys and 0.44 for girls, which implies zero shared environment effects for boys but 7% for girls. We are reminded again that heritability estimates are not the extent to which a person's traits are due to genes, but to the extent to which variance in those traits among people in the particular population studied is due to genes. Nurture is also important: "One of the nurture risk factors that has been most studied specifically with regard to CU traits is parenting. A growing literature links harsh parenting and parenting that is low in warmth and involvement to CU traits" (Hyde & Dotterer, 2022, p. 549). However, Hyde and Dotterer (2022) note that the association between parenting and CU traits could exist because parents and children share common genes (passive rGE), and harsh parenting may reflect parent's CU traits. Alternatively, they suggest that children's CU traits elicit negative reactions from their parents (evocative rGE). It has been shown that harsh parenting is moderated by inherited risk for CU, especially among children with elevated genetic risk (Trentacosta et al., 2019).

Lack of warm nurturing in a child's early years impacts their neuroarchitecture. Chugani et al. (2001) used positron emission tomography (PET)-to scan a sample of Romanian orphanage children after they had resided in American foster homes for an average of 5.6 years. Compared with control subjects, these children showed significantly decreased metabolism in areas most related to psychopathy and CU—the PFC and the amygdala. Eluvathingal et al. (2006) examined the UF in Romanian orphanage children matched with controls using DTI. FA values were significantly smaller ($p = .003$) in the left uncinate in the orphan children compared with controls. This study shows that children who suffer early emotional deprivation may develop a number of the neurobiological abnormalities seen in CU and psychopathy.

Youths with CU are often found to have bold and fearless temperaments and low fear may be expected to lead to high levels of approach behavior, reward dominance, and low sensitivity to punishment (Berluti, Ploe, & Marsh, 2023; Trentacosta et al., 2019). Fear is a vital evolved response to danger; if we didn't experience it, we wouldn't be able to take steps to protect ourselves from threats. According to Lykken (1995, p. 144): "Like the ability to experience pain, the fear mechanism is especially useful early in life before the individual's judgment and reason are sufficiently dependable guides to behavior." Reasonable levels of fear are useful in viscerally guiding children's behavior in the desired direction before their cognitive understanding of what kinds of behavior are expected of them, but relative fearlessness makes it difficult to appreciate danger and gives rise to the tendency to take risks and to favor approach over avoidance behavior in potentially rewarding situations.

The Autonomic Nervous System and Conscience

Robert Levenson has remarked: "When it comes to emotion, all roads lead to the autonomic nervous system (ANS). Whether it is the generation, expression, experience, or recognition of emotion, the role of the ANS is critical" (2014, p. 100). Each emotional episode we experience involves the ANS activity, and the strength of an emotion depends on both innate temperament and classical conditioning. The ANS coordinates a complex network of nerves, organs, and sensors distributed throughout the body. It is a major control system that functions unconsciously to automatically maintain homeostasis in the viscera such as the heart, lungs, kidneys, and other internal organs, but we are only concerned here with its role in helping to determine the strength of the conscience. The ANS has two branches: the sympathetic system ("fight or flight") and the parasympathetic system ("rest and digest"). When we perceive a threat, amygdala-associated networks send signals to the sympathetic branch to mobilize the body to fight, flee, or sometimes freeze. The body pumps out epinephrine and norepinephrine to dilate the pupils and lungs, increase the heart rate, and many other things. When the threat is over, the parasympathetic system restores the body to homeostasis.

Humans are not born with a desire to behave according to social norms and live in their limbic worlds for much of their early childhood. They throw temper tantrums, strike out, and take what they like whenever the urge strikes them because nothing matters except their immediate desires. In Freudian terms, they are controlled by the raw energy of the id, but most slowly come to realize and appreciate the rights and feelings of others. Parents must teach their children to behave in socially acceptable ways by providing positive and negative consequences for their actions. The success of this endeavor depends on many things, including parental willingness and ability to monitor their children's behavior, the warmth of the attachment relationships children have with parents, and how effectively children have been reinforced for good behavior and punished for bad behavior during the socialization process. The best predictor of how well a child learns moral lessons is the physiology he or she brings to the socialization process (Choy, Farrington, & Raine, 2015).

The ratio of rewards to punishments a child experiences engages operant conditioning, but classical conditioning is most salient in the early stages of conscience development (Choy, Farrington, & Raine, 2015). Classical conditioning is mostly passive and visceral as opposed to operant conditioning which is active in forming mental associations between behavior and its consequences. Classical conditioning forms subconscious associations between our behavior and our visceral responses. For instance, if a child behaves aggressively toward another and receives parental rebuke, it should produce internal unpleasant affective states such as anxiety, guilt, or shame. These unpleasant feelings should lead to the decision to desist from similar behavior in the future, but these feelings are not experienced as equally unpleasant for everyone. How well our moral lessons are learned depends primarily on the level of our ANS arousal—how quickly and strongly it reacts to clues of immanent disciplinary responses to our behavior. Choy, Farrington, and Raine (2015, p. 190) explain the route from low ANS arousal to conscience:

> Lower levels of arousal cause poorer conditioning to environmental stimuli. It is assumed that the strength of the conscience depends on children's passive avoidance conditioning by parents. Impaired conditioning may result in the absence of or decrease in anticipatory anxiety regarding the consequences of a criminal or antisocial act, which causes a weak conscience.

ANS arousal thresholds are often measured by heart rate. A low resting heart rate (<60 beats per minute) has been called the "best-replicated biological correlate of antisocial behavior in child and adolescent populations" (Ortiz & Raine, 2004, p. 159). Choy, Farrington, and Raine (2015, p. 194) report that "lower heart rate was strongly and consistently associated with active disregard reflected by negative and aggressive responses to others distress and higher heart rate was associated with greater empathy and likelihood of intervening to help."

ANS arousal measures are normally distributed, with most individuals clustered around the mean. Individuals at the *hyper*arousable tail of the distribution are easily aroused by punishment cues (fear) and will thus avoid behaving in ways that signal those cues. They learn their prosocial lessons well because arousal produces punishing visceral feelings indicative of anxiety, fear, and shame (rapid heart rate, flushing, "butterflies" in the stomach). When hyperarousable individuals contemplate behaving contrary to social expectations, memories of the consequences they experienced in childhood when they behaved badly flood the amygdala and engage the ANS to produce anxiety or fear. When they subconsciously decide not to act on their impulse the parasympathetic system engages to restore the ANS to homeostasis, which amounts to physiological reinforcement (reward) for conforming behavior. Barkow (1989, p. 121) describes the emotional component of the conscience as an involuntary "limbic system override" that adjusts our behavior in conforming ways.

Thus, the degree to which the sympathetic ANS is activated in the face of threat and/or the speed at which the parasympathetic returns the body to homeostasis is a major determinant of conscience development (Gao et al., 2010). The development of conscience involves more than cognitive mechanisms since a developed conscience typically moves us to do the "right" thing before we have had an opportunity to cognitively assess our options (Barkow's "limbic system override"). People with strong moral consciences habitually ignore criminal opportunities; they do not consciously calculate cost:benefit ratios before ignoring them. Rational contemplation provides the content of our conscience; that is, the lessons we learn relating to what things we should feel guilty, ashamed, and embarrassed about, and what things we should feel good about, but the conscience's strength, power, and resilience are provided by emotion.

Conscience is thus the cooperative output of limbic emotional and prefrontal rational cognitive mechanisms, which enables us to internalize the moral norms of our society. Simply being cognitively aware of what is right or wrong is not enough; that knowledge must be paired with emotional salience for it to be effective. Even the worst criminals of sound mind know the rational words of the social contract, but their poor emotional voices render them unsuited for the social choir. Individuals with a strong conscience will feel guilt, shame, and anxiety when they violate social norms, but those with a weak conscience will not experience these emotions. As Kochanska and Aksan (2004, p. 304) put it: "An impaired conscience is the core aspect of conduct disorders, antisocial development, and psychopathy. Conversely, the capacity for remorse and empathy, an appreciation of right and wrong, and engaging in behavior compatible with rules all mark successful adaptation."

Several studies have shown that young males living in criminogenic environments who remain free of their influence show hyperactive ANS arousal under conditions of threat (Lacourse et al., 2006). Youths with highly reactive ANSs reared in criminogenic environments are less likely to commit antisocial acts than youths with hyporeactive ANS arousal reared in non-criminogenic environments (Brennan et al., 1997). A longitudinal study of a birth cohort found that measures of poor ANS conditioning (measured electro-dermally) at age 3 successfully predicted criminal offending (official records) at age 23 independent of controls for a variety of social adversities (Gao et al., 2010). Moffitt and Walsh (2003) attribute hyperactive ANSs to those rare individuals who abstained from antisocial behavior altogether during adolescence. Individuals with hypoactive ANSs, on the other hand, are not viscerally reinforced for conforming behavior because they are not aroused to fear in the first place and thus cannot receive positive reinforcement for conforming behavior by way of a return to ANS homeostasis.

Our discussion of conscience and physiological arousal levels leads us to what Walsh and Vaske (2015, p. 168) call "the natural enemies of crime"—fear and empathy:

> Empathy is other-oriented and prevents one from committing acts injurious to others because one has an emotional and cognitive investment in the well-being of others. Fear is self-oriented and prevents one from committing acts injurious to others out of fear of the consequences to one's self. Many other prosocial tendencies flow from these two basic foundations, such as a strong conscience, altruism, self-control, and agreeableness.

Treatment Protocols

Treatment protocols for delinquents and criminals that specifically address their low fear and low empathy are, to my knowledge, non-existent. How do we normalize physiological fear responses in low-fear delinquents and criminals to decrease their offending and increase their empathy? If anything can be done, these individuals have to be identified via various physiological measures such as heart rate and stress response, which are rarely, if ever, done by correctional treatment personnel. Differentiating offenders according to their biopsychosocial profiles can lead to individualized treatment plans akin to individualized medical treatment plans rather than forging ahead with a one-size-fits-all mentality and may enhance treatment outcomes. The task is daunting, but not impossible if clinicians integrate biopsychosocial measures into their treatment designs as outlined in Chapter 16. However, biopsychosocial markers are not necessarily more determinant of crime than social risk factors, and prevention is always better than treatment so, for now, we reiterate what was said in Chapter 1—the best cure for crime is a stable two-parent family in which children are provided with warm and loving nurturing and consistent disciplinary practices.

PART III

Traditional Criminology Theories and Prevention and Treatment Policies

6

HUMAN ECOLOGY/SOCIAL DISORGANIZATION THEORY AND POLICY

Human Ecology

All crime prevention policies are premised on a theory or theories that purport to explain why crime occurs, and the theory most often chosen to guide policymakers is understandably the theory that is most in vogue among criminologists at the time. The first real effort at crime prevention aimed at something other than building more prisons was animated by human ecology theory. This theory was the first criminological theory to be developed in the United States and formulated primarily by Clifford Shaw and Henry McKay (1972) at the University of Chicago during the 1920s and 1930s. Human ecology borrowed from biology the idea of the relationship between organisms and their environments with intentions of "achieving a thorough-going natural science treatment of human behavior" (Hawley, 1944, p. 400). *Ecology* describes the interrelationships of plants and animals and their environment—how each affects and is affected by the other. However, because Shaw and McKay were schooled in the sociological tradition that does not like gazing below social facts to look at more fundamental mechanisms, they looked only at how environments affect people and neglected how people affect their environments.

Long-term occupation of a particular ecological niche implies a high level of adaptation to it among the organisms occupying it. Over time, the niche becomes a "natural area" for them, and organisms enjoy symbiotic relationships with it. However, if non-native species invade these niches, they may eventually come to dominate them and drive native species to extinction. An example is the problems in the southeastern United States

DOI: 10.4324/9781003642268-9

caused by an alien plant introduced from Japan called kudzu. Kudzu is a fast-growing semi-woody vine that grows at a rate of about a foot per day. It outcompetes all native flora by growing around them, blocking sunlight, siphoning off their moisture, and suffocating them, leading to cascading negative effects throughout an ecosystem. This process of invasion, dominance, and succession, describing the occupation of ecological niches by a species of plant or animal life previously occupied by other species, was borrowed whole and imported into human ecology.

Human ecology describes the relations of humans and the environments in which they live and views neighborhoods as "natural areas" differentially adaptive for different ethnic groups (e.g., Little Italy, Chinatown, Pole Town, and so forth). When these natural areas are invaded by alien racial or ethnic groups (human kudzu, so to speak), it also leads to cascading negative effects throughout these neighborhoods, including large increases in antisocial behavior. To address this phenomenon, Shaw and McKay (1972) began by analyzing Cook County Juvenile Court records spanning the years from 1900 to 1933 and noted that the rates of crime and delinquency were always found in these invaded neighborhoods. This suggested to them that there existed natural areas that facilitated crime and delinquency independent of their inhabitants. That is, crime was heavily concentrated in certain slum neighborhoods regardless of the ethnic identities of their residents. Shaw and McKay's findings were welcomed by sociologists because they increased confidence in their belief that the environment is more important than the traits individuals bring with them to it in explaining antisocial behavior.

Human ecology researchers characterized the spatial patterns existing in U.S. cities as radiating outward from the central business and industrial areas in a series of concentric circles or ecological zones. Zone I was the loop area of Chicago and Zone II was the factory zone around which Chicago residents had previously resided, but when Shaw and McKay conducted their research, they were inhabited by the poorest residents. This was the so-called transition zone where population changes leading to crime and delinquency mostly occurred. The transition zone was populated by poor native and foreign immigrants to Chicago because the cheapest rents were to be found there.

In response to increasing immigration and factory expansion, some residents of the transition zone moved to Zone III, the zone of working-class homes, making neighborhoods in this zone less desirable. Consequently, those who could afford to do so moved to the next desirable zone. Successive waves of immigrants arrived and occupied older inner-city neighborhoods, precipitating a rippling effect like a stone dropped in a pond and rippling outward. Each successive wave of newcomers to the poorest neighborhoods generated constant movement from zone to zone as members of more established groups sought to escape the intrusion of the newcomers. Urban decay and crime are consequences of this population movement. Delinquency rates decreased linearly from 11.9 incidents per 100 juveniles in the poorest zone to 1.8 per 100 in the most affluent zone (Zone V).

Social Disorganization

That crime and delinquency declines moving from the inner-city outward toward more affluent neighborhoods was not itself theoretically significant. European studies have long shown this to be the case in their cities. Shaw and McKay knew ecology per se was insufficient to explain the crime phenomenon and that they needed a mechanism to explain how population displacement and replacement translated into crime and delinquency. The mechanism formulated was *social disorganization*, which meant the inability of neighborhood residents to recognize common values and goals led to the breakdown of the power of informal community norms that regulated conduct. Social disorganization is created by the continuous redistribution of neighborhood populations, bringing with them a variety of cultural traditions that were often at odds with traditional neighborhood norms of behavior. Neighborhoods invaded by members of alien racial or ethnic groups became rife with conflicting values and conduct norms and soon lost their sense of community. In these areas, there is little to no consensus on how things ought to be or how things ought to be done. The movie *Gran Torino* highlights the alienation felt by Clint Eastwood's character as his neighborhood, formerly populated by White working-class families, became populated by Asian immigrants.

Robert Putnam (2007) conducted the largest study of the effects of racial/ethnic diversity on neighborhood cohesion using the Social Capital Benchmark Survey of close to 30,000 interviews in 41 locations across the United States. His concern was the effects of racial/ethnic diversity on social capital. Social capital refers to the web of social networks that connect people to others in the neighborhood and breed norms of reciprocity, trustworthiness, and a sense of belonging. Putnam's research showed that population diversity has devastating effects on neighborhoods by reducing social capital, which reduces the kind of informal social controls that prevent criminal activity as Shaw and McKay had hypothesized. He concluded that the greater the diversity, the greater the distrust of strangers and even members of one's own ethnic or racial group. In neighborhoods characterized by high ethnic/racial diversity only about 30% of respondents said they trusted their neighbors "a lot" whereas in low-diversity neighborhoods 70–80% said they trusted their neighbors "a lot." Putnam concluded:

> Inhabitants of diverse communities tend to withdraw from collective life, to distrust their neighbors regardless of the color of their skin, to withdraw even from close friends, to expect the worst from their community and its leaders, to volunteer less, give less to charity and work on community projects less often, to register to vote less, to agitate for social reform more but have less faith they can actually make a difference.
>
> *(2007, p. 151)*

Shaw and McKay concluded that social disorganization impacts crime and delinquency in two ways. First, the lack of informal social controls (the reduction of social capital) within neighborhoods facilitates crime by failing to inhibit it. Second, in the absence or weakening of prosocial values, a set of values supporting antisocial behavior is likely to develop to fill the vacuum. Youths in slum neighborhoods thus have both negative and positive inducements to crime and delinquency represented by the absence of effective social controls and the presence of delinquent values, respectively. These conditions are transmitted across generations until they become intrinsic properties of the neighborhood culture.

The units of analysis in human ecology theory are communities and crime rates; that is, it looks at how crime rates vary by neighborhood-level culture and structure. The theory pays scant attention to individuals and their characteristics except to note how they may respond to social disorganization and decreases in social capital. However, whatever the environmental factors that contribute to criminal behavior may be, they must influence individuals before they can affect behavior. People vary greatly in how they respond to environmental conditions according to the characteristics they bring with them (G*x*E and rGE processes) as exemplified in the saying, "The fire that melts the butter hardens the egg."

Shaw and McKay's theory maintains that crime is concentrated in socially disorganized slum areas because economically deprived people are concentrated there and see the concentrated disadvantage of the neighborhood as the cause of high levels of crime. However, they never entertained the notion that crime and concentrated disadvantage are mutually causative, which a true ecology should have led them to posit. Velez (2018, p. 39) notes how high crime levels strengthen the subcultural values that lead to more concentrated disadvantage: "High crime areas also can increase cultural adaptations that make criminal behavior more likely." Likewise, Hipp's (2010) study of 2,534 census tracts in 13 cities found that neighborhoods with high violent crime rates experience significant increases in concentrated disadvantage, thus creating a vicious cycle of concentrated disadvantage and crime feeding on each other. In other words, people are actors, not just reactors, and they affect their environments just as environments affect them.

The People Versus Places Issue

The causal direction has always been a problem for sociological theory, which always appears to posit one-way causality such as poverty causes crime, accident of birth causes socioeconomic status, or gender socialization causes gender differences in behavior. Noting that human ecology theory offers "structure-only" accounts of crime, Ruth Kornhauser (1978, p. 104) posed the question: "How do we know that area differences in delinquency rates result from the aggregated characteristics of communities rather than the characteristics of individuals selectively aggregated into communities?" In other words, are neighborhoods run down and criminogenic because there are many people with personal characteristics conducive to antisocial behavior and poverty populating them, or do neighborhoods somehow cause crime independent of the characteristics of people living there? One way of looking at this question is to note that when formerly blighted areas become "gentrified" and better-behaved people move in, the neighborhood is no longer criminogenic—neighborhoods do not trash themselves any more than they gentrify themselves. Ecology is about the dynamic interrelationships of organisms and their environment, so if the theory is to be consistent with the concept it imported from biology, Kornhauser's question is essentially a non-question because they are mutually constitutive. Unfortunately, human ecology theory concentrates only on how environments affect people and turns a blind eye to the other half of the equation. While choices people make are often made under circumstances beyond their control, they must bear some responsibility for the state of their environments.

Just as crime rates are the aggregate of crimes committed by individuals; a neighborhood is an aggregated reflection of the behavior of its inhabitants. As John Paul Wright (2009, p. 148) notes:

> It should be expected that individuals with similar traits and abilities, who have made many of the same choices over their life-course, should tend to cluster together within economic and social spheres. In other words, a degree of homogeneity should exist within neighborhoods, within networks in those neighborhoods, and within families in those neighborhoods.

Prominent ecological theorists Sampson and Bean (2006, p. 29) also maintain that structure (the condition of the neighborhood) versus culture (neighborhood norm and values) argument produces a false dichotomy because each is created by and creates the other: "The relational approach understands culture not as a simplistic adaptation to structure in a one-way causal flow, but an intrasubjective organizing mechanism that shapes unfolding social processes and that is constituent of social structure." Moffitt and Beckley (2015, p. 122) also argue that criminogenic neighborhoods are both created and sustained by their inhabitants: "People who have behaved antisocially 'end up in' criminogenic environments selectively. ...Thus, selection effects account for much of the observed correlations between crime and many of its putative environmental risk factors."

This may be seen as extreme methodological individualism because biopsychosocial criminology posits that there are independent and joint contributions of all individual, social, and contextual factors. Oberwittler's (2004, p. 228) study of delinquency in Germany concluded:

> Ecological contextual effects are likely to exist, and the neighborhood context appears to play an important role in these effects. However, as has been shown in previous research in U.S. cities, contextual effects on adolescent behavior are generally rather small compared with individual-level influences.

Another study looking at both the effects of neighborhoods and individual influences on crime (Wikstrom & Loeber, 2000) concluded that neighborhood effects were related to delinquency only for boys who began committing delinquent acts during adolescence (Terrie Moffitt's [1993] adolescent-limited offenders) and that boys who did so before adolescence (Moffitt's life course-persistent offenders) were equally delinquent across all 90 of the Pittsburgh neighborhoods they studied.

Osgood and Chambers (2003) conducted a large study of criminal behavior in socially disorganized rural settings. They pitted neighborhood effects against the behavioral choices people make. They traced social disorganization to high population turnover and ethnic diversity but identified high rates of female-headed households, which is a result of choices people make, as the most important factor in explaining crime rates. The most notable finding of the study was that: "A 10 percent increase in female-headed households was associated with a 73 to 100 percent higher rate of arrest for all offenses except homicide [a 10% increase in female-headed households was associated with a 33% increase in homicide]" (p. 6). Messner and Sampson's (1991) study of 153 American cities likewise found that the proportion of female-headed households was the best predictor of crime. McLaughlin and Mackey (2008) also examined the relationship between non-marital births and violent crime in all 50 states from 1980 to 2004 and found for a generation lag of 20 years, non-marital births explained 65.1% of the variance in crime. Likewise, Mackey and Immerman (2007, p. 128) found that: "Over 75% of the variability in rates of violent crime can be explained by differential rates of out-of-wedlock births." Finally, Errol, Madsen, and Moslehi looked at crime rates in 16 advanced countries over 200 years and concluded: "Our results suggest that family structure, measured by divorce rates and out-of-wedlock births, is a significantly positive determinant of violent crime, property crime, assaults, homicide and robbery over the past two centuries" (2021, p. 535).

Human ecology theory cannot account for why most people in disorganized neighborhoods presumably do not commit serious crimes or why among those who do a small minority commits the majority of them. The ecological fallacy states that we cannot make inferences about individuals and groups based on information derived from the larger population of which they are a part. Shaw and McKay (1972) showed that Asians and Jews living in high-crime areas had low crime rates. To find high crime rates in a neighborhood with large Asian or Jewish populations and then to assume that Asians and Jews commit crimes at the neighborhood rate is an example of the ecological fallacy (a faulty inference made about an individual or subset of a population based on aggregate data from the population as a whole). Low Asian and Jewish crime rates in high-crime neighborhoods suggested that the human ecologists' rejection of group and individual differences as explanations for crime and delinquency was misplaced.

Policy: The Chicago Area Project

If socially disorganized slum neighborhoods are the "root cause" of crime, what feasible prevention policy can be derived from the theory? The unit of analysis in human ecology theory is the community, and thus the unit of intervention is the community. But communities are aggregates of individuals, so if neighborhoods are chaotic and inhabited by people with antisocial codes of conduct, the first thing that comes to mind is the strengthening of community life and the inculcation of prosocial norms and values in the individuals who live there. That is easy to say, but how do we go about it? Clifford Shaw saw the problem in the 1930s and started securing funds for the Chicago Area Project (CAP). This project is still in operation almost a century later, and its website describes the project thusly:

> Chicago Area Project is at the forefront of community development, empowering all walks of life. We stand by our mission of reducing juvenile delinquency and providing tools to promote self-efficacy in overlooked communities. Using a three-pronged approach to addressing delinquency and its root causes-community organizing, direct services, and advocacy-CAP empowers a broad base of community stakeholders to improve neighborhood conditions, hold institutions accountable, reduce anti-social behavior of young people, protect children from inappropriate institutionalization, and provide youth with positive role models for personal development.

CAP funds several programs to generate or strengthen a sense of community in neighborhoods with the help and cooperation of schools, churches, recreational clubs, trade unions, and businesses. Athletic leagues, various kinds of clubs, summer camps, and many other activities are instituted to occupy the idle hands of the young. "Street Corner" counselors are hired to offer advice to youths and to mediate with the police on their behalf when they get into minor troubles and residents are encouraged to form committees to resolve neighborhood problems such as cleaning up the neighborhood. CAP counselors appealed for help to street gangs which held the power in the neighborhoods under the assumption that young street gang members would respond favorably to sympathy, affection, and understanding when reached out to by others who could approach them on their level.

CAP has thus always worked with Chicago's gangs from its inception to the present day. Its workers identify and meet with agreeable gang leaders to discuss community and individual needs in efforts to create positive changes in neighborhoods and individuals, but gang leaders could not be expected to be cooperative with people whose agenda was to challenge their way of life except in ways they see as profitable to themselves. Unfortunately, despite the valiant efforts of CAP and the flood of dollars supporting it, gang violence in Chicago today appears to be as bad, or worse, than it ever was. DaViera et al. (2020, p. 65) note that:

> Community violence proliferates in the lives and neighborhoods of a substantial portion of Chicago youth. Between 2015 and 2016, there was a 58% increase in homicide rates and a 43% increase in non-fatal shootings, specifically concentrated in several disproportionately low-income neighborhoods on the south and west sides of Chicago.

Sorrentino and Whittaker express some positive aspects of the CAP:

> As residents work on behalf of their children, positive attitudes are reinforced. The children begin to live in a better environment and respond to constructive social influences. These influences, as well as the improvements in general living conditions that the residents effect, advance both the prevention of delinquency and the treatment of delinquents. In fact, in those communities where area projects have been in operation for a number of years, incidents of crime and delinquency have decreased.
>
> *(1994, p. 10)*

Sorrentino and Whittaker, however, did not empirically demonstrate where and when crime and delinquency have decreased. In fact, despite the money and energy invested in CAP, its effects have never been empirically evaluated in systematic ways. Google Scholar searches spit out 1,620 hits for "Chicago Area Project" but not one purports to assess its efficacy empirically. All the evidence of positive effects that I have read in books and articles has been anecdotal. Similar programs in other cities had some positive outcomes, but their impact on crime and delinquency rates has been negligible. Writing about the impact of CAP-type programs in these cities, Rosenbaum, Lurigio, and Davis (1998) concluded that there were: "few positive program effects. The local programs did not affect official crime rates and in some cases were associated with adverse change in survey-based victimization rates" (p. 214). Nevertheless, despite this pessimistic note, it is doubtless true that many young persons have been rescued from a life of crime by programs such as CAP.

Policy: Moving to Opportunity

If you can't take the neighborhood out of the person, perhaps we can take the person out of the neighborhood and move him or her to a better one. Crime prevention policies are often aimed at reducing intergenerational poverty. One possible way of achieving this is to remove children from poverty-stricken areas and disperse them among more affluent neighborhoods in the hope that they may conform to the behavioral standards of their new neighborhoods. The Moving to Opportunity (MtO) program was such a program. The MtO program was a voluntary program designed to give low-income people opportunities to forge better lives. Like the CAP, the MtO program was premised on human ecology theory's notion that better neighborhoods produce better-behaving people, and was meant primarily to increase economic opportunities for the dispersed families, and not as a crime prevention policy per se. MtO was a HUD-funded experiment that began in 1994 in five cities and ended in 2010. The program randomly assigned low-income families, 93% of which were female-headed (Jackson et al., 2009), to receive either a standard Section 8 voucher or a voucher to relocate to low-poverty neighborhoods, which were defined as neighborhoods with fewer than 10% of its residents living in poverty. Thus, social scientists were provided with three groups to conduct their studies: the experimental (MtO families), Section 8 families, and control groups composed of those families not assigned to the program but were eligible.

Unlike the CAP, there have been numerous MtO studies empirically assessing its effect on various forms of antisocial behavior. MtO studies have found that generally, the receipt of a voucher results in better mental health and less risky behavior for girls, but worse outcomes for boys, especially concerning delinquency (Kling, Liebman, & Katz, 2007). Sciandra et al. (2013) found that arrest rates for violent crime among women in the MtO program fell by 33% and property crime rates fell by 32% ten years after relocation compared to a control group remaining in the old neighborhood. However, ten years after men were relocated, their arrests for property crime increased by 32% compared to the control group but no difference between them and the control group (members who remained in the same neighborhoods as those who moved) was found for violent crime.

Such findings relating to sex differences as those above are consistently found. Kim et al. (2022, p. 79) looked at four other studies that tested sex differences among MtO-relocated adolescents in terms of their engagement in a variety of behavioral problems. They concluded:

> These studies consistently found that moving out of high-poverty public housing neighborhoods was associated with increased substance use, binge drinking, risky behavior, and delinquency among boys, while MtO relocation significantly reduced rates of conduct disorders and improved nonfamily social networks among girls.

There are no explanations for why these opposite effects between males and females are seen when they move to better neighborhoods. Perhaps more males chose to remain connected to their old peer networks and schools than did females, or males find moving to be a more stressful experience than females, or perhaps girls, in general, are more durable and receptive to positive changes in their environment.

We may conclude that MtO studies find mixed results; sometimes moving to better neighborhoods matters and sometimes it does not. Why do they sometimes have positive effects and sometimes negative effects? Robert Sampson notes that while experiments are the gold standard in social science because they inform us with a great deal of confidence that experimental and control groups differ, they cannot tell us why the putative cause has the effect that it does: "Experiments do not answer the 'why' question. The causes of neighborhood effects and social mechanisms have been a black box, and neighborhood-level interventions have been neglected" (2008, pp. 226–227).

One important "why" mechanism is highlighted by Chetty, Hendren, and Katz (2016). They report that the beneficial gains from moving to better neighborhoods are inversely related to the age when children move, with benefits diminishing as age at the time of entry into the program increases, with adolescent participants who were older when they moved, especially boys, experiencing more negative outcomes. That is, the biggest positive results occur when children are less than 13 years old when they move and diminish thereafter. This has important implications for policy because brain plasticity (a "black box" from Sampson's sociological ecological perspective) is high during early childhood, peaks during adolescence, and slowly declines thereafter (Laube, van den Bos, & Fandakova, 2020). Children's developing brains have higher malleability in response to changing experiences compared to adults, and thus those who moved earlier in life fared better in their improved environments than those who moved later. This neuroscience insight offers a compelling argument for taking note of biological as well as social science evidence when formulating policies relating to crime because such evidence provides levers to pry open more black boxes.

7

THE ANOMIE TRADITION AND POLICY

The Variety of Anomie Theories

Sociology-based criminological theories are not easy to classify, but we can broadly categorize them into social structure and social process theories. Social structure theories direct our attention to how people behave determined by their social roles and social positions in the social structure and express ideas of social continuity, regularity, and interrelatedness in social life. Human ecology theory is an example of such a theory. Social process theories afford people more autonomy and urge an understanding of how individuals subjectively perceive their social reality and react accordingly. The social process perspective is summed up in the Thomas theorem: "If men define situations as real, they are real in their consequences" (Nettler, 1978, p. 272). To various extents, all social process theories represent the joining of sociology and psychology. We first look at anomie theory and what crime prevention policy recommendations can be derived from it.

Anomie theory is a rather difficult creature to grasp because it has been couched in structural-cultural terms by Merton (1938) and Messner and Rosenfeld (2001), in broadly psychological terms by Agnew (1992), and later in biopsychosocial terms (Agnew, 2005; Walsh, 2000), and in hybrid terms by Durkheim (1951; 1982). French sociologist Émile Durkheim introduced the term anomie ("a-normative" or "without norms') into criminology. He meant by this the breakdown or weakening of norms because a society without norms of behavior is not viable. Social norms are weakened when an excess of contradictory norms exist in society.

DOI: 10.4324/9781003642268-10

In our discussion of human ecology in Chapter 6, we saw that such a situation exists when people from different cultural backgrounds live side by side. Norms are also threatened by periods of rapid social change, which Durkheim saw as weakening social solidarity. We saw this in the United States with the back-to-back elections of two of the most divisive presidents in our history—Barack Obama and Donald Trump.

Structural-Cultural Anomie

Durkheim identified two forms of social solidarity: mechanical and organic. Mechanical solidarity exists in small pre-state societies in which members share strong emotional ties to the collectivity because they share common experiences and circumstances and thus share common values and a "collective conscience." This is the same idea at the societal level that Shaw and McKay's human ecology theory emphasized at the neighborhood level. In a society characterized by mechanical solidarity, informal social controls are strong, and antisocial behavior is minimal. Large modern societies are characterized by organic solidarity due to high levels of occupational specialization (the division of labor) and diversity of experiences and circumstances. This tends to weaken common values, social capital, and social bonds; consequentially, antisocial behavior grows.

Durkheim argued that because crime is found at all times and in all societies, it is a normal and inevitable social phenomenon and even functional because it serves to identify the limits of acceptable behavior and may serve as a socially unifying force when the community at large comes together to express opposition to criminal behavior. He also stressed that too much repression of deviant behavior would lead to pathological conformity that stifles creativity, progress, and personal freedom. For Durkheim, crime is one of the prices we pay for freedom and social progress. Durkheim (1982) asserted that when crime drops significantly below average levels, such as during wartime, it is a sign that something is wrong.

Durkheim (1982) believed that crime was "a normal phenomenon of normal sociology," but also that the criminal "is an individual normally constituted from the biological and psychological points of view" (pp. 106–107). He also asserted that in any society there are always individuals who "diverge to some extent from the collective type," and among them is the "criminal character" (p. 101). Durkheim also set the stage for later extensions of anomie theory by addressing "strains" when he wrote that although humans are similar in their "essential qualities, one sort of hereditary will always exist, that of natural talent" (1951, p. 251). The crux of the crime problem at the individual level is that "human activity naturally aspires beyond assignable limits and sets itself unattainable goals" (p. 247). When some people get less than they expect, they are ripe for criminal behavior.

Robert Merton (1938) agreed with Durkheim's notion that the inability to attain resources legitimately generates unhappiness, or strain, which sometimes leads to efforts to obtain them illegitimately. Whereas human ecology/social disorganization theory assumes that *rejections of* conventional middle-class values via the intergenerational transmission of deviant values were productive of crime, Merton argued that it was *acceptance* of middle-class values that was productive of crime by placing an overweening emphasis on financial success. The core of Merton's theory is that American culture defines monetary success (the "American Dream") as the predominant cultural goal all its citizens should be encouraged to achieve. However, he maintained that America's social structure restricts access to legitimate means of attaining it to certain segments of the population. This disjunction between cultural goals and the structural impediments to achieving them is the strain-inducing anomic gap in which crime percolates.

Durkheim's naturalistic view of human nature led him to posit that the freeing of natural greed, acquisitiveness, egoism, deviance, and crime are *consequences* of anomie, whereas Merton's social constructivist view of human nature led him to believe these traits are socially constructed and *cause* anomie (Passas, 1995). In Merton's view, America's capitalist society is a negative force that *motivates* criminal behavior and anomie, rather than an occasional condition arising from rapid social change as Durkheim saw it. For Merton, anomie is a permanent condition caused by the disjunction between cultural success goals and the lack of legitimate opportunities for some segments of society by which to accomplish them. He saw crime as woven into the fabric of American society and arises from conformity to American values—a way disadvantaged people who have been blocked from getting what they have been taught to want (economic success) through legitimate means (education, good-paying job)—not from deviation from its values due to weakening of social bonds.

Merton identified five modes of adaptation to this alleged disjunction between cultural success goals and the lack of legitimate opportunities people may perceive, although he never systematically explored why individuals take on one adaptation rather than another. They are:

Conformity. This is the most common mode because most people have legally prescribed means of attaining cultural success goals at their disposal.

Ritualism. This is adopted by people who have given up on achieving the "American dream" but continue to work within legal boundaries because they accept the system's legitimacy.

Innovation. This is the mode most associated with crime, which is an avenue to success—a means by which deprived people get what they have been taught by their culture to want.

Retreatism. This is adopted by those who reject both the cultural goals and the means of attaining them. They drop out of society and take refuge in substance abuse.

Rebellion. This is the adaptation of those who reject both the goals and the means but wish to substitute alternative legitimate goals and alternative legitimate means such as socialism.

Institutional Anomie Theory

An extension of Merton's theory is institutional anomie theory (IAT) which claims that "high crime rates are intrinsic to American society: in short, at all social levels America is organized for crime" (Messner & Rosenfeld, 2001, p. 5). Messner and Rosenfeld purport to show that inequality in the United States is not an aberration of the American Dream but rather an expression of it: "A competitive allocation of monetary rewards requires both winners and losers, and winning and losing have meaning only when rewards are distributed unequally" (p. 9). From this position American meritocracy is both criminogenic and unfair: "People are born with different genetic endowments and are raised in different families over which they have no control, raising fundamental questions about the fairness of even a perfectly functioning meritocracy" (Sawhill & Morton, 2007, p. 4).

IAT notes that the main institutions of society that influence or control our behavior are the economy, family, religion, education, law, and government. These integrated institutions provide society with the rules of the game, and each has its spheres of influence. Although integrated, when one institution intrudes excessively on the others it impedes them from functioning in ways they are meant to. IAT avers that when the power between the institutions is balanced, society is stable and crime rates are low. However, when there is an imbalance, society becomes anomic, institutions lose their capacity to control behavior, and crime rates are high. The essence of IAT is that the imbalance of power over people's lives in the United States is tipped heavily toward the economy so that all other social institutions are subjugated to it. That is, American culture devalues the functions of other social institutions and obliges them to accommodate themselves to the dominance of the economy. IAT maintains that a great deal of the focus of the family, religion, education, law, and government is brought to bear on instilling the beliefs and values of the marketplace to the detriment of the institution-specific beliefs and values they are supposed to inculcate. The dominance of the economy disrupts the prosocial functioning of the other institutions and substitutes an overweening concern for financial success, which is seen as profoundly criminogenic.

Messner and Rosenfeld (2001) see the transformation of social relationships tainted by economic considerations into commodities and thus decommodification *is* the answer. Research shows that the institutions of religion and the family have the greatest impact on crime prevention (Pratt & Cullen, 2005; Salas-Wright, Vaughn, & Maynard, 2014). The social relationships in those institutions, particularly the family, require freeing from the economy. For Messner and Rosenfeld, freeing people from economic domination would allow them to construct their lives unconstrained by market considerations and cutthroat competition would reduce crime. This would first require identification and analysis of the linkages between macro-level social systems and the micro-level of individual traits and the behaviors they lead to. According to Messner, Thome, and Rosenfeld (2008, p. 164), the linkage requirement is: "Durkheim's distinction between 'moral' and 'egoistic' individualism," which brings psychology into IAT and proposes that "the egoistic type characterizes societies in which the economy dominates the institutional structure, anomie is rampant, and levels of violent crime are high." Egoistic individuals are narcissistic, self-absorbed, and self-centered people who believe the world owes them a living and will often take anything they feel they are entitled to.

Psychological and Biopsychosocial Anomie

A move toward including individual psychological characteristics in the anomie tradition is Robert Agnew's general strain theory. Agnew identifies several sources of strain besides the disjunction between cultural expectations and structural barriers. Strain arises from the presentation of negative stimuli such as child abuse or neglect and negative school experiences such as bullying. These can lead to delinquency and crime via efforts to escape negative stimuli by running away from home and truancy. Strain can also result from removing positive effects on one's life, such as losing a boyfriend, girlfriend, or job. Losses such as these may induce delinquency and crime by efforts to prevent or regain the loss by illegal means or by seeking revenge on those one holds responsible for the loss.

Everyone experiences many strains throughout their lives, but their impact differs according to their magnitude, recency, duration, and clustering. That is, miseries multiply and cluster together to produce a whole greater than the sum of its parts and may overwhelm a person's coping abilities. Agnew maintains that strain results in crime and delinquency by the developing of a negative attitude about other people among those who experience chronic strains (or among those who are already egoistic): "Repeated or chronic strain may lead to a hostile attitude—a general dislike and suspicion of others and an associated tendency to respond in an aggressive manner" (2002, p. 119). Agnew thus views crime and delinquency as primarily the result of negative emotions that arise from strains, particularly from negative relationships with others, as is often the case among egotists. He sees anger as the negative emotion most strongly involved in crime. Agnew asserts that people are most likely to react with anger when they blame their negative situations or relationships on others because anger leads to a desire for revenge, particularly among males.

Broidy and Agnew (1997) find that males and females are burdened with different concerns and respond differently emotionally to failures to deal with these concerns satisfactorily. Whereas males are more concerned with financial success, females are more concerned with maintaining close relationships. Male concerns with material things may lead to property crimes to fulfill them, but female concerns with relationships cannot be fulfilled by crime. They also find that males are more likely to respond to strain with anger, while females are more likely to respond with both depression and anger. Male anger is accompanied by moral outrage and placing the blame on others, to which they might respond with violence. Female anger, on the other hand, is likely to be accompanied by guilt and shame, and they are less likely to blame others for their anger.

Agnew's greatest contribution is to insist that the most important factor in how our lives are shaped is not strain per se but *how we cope with it.* None of us are happy when strain intrudes on our lives and may curse and throw things around, but few cope with it by committing crimes. How we cope with strain depends on things such as the level of social support we enjoy; the number, frequency, duration, and intensity of the strain-inducing circumstances we face; and what kind of persons we are. According to Agnew, the individual traits that differentiate people who cope poorly with strain from others who cope well include, "temperament, intelligence, creativity, problem-solving skills, interpersonal skills, self-efficacy, and self-esteem" and "these traits affect the selection of coping strategies by influencing the individual's sensitivity to objective strains and the ability to engage in cognitive, emotional, and behavioral coping" (2002, p. 123).

People who cope poorly with the inevitable strains of life are those with inadequate levels of positive psychological and cognitive traits.

Crime is thus more likely when individuals have personality traits that render them intolerant of strain. Agnew (2002) found that youths with high levels of negative emotionality (the tendency to react to strain situations with anger and irritation) and low constraint (low self-control) were more likely than other youths to respond to strain with criminal behavior. These and the other traits that Agnew identifies may also be the traits that move people into their particular Mertonian mode of adaptation—negative and impulsive people with low intelligence and poor coping skills are not likely to achieve legitimate financial success.

DeLisi and Vaughn (2014) have shown that most antisocial behavior can be traced to two of the traits Agnew identifies—weak effortful control (low self-control) and negative emotionality. By adding these personality traits, Agnew has moved the anomie/strain tradition away from its pure sociological origins toward a more interdisciplinary future, as indicated by his statement: "Most notably, crime is most likely when individuals with certain bio-psychological characteristics are in environments where strain is common" (Agnew, 2014, p. 186). Furthermore, Stogner (2014, p. 199) opines: "Perhaps none of the major theoretical models in the field of criminology have the potential to be as intricately and effectively linked to biosocial research as Agnew's general strain theory (GST)." Stogner is correct because the personality traits Agnew identifies as those that most strongly affect one's ability to cope positively with strain are heritable and have strong neurobiological roots.

In his general (as distinguished from his general strain theory) or "super traits" theory, Agnew (2005) engages with social, psychological, and biological variables. The theory begins with the fundamental notion that crime is most likely to occur when constraints against it are low and the motivations for it are high. At the heart of the theory are five age-graded life domains that are proven robust correlates of crime: personality, family, school, peers, and work. The theory is developmental because these domains interact and feedback on one another across the life course. The theory posits that personality traits set individuals on a developmental trajectory that influences how others in the family, school, peer group, and workgroup domains react to them. That is, personality variables condition the effect of social variables on crime. Agnew notes that personality traits such as sensation seeking, impulsivity, inattentiveness, and low empathy cluster together to produce the key "super traits" of low self-control and irritability (a feature of negative emotionality). People saddled with low self-control are impulsive, risk-taking, lacking in perseverance, and have little concern about the long-term consequences of their behavior. People with irritable temperaments are antagonistic and adversarial in their interaction style, which makes them likely to evoke negative responses from family members, school teachers, peers, workmates, and other people in general that feedback and make those tendencies worse than they would have otherwise been in the process of evocative rGE.

Agnew states that "biological factors have a direct effect on irritability/low self-control and an indirect effect on the other life domains through irritability/low self-control" (p. 213) and acknowledges the role of serotonin and the ANS in irritability and self-control (2005, pp. 141–142). However, he appears to favor parental treatment as the primary reason children become irritable and/or lack self-control (p. 71) even though the behavioral genetic literature consistently notes that the shared environment (which includes parenting) contributes very little to adult personality differences. Previous work has shown that constraint (self-control) is inversely related to negative emotionality and that negative emotionality is strongly related to criminality "across countries, genders, races, and methods" (Caspi et al., 1994, p. 163). Caspi et al. state that low levels of serotonin underlie both high levels of negative emotionality and low levels of self-control, and claim that low serotonin "may be a heritable diathesis for a personality style involving high levels of negative affect and low levels of constraint, which generates in turn a vulnerability to criminal behavior" (1994, p. 188). Boisvert et al. (2018) and Lesch et al. (2012) provide good examples of how serotonin underlies self-control and negative emotionality, respectively.

Agnew claims his theory can explain sex, race, SES, and age effects on criminal behavior. He argues that males are more likely to inherit irritability-low self-control than females because in evolutionary terms these traits aided male reproductive success by enhancing male aggressiveness and competitiveness. As for race differences, Agnew argues that African Americans are more likely to be poor and to receive discriminatory treatment, which may increase irritability and perceptions of poor job prospects may lead to the adoption of an impulsive "live-for-today" lifestyle. In terms of SES, he states that "individuals from low-SES families may be more likely to inherit these traits, as these traits may be more common among low-SES individuals" (2005, p. 143). He also notes that low-SES individuals not only may be more likely to inherit alleles related to such traits but also are more likely than higher-SES individuals to suffer biological insults such as prenatal exposure to toxic substances and birth complications that contribute environmentally to low self-control and negative emotionality.

As for age-related factors, Agnew notes that the immaturity of adolescent behavior reflects the immaturity of adolescent's brains and that adolescents tend to become more irritable because their brains undergo a period of intense "remodeling." At the same time their brains are changing, adolescents experience massive hormonal surges that tend to facilitate aggression and competitiveness. Thus, the neurological and endocrine changes during adolescence *temporarily* increase irritability-low self-control among adolescents who limit their offending to their adolescence, while for those who continue to offend well into adulthood, irritability-low self-control is a *stable* characteristic. Summing up the theory, Ngo and Paternoster (2014, p. 18) state: "While clearly not a homage to parsimony, Agnew's general theory does hold promise of uniting diverse theoretical perspectives into an organized framework for understanding crime."

Policy Recommendations Derived from the Anomie Tradition

The ideas of Merton's anomie theory had a tremendous impact on public policy via President Lyndon Johnson's War on Poverty. The reasoning was that since crime is perceived as an activity engaged in mostly by the poor, fewer poor people would mean fewer crimes. The poverty rate fell minimally but, as we have seen the expected bonus of crime reduction did not materialize. If crime is caused by the Mertonian notion of a disjunction between cultural values emphasizing success for all and a social structure denying access to legitimate means of achieving it to some, rather than poverty per se, the cure for crime is to increase opportunities or dampening aspirations. The dampening of aspiration would not be acceptable to policymakers of any ideological persuasion, so the answer is to increase opportunities.

Following in the footsteps of CAP, in the early 1960s Richard Cloward and Lloyd Ohlin developed a delinquency prevention project known as Mobilization for Youth (MOBY), which mobilized the community to support change in outcomes and conditions that support healthy youth development. It concentrated on expanding legitimate opportunities for disadvantaged youths via several educational, training, and job placement programs. MOBY programs received generous private, state, and federal funds and served as models for such federal government programs as Head Start, the Job Corps, the Comprehensive Employment and Training Act (CETA), and affirmative action (LaFree, Drass, & O'Day, 1992). As these many programs attest, far from blocking opportunities to economic success, the state goes to great lengths to ensure that all may have opportunities to get into the game.

Although many young people were doubtless diverted from a life of crime because of the opportunities presented to them by such programs, unfortunately, their heyday occurred at the same time the United States was undergoing a huge jump in crime from 1965 to 1980, putting a damper on enthusiasm for them among politicians. In common with CAP, although touted as a delinquency-crime prevention program, its effects on crime and delinquency have never been empirically evaluated. As Welsh and Pfeffer (2013, p. 538) note:

> Based on Richard Cloward and Lloyd Ohlin's concept of providing opportunities for legitimate success, MOBY created employment opportunities in the community, coordinated social services, and sponsored social action groups such as tenants' committees, legal action services, and voter registration. Unfortunately, the program was never evaluated to assess its impact on delinquency.

This is a problem often associated with large programs such as MOBY. The best we can do is to observe that they either are or are not successful in reducing factors that are correlated with crime and delinquency and infer from this that they probably did or did not have the effect of reducing them.

The policy recommendation of IAT would be to tame the power of the market via decommodification. For instance, the decision to have children could be freed from economic considerations by granting government-guaranteed maternity leave benefits and family allowances/income support, and higher education should be accessible to all people with talent without regard for the financial ability to pay. In other words, policies that ensure an adequate level of material well-being does not completely depend on an individual's performance in the marketplace. Rudolph and Starke (2020) tested IAT and social support theories among 18 economically highly developed countries (excluding the United States as an outlier with both high homicide rates and low government social support) that have extensive social security systems for homicide rates between 1990 and 2011. They found that the welfare state suppresses crime, particularly through social support via generous unemployment benefits, but IAT's key concept—decommodification—does not have any effect. They concluded:

> Although we find a statistically significant negative effect of total spending on homicide, this does not mean that more generous welfare programs are necessarily better at fighting crime. First, raising overall levels of decommodification—which reflects the inclusiveness and generosity of social policy across several areas—does not seem to have an effect, either. Second, when looking at effects for sub-areas of social policy, it becomes clear that some areas, including family policy spending and general social assistance do not have the expected effect.
>
> *(2020, p. 8)*

Cochran and Bjerregaard (2012) tested IAT among 49 diverse countries. They developed a composite index of institutional anomie consisting of the economic freedom index as their measure of cultural emphasis on the accumulation of wealth for citizens, the gross domestic product (GDP) as their measure of a nation's economic strength, and the Gini coefficient of economic inequality as their measure of blocked opportunities. They found that societies high in structural anomie (societies with high economic freedom, GDP, and economic inequality) had the highest rates of instrumental crimes such as theft offenses (more to steal). The strength of the economy in these nations is sufficient to sustain opportunities to gain wealth, but only for those with the ability to successfully engage with the meritocracy; others innovate. On the other hand, the highest rates of expressive crimes such as homicide were found in nations that place a strong emphasis on economic success (high on the economic freedom index) but with an economy not strong enough to sustain the desires of all (a low GDP).

Cochran and Bjerregaard's study is an excellent one that reveals how crime rates are tied to three basic structural measures, but what are the policy recommendations? No one wants economic freedom curtailed or GDP reduced. The only thing left is to reduce economic inequality because this "want among plenty" is seen as a cause of crime in both Merton's and Messner and Rosenfeld's anomie theories. But we have seen that Sawhill and Morton view those in want as cursed with genetic and/or family deficiencies that prevent them from competing successfully in a meritocracy which they see as "unfair" (2007, p. 4). Fairness is a philosophical issue suffused with contradictory notions. We may rightly feel sorry for individuals burdened with genetic and environmental burdens not of their own making, but how does the moral issue of fairness fit into this? Those of a conservative bent view economic fairness as an equal opportunity *process*—a non-discriminatory chance to enter the race—which governments can guarantee via law. Those with a liberal/progressive bent tend to view fairness as equality of *outcome*—which no power on earth can guarantee. Former Federal Reserve chairman Ben Bernanke echoes Messner and Rosenfeld's concerning the system requiring unequal outcomes, but he draws the opposite conclusion from it:

> Although we Americans strive to provide equality of economic opportunity, we do not guarantee equality of economic outcomes, nor should we. Indeed, without the possibility of unequal outcomes tied to differences in effort and skill, the economic incentives for productive behavior would be eliminated and our market-based economy—which

> encourages productive activity primarily through the promise of financial reward—would function far less effectively.
>
> *(Sawhill & Morton, 2007, p. 1)*

However, there is room for enhanced means-tested government support for people at the bottom of the socioeconomic ladder without sacrificing the economic freedom of our meritocratic system. Economic freedom is "the absence of government coercion or constraint on the production, distribution, or consumption of goods and services beyond the extent necessary for citizens to protect and maintain liberty itself" (Beach & O'Driscoll, 2003, p. 2). Few of us would want to exchange that freedom for a state command economy which, as the history of the 20th century revealed, is the road to ruin. However, if strengthening government social support policies sounds too socialistic, we should remind ourselves that the United States has already adopted many socialist policies demanded by the American public such as the 40-hour workweek, unemployment benefits, social security, Medicare, public works, legal trade unions, and child labor laws. These programs were part of the 1928 platform of the American Socialist Party (Walsh, 2009). Other reforms predating 1928, such as a graduated income tax, free education for all children, and the abolition of child labor, are so integrated into American life that few today would call them socialist, although they were previously perceived as such. Of course, these are across the board policies we all benefit from, not targeted policies aimed at individuals at-risk for criminal behavior.

8

SUBCULTURAL THEORIES AND POVERTY

Early Subcultural Theories

Several scholars, including some of Robert Merton's former students, took his modes of adaptation concept and developed several subcultural theories. Subcultural theories posit that crime is rooted in criminal subcultures and identify cultural values, attitudes, codes, and behaviors that exist in them. Subcultures are formed when a significant number of people (mostly people of lower socioeconomic status [SES]) feel alienated from the parent culture and forge a lifestyle different from it that involves values, attitudes, and behavior at odds with it (Merton's innovators and retreatists). Subcultural theories of crime aver that people who perceive that they have been victimized by mainstream culture will reject it and will create their own norms and values that are oppositional and confrontational to it.

Marvin Wolfgang and Franco Ferracuti's (1967) subculture of violence thesis is an early example that has influenced much subsequent work. A subculture of violence is one in which norms, values, and attitudes existing in it legitimize the use of violence to resolve conflicts and which is supportive of all forms of crime and deviance. In formulating their theory, Wolfgang and Ferracuti reasoned that "by identifying the groups with the highest rates of homicide, we should find in the most intense degree a subculture of violence" (p. 153). They found such subcultures in Philadelphia's Black communities of concentrated disadvantage in the mid-1950s. They found that the homicide rate for young Black males in those communities was 27 times higher than that for young White males, and the Black female rate was 23 times greater than that for White females. Unnever

DOI: 10.4324/9781003642268-11

and Gabbidon (2011, p. 1) also note the large overrepresentation of Blacks in violent crime and explain it as a response to "living within a conflicted racially stratified society," Black male perceptions of racial discrimination, and the extent to which they embrace the *criminalblackman* stereotype. Subcultural theories largely absolve individuals from responsibility for their actions and place it on society's shoulders.

Norms existing in subcultures of violence dictate that males are expected to settle matters "like a man" and to take care of their own beefs (don't involve the police). "Taking care of business" may involve violence in subcultures where it is not viewed as illicit, and young men are hypersensitive to insult and willing to defend their reputations vigorously (Mazur, 2023). It is part of the street code that "emerges where the influence of the police ends and where personal responsibility for one's safety is felt to begin" (Anderson, 1999, p. 33). The successful application of violent aggression—a manifestation of subcultural values *and* a disavowal of mainstream cultural values—is a source of pride (Anderson, 1999). Cao, Adams, and Jensen (1997, p. 367) opine that the subculture of violence thesis "remains *the* definitive argument for society's role in creating violent criminal behavior."

Albert Cohen's (1955) subcultural theory seeks to explain how low-income youths adapt to their limited avenues of legitimate success. Cohen noted that most criminal behavior in low-SES neighborhoods is not, as Merton claimed, a rational method of securing financial assets, but rather an expression of short-run hedonism. Short-run hedonism is impulsively seeking immediate gratification of desires without regard for long-term consequences. He maintained that most delinquent behavior is nonutilitarian, malicious, destructive, and negative and turns middle-class norms of behavior upside down. Cohen stated that because many youths in low-income areas cannot live up to middle-class measuring rods, they experience status frustration that leads them to embrace their oppositional subculture which stresses behavioral norms contrary to the middle class. Cohen saw criminal subcultures as a mass reaction to the problem of blocked opportunities, although he saw status frustration as the primary cause. All people desire status, including low-SES youths, but they desire "juice," "street cred," and "rep" and seek it through means at odds with middle-class means. To gain their kind of status and respect, members of criminal subcultures establish "new norms, new criteria of status which define as meritorious the characteristics they *do* possess, the kinds of conduct of which they *are* capable" (Cohen, 1955, p. 66).

Another extension of Merton's strain theory is Richard Cloward and Lloyd Ohlin's (1960) differential opportunity theory. Cloward and Ohlin noted that delinquents and criminals want the American dream but have no interest in middle-class means of attaining it, preferring "big cars," "flashy clothes," and "swell dames" (p. 96). However, they pointed out that just as there are barriers to legitimate success, there are barriers to achieving illegitimate success. It takes more than talent and motivation to make it within the legitimate or illegitimate opportunity structure. They noted that there were three types of gangs; some focusing on criminal enterprises, some on conflict, and some on escapism, or what Merton described as retreatist. While conflict and escapist gangs tend to form spontaneously, criminal gangs are difficult to enter. Wannabe gang members need a friend, relative, or acquaintance as a sponsor who can show them the ropes to become part of a criminal gang. Youths living in neighborhoods with an established illegitimate opportunity structure have an advantage over youths living in areas that do not. Individuals within an illegitimate opportunity structure may join criminal gangs, such as Mafia-type gangs, which have a pool of aspiring sponsored recruits if they so desire and can establish their worth to it.

Cloward and Ohlin's conflict and escapist gang develop from the frustration of living in low-SES cultures. Conflict gangs are generated in neighborhoods with a high degree of transience and instability (social disorganization) as opposed to stable areas with an established illegitimate opportunity structure. Members of these loose-knit gangs commit senseless acts of violence to dominate territory in their efforts to make a living from criminal activity and tend to be "individualistic, unorganized, petty, poorly paid and unprotected" (Cloward & Ohlin, 1960, p. 73). Escapist gangs are composed of what Cloward and Ohlin call "double failures" and "retreatist" in their attitudes and turn to alcohol and drugs "as a solution to their status dilemma" (p. 183). Both conflict and escapist gangs are concerned with the immediate gratification of their wants and needs.

Walter Miller's focal concerns theory (1958), developed during 13 years of ethnographic work with various colleagues, takes issue with the idea that delinquent gangs are formed as a reaction to status deprivation. Criminals in subcultures may resent the middle class, but it is not simply a matter of "If you can't join 'em, lick 'em" because their resentment is born out of envy for what middle-class people have, not for what they are. Middle-class habits of hard work, personal responsibility, and an orientation to the future have no appeal to them. Miller asserted that low-SES subcultural values must be viewed on their own terms and not as simple negations of those of the middle class. He identified six interrelated focal concerns that dominate the values that animate the lifestyle of those at the bottom SES rung of society.

1 Trouble: Trouble is something you don't want, but if it is the right kind where you can show that you can handle yourself, it validates your status.

2 Toughness: Toughness is valued very highly for the status it confers on low-SES males. A reputation for toughness helps to avoid trouble with others in the subculture.
3 Smartness: Smartness refers to street smarts; the ability to con others and to survive on the streets using your wits.
4 Excitement: Excitement is the search for such things as committing crimes and getting away with it; sexual adventurism, gambling, and getting drunk or high.
5 Fate: Fate is believing that one's life is controlled by others: "What will be, will be".
6 Autonomy: Autonomy refers to the desire to be free of the control of authority figures such as teachers, employers, and the police, and able to "do my own thing."

The lifestyle typified by these focal concerns catches people in a web of circumstances that virtually guarantee that they will be engaged in antisocial activities. The search for *excitement* leads to vandalism, fights, drug and alcohol abuse, and sexual adventures in which little preventative care is taken (*fate*), and the desire for personal freedom (*autonomy*) precludes marriage (which may hinder the future excitement and put a damper on one's autonomy) if pregnancy results. Given this, Miller was concerned that many males in low-SES neighborhoods would grow up in fatherless homes with little supervision and seek their male identities in gangs, which he calls "one-sex peer units" (1958, p. 14).

Elijah Anderson's (1999) ethnographic work in Black neighborhoods in Philadelphia supports Miller's idea of focal concerns. Anderson notes that the concentrated disadvantages in Black low-SES neighborhoods spawn a hostile oppositional subculture that spurns things valued by middle-class America, as in "rap music that encourages its young listeners to kill cops, to rape, and the like" (p. 107). He also notes that many "decent" families privately subscribe to traditional values in such neighborhoods but the ambiance is determined by "street" families, which often requires decent people to "code switch" (adopt street values) to survive in them. Striving for legitimate success via education and legitimate employment is viewed as "dissing" the neighborhood, and street people do what they can to prevent their "decent counterparts from... acting white" (p. 65). The street code is primarily a campaign for respect achieved by exaggerated displays of hyperinflated manhood, defined in terms of toughness and sexuality in a gang context.

Cultural Criminology and Cultural Debasement

Cultural, or anarchic, criminology is the latest iteration of subcultural theory and stresses the emotional nature of crime. It has done criminology a favor by introducing the much-neglected idea of emotions. Cultural criminology is more interested in how committing crimes makes criminals *feel* rather than what material benefits they may gain, and they tend to be left-wing radical Marxists who attack theories favored by both conservatives and liberals. They have a special distaste for viewing criminals as rational calculators: "The enemy of cultural criminology is the state and an administrative criminology that advocates rational choice theory" (Lilly, Cullen, & Ball, 2011, p. 226). The theory views crime as the result of the breakdown of the values of traditional culture which has become obsessed with consumerism, hedonism, sex, and violence (Young, 2003).

Cultural criminologists introduced the concept of *anelpis* (a Greek term meaning "without hope") to explain the mindset of a segment of society that is "a historically unique section of humanity, which cannot be described as an 'underclass' in the structural sense because their wage needs have been priced out of the global market" (Hall & Winlow, 2004, p. 277). Economic globalization has caused the loss of millions of well-paying manufacturing jobs formerly available to those with limited credentials in the United States. The state of mind of these people "without hope" living in a morally debased culture is described as "the presence of virtually total cynicism and nihilism: virtually no opinion, no realistic expectations, no hope and no fear of authority" (Hall & Winlow, 2004, p. 277). This image is of people trapped in permanent economic depression who have abandoned all rational thought and reverted to a more primitive state animated primarily by negative emotions such as humiliation, anger, resentment, and rage. Cultural criminologists view criminal behavior as attempts to escape these negative emotions and to assert their humanity. For the *anelpis*, "rules are transgressed because they are there, risk is a challenge, not a deterrent" (Young, 2003, p. 319).

The cultural degradation view of cultural criminology is shared by conservative criminologists. They see it as emerging from the dominance of a liberal/progressive worldview that has "undermined traditional values and authority. A culture that had emphasized self-control and discipline was replaced by a culture trumpeting moral relativism and an insidious permissiveness" (Cullen & Agnew, 2011, p. 459). The difference is that cultural criminologists trace cultural degradation to relentless poverty caused by the loss of many good jobs while conservative criminologists trace poverty (both economic and moral poverty) to cultural degradation. As described by Bennett, DiIulio, and Walters (1996, p. 13):

> [Moral poverty] is the poverty of being without loving, capable, responsible adults who teach you right from wrong. It is the poverty of being without parents and other authorities who habituate you to feel

> joy at others' joy, pain at others' pain, happiness when you do right, remorse when you do wrong. It is the poverty of growing up in the virtual absence of people who teach morality by their own everyday example and who insist that you follow suit.

Poverty: What Causes It?

All subcultural theories focus on poverty as the fundamental cause of both subcultural formation and crime. Crime and poverty are correlated, but does poverty cause crime, or does crime cause poverty? It is an article of faith among most sociologists that the former is the case, but prominent sociologist and criminologist Robert Sampson (2000, p. 711) notes that:

> everyone believes that "poverty causes crime" it seems; in fact, I have heard many a senior sociologist express frustration as to why criminologists would waste time with theories outside the poverty paradigm. The reason we do... is that the facts demand it.

Frank Schmalleger (2004, p. 223) also notes that the underlying assumption of all structural and subcultural theories is that the "root cause" of crime is poverty, but notes that: "Some now argue the inverse of the 'root causes' argument, saying that poverty and what appear to be social injustices are produced by crime, rather than the other way around." This is an important issue that points to different policy implications. Of course, neither may directly cause the other because some third set of variables may cause both crime and poverty or the effect may be bidirectional suggesting that poverty causes crime but crime also causes poverty; that is, poverty and crime are mutually reinforcing (Hipp, 2010). This is not to say that most people in poverty are criminals or that all criminals are in poverty.

One variable highly correlated with both poverty and crime is intelligence, as measured by IQ tests (Frisell, Pawitan, & Långström; 2012; Schwartz et al., 2015). IQ is highly heritable, with estimates ranging from 0.50 in childhood to 0.80 among older adults (Deary, Cox, & Hill, 2022). The change in these estimates over time reflects the fact that the correlations between pairs of DZ twins fall dramatically from childhood to adulthood as the influence of shared environment decreases while correlations between pairs of MZ twins, regardless of whether they were reared together or apart, remain stable from childhood to adulthood. The adolescent IQ correlation between MZ twins *reared apart* (0.72) is significantly larger than that between DZ twins *reared together* (0.60), and the weighted correlation across diverse studies between adult DZ twins is only 0.22 (Bouchard & McGue, 2003). Genes confer IQ levels, and their effects are amplified over time through G*x*E and rGE processes as people select environments correlated with their genetic propensities.

Intelligence predicts many life outcomes associated with criminal behavior such as poverty, low education, out-of-wedlock birth, and unemployment. For instance, the National Longitudinal Study of Youth (NLSY) assessed the IQ of 12,686 Whites in 1979 when subjects were between 14 and 17 years old and interviewed them about various life outcomes when they were between 24 and 27 years old. Dividing the sample between the bottom 20% on IQ (87 and below) and the top 20% (113 and above), Herrnstein and Murray (1994) looked at life outcomes between these groups. They found that 66% of the low-IQ group dropped out of school versus 2% of the high-IQ group. Some other outcomes between the two groups were "Living below the poverty level" (48% low vs. 5% high), "Males unemployed the entire previous year" (64% low vs. 4% high), "Females who had a child out of wedlock" (52% low vs. 2% high), and "Ever interviewed in jail or prison" (62% low vs. 2% high). The 33:1 ratio of the latter outcome speaks volumes about the role of IQ in accounting for crime.

Income levels are one measure of one's SES. Sociologists tend to view children's SES as leading directly to their adult SES, and thus to poverty, affluence, and everything in between. But what causes SES? From the above NLSY data, IQ has to be an obvious factor since almost ten times as many low IQ people (48%) were in poverty versus 5% of high IQ people at age 27. So, the next question is what causes IQ? When sociologists consider the correlation between IQ and SES, they tend to view children's IQ as an effect only of parental SES. This kind of naïve environmentalism assumes that any correlation between parents and children is due to parental effects. Noting that the IQs of parents and offspring are correlated, which is to be expected since parents provide their children's genes, Spirtes, Glymour, and Scheines (2000, p. 112) remark: "It seems very unlikely that the child's intelligence causes the family socioeconomic status, and the only sensible interpretation is that SES causes IQ, or they have a common unmeasured cause." The first clause in that sentence is an obvious truism, the second is demonstrably false, and as for the third, genes are the "unmeasured cause" they ignore.

Plomin and von Stumm (2018, p. 3) note that:

> Across studies, parents' education correlates 0.30 with children's intelligence, implying that it accounts for 9% of the variance in children's intelligence. This association is, however, confounded by genetics, because children inherit the DNA differences that predict their intelligence from their parents.

The real test is not the correlation between parental SES and children's IQ, but rather the correlation between children's IQ and their adult SES. As Jensen notes: "If SES were the cause of IQ, the correlations between adults' IQ and their attained SES would not be markedly higher than the correlation between children's IQ and their parents' SES" (1998, p. 491). He also notes that across numerous studies, the correlations between adult IQ and their SES are in the range from 0.50 to 0.70 (Jensen, 1998). The variance explained in adult SES by offspring IQ is thus roughly three to five times higher than the variance accounted for by parental SES and offspring IQ.

Nettle's (2003) study of all children born in Britain in one week in 1958 and followed to age 42 found that IQ is associated with class mobility in adulthood across all social classes of origin. An IQ difference of 24.1 points was found between those who attained professional class and those in the unskilled class, regardless of the class of origin or anything else. He concluded that "intelligence is the strongest single factor causing class mobility in contemporary societies that has been identified" (2003, p. 560). Another longitudinal study of 4,298 British males ages 11 to 33 using data from the National Child Development Study (Bond & Saunders, 1999) tested the child SES-determines-SES position against the meritocratic position (individual ability determines adult SES). They found that meritocratic (cognitive ability, ambition, and hardworking) factors assessed when subjects were seven accounted for 48% of the variance in occupational status, a major measure of SES, at age 33. All background variables combined, including parental SES, accounted for only 8%. Bond and Saunders concluded: "Occupational selection in Britain appears to take place largely on meritocratic principles" (1999, p. 217). They note a persisting association between class or origin and class of destination, but that persistence is mediated by meritocratic factors (p. 234).

Policy Recommendations of Subcultural Theories

Policy recommendations derived from subcultural theories do not differ from those derived from ecological or anomie/strain theories. Programs such as PRWORA, the Chicago Area Project, and the Mobilization for Youth, however, concentrated on changing the behavior of individuals not the patterns of subcultures. Changing a subculture is next to impossible insofar as a subculture is a patterned way of life, we cannot attack the problem in parts and expect to effect much change in the whole. One possible strategy would be to disperse "problem families" throughout a city rather than concentrating them in block-type projects as is typically done. We have seen that this was done with the MoT program with mixed results. In some cases, rather than breaking up the subculture and its values, it may result in its displaced carriers "infecting" areas previously insulated from the values they brought with them.

We saw an example when Hurricane Katrina hit New Orleans in 2005. It disrupted gangs, scattered drug customers, and an uneasy peace settled over the city. However, gang members took their attitudes and behaviors to their new cities. After only a few months, New Orleans criminals who had moved to other cities had committed 39 murders and were suspects in 42 others (Ripley, 2006). Ripley goes on to note:

> For the first time in modern history, we now know what criminals will do after a mass exodus: just like everyone else, they will spend a couple of months getting their bearings. They will apply for aid and call people they care about on their cell phones. Then they will find one another and start killing one another again. They will go where the housing and the drug users are. Perhaps most important of all, they will carry with them the petty disputes of the past, along with their assumptions about the consequences.
>
> *(2006, np)*

Routine Activities Theory

Rather than ending on this pessimistic note, we might better look at the crime prevention policies suggested by Cohen and Felson's (1979) routine activities theory. This theory maintains that crime results when a motivated offender meets a suitable target (a person walking down a dark alley, a darkened house, etc.) lacking a capable guardian (companions, watchful neighbors, patrolling police, etc.). Routine activities theory takes motivated offenders for granted in lower SES areas. Thus, the key to preventing crime from this theory is reducing criminal opportunities by minimizing the occasions in which potential offenders and suitable targets come together by arranging the environment to make offending more difficult and riskier. If you were a motivated criminal with even a modicum of rationality, before deciding to commit a crime you would consider certain questions such as: "Is there a fast way out of the area after the job is done?" "How vulnerable is the target (is the car unlocked, is the girl alone)?" "What are my chances of being seen by others?" "If I am seen, are the witnesses likely to intervene or call the police?" These are questions most potential lawbreakers ask themselves all the time.

These policy implications of routine activities theory boil down to arranging the local environment so that criminals will dissuade themselves from committing crimes by maximizing the probability that the answers to questions such as those above will lead them to conclude that committing a criminal act is not worth the risk. The focus is thus on environmental design. Environmental design concerns itself with the concept of defensible space, which is "a model for residential environments which inhibit crime by creating the physical expression of a social fabric that defends itself" (Newman, 1972, p. 3). Environmental design refers to removing certain physical features of the environment to make natural surveillance easier, thus reducing criminal opportunities. The best physical environment for the growth of crime is the large barracks-like blocks of apartments with few entrances, few private spaces, and few demarcation barriers that say "This space is mine." Families must be given back a sense of ownership, for if everything is "owned" in common (e.g., elevators, walkways and staircases, balconies, grass, and shrubbery), then no one takes care of these things and they deteriorate rapidly. A situation such as this is known in economics as "The tragedy of the commons." Streets must be strategically arranged to generate a sense of belonging to "My special neighborhood" and spatially arranged so criminals cannot easily access or escape from the neighborhood.

Individuals, businesses, and local governments can reduce crime by target hardening. Examples of target hardening include people investing in antitheft devices on automobiles, home alarms, and large aggressive dogs, and governments investing in vandal-resistant materials on public property, improved city lighting, surveillance cameras in stores and public gathering places, removing signs from convenience store windows to enhance natural surveillance, having more than one clerk in a store to enhance guardianship, check guarantee cards, banning the sale of alcohol at sporting events, neighborhood watches, and teenage curfews.

Crime is highly concentrated at a small number of specific "hot spot" locations in cities where the police are constantly called. For instance, Andresen, Curman, and Linning (2017) found that in Vancouver, between 5% and 7% of the street segments and intersections accounted for 100% of the robberies, and between 14% and 17% of much the same areas accounted for 100% of street assaults incidents between 1991 and 2006. Schnell, Grossman, and Braga (2019) found that less than 4% of Newark, NJ street segments generated almost 25% of street violence incidents between 2008 and 2013. Thus, routine activities theorists are likely to recommend that the police concentrate their efforts on so-called hot spots where that act both as deterrents by arresting lawbreakers and as sentinels (capable guardians) as recommended by intelligence-based policing made possible by CompStat programs across the nation (Zimring, 2013). Hot spots are places identified by crime mapping where crime clusters. However, it is not only serious crimes that occur in hotspots but also numerous minor antisocial acts such as public drunkenness and urination, fights, and vandalism. Routine activities theorists argue that such acts should not be ignored because they contribute to the further deterioration of a neighborhood and invite more and worse crimes.

As a highly politicized theory, cultural criminologists tend to discount crime prevention efforts (Farrell, 2010). After all, cultural criminology is not interested in primary crime prevention, but rather in understanding the emotionally expressive motives of a certain class of offender—those who supposedly have given up hope of ever effectively participating successfully in mainstream society. While cultural criminologists are unable to draw any practical applications from their theory, understanding the minds and motives of motivated offenders, even offenders primarily moved by emotions and "damn the consequences" rather than rationality, others may be led to devise ways of effectively dealing with them in the future. Cultural criminologists emphasize the highly emotional nature of crime rather than its material gain and discount risks. To quote Jock Young again, for the *anelpis*, "rules are transgressed because they are there, risk is a challenge, not a deterrent" (2003, p. 319).

If cultural criminologists think about crime prevention at all, they point out the pitfalls of things such as defensible space and target hardening rather than offer any preventative suggestions. They maintain that with such obstacles in place, criminals will move to less guarded areas to ply their trade—crime displacement—or when a target is hardened, such as antitheft devices on automobiles, they will resort to the more dangerous business of carjacking. Thus, Graham Farrell (2010, p. 60) asserts that cultural criminology offers "little, if anything, useful to inform crime reduction efforts." Since much of the blame for predatory criminality is placed at the door of capitalism, the only solution to the crime problem for cultural criminologists seems to be to replace the American free market economy with a government-controlled command economy, which is a policy that is highly unlikely to resonate with most Americans.

9

SOCIAL LEARNING THEORIES

Differential Association Theory

All social learning theories posit that criminal behavior is learned behavior that is learned in the same way any other behavior is learned; that is, by interpersonal communication and social interaction in small intimate groups such as the family, school, and—predominantly during adolescence—peers. That is, learning criminal behavior involves the same culturally transmitted mechanisms involved in any other learning and includes specific skills and techniques for committing crimes and the motives, rationalizations, justifications, and attitudes of criminals. Many different animal species learn by instinctively mimicking others, but humans are the learning species par excellence because their highly evolved social intelligence has allowed them to build heavily on what they have learned, and it is this that has made our species the masters of the planet. The most long-lived learning theory is Edwin Sutherland's differential association theory (DAT) which he formulated at the University of Chicago around the same time (the 1920s–1930s) as Shaw and McKay were formulating their human ecology theory.

In common with Walter Miller's (1958) focal concerns theory, Sutherland maintained that lower-status cultures have their own integrity and organization, and disdained the phrase *social disorganization* as insulting and substituted *differential social organization* for it. Sutherland's ambition was to develop a universal theory of delinquency that could explain both individual criminality and aggregate crime rates by identifying conditions that must be present for crime to occur and are absent when crime is absent.

DOI: 10.4324/9781003642268-12

He stressed that the social context in which people are embedded largely determines the behavioral patterns they exhibit and attempted to provide mechanisms by which factors lead to crime. Sutherland explicitly denied the role of psychology or biology in crime and delinquency, but his theory is implicitly psychological in that it focuses on the process of becoming delinquent via social definitions of reality and attitude formation, and one can hardly say that the genetic and physiological profiles people bring with them to social situations do not matter. Sutherland's theory consists of the following nine propositions:

Criminal behavior is learned.
Criminal behavior is learned in interaction with other persons during a process of communication.
The principal part of the learning of criminal behavior occurs within intimate personal groups.
When criminal behavior is learned, the learning includes techniques of committing the crime, which are sometimes complicated and sometimes simple, and the specific direction of motives, drives, rationalizations, and attitudes.
The specific direction of motives and drives is learned from definitions of the legal codes as favorable or unfavorable.
A person becomes delinquent because of an excess of definitions favorable to violation of law over definitions unfavorable to violation of law.
Differential associations may vary in frequency, duration, priority, and intensity.
The process of learning criminal behavior by association with criminal and noncriminal patterns involves all the mechanisms in any other learning.
While criminal behavior is an expression of general needs and values, it is not explained by those needs and values since noncriminal behavior is an expression of the same needs and values (Sutherland & Cressey, 1974, p. 75).

The key proposition is "A person becomes delinquent because of an excess of definitions favorable to violations of law over definitions unfavorable to violations of law." This proposition is trivially true and tautologous because "an excess of definitions favorable to violations of law" and "delinquent" are the same thing—if we know one, we automatically know the other. But the tautology charge will lose its power if we include biopsychosocial insights to specify how and why some people in the same environment learn excess of definitions favorable to violations of law and others do not because all behavior involves G*x*E and rGE processes. Definitions refer to the meaning our experiences have for us and how our attitudes, values, and habitual ways of viewing the world are derived from them. DAT argues that learning criminal conduct is a process of modeling the self after and identifying with individuals we respect and value. Definitions are favorable to law violations in proportion to the frequency, duration, priority, and intensity of exposure to them. Definitions favorable to law violation are most likely learned in disorganized low-SES neighborhoods where children are surrounded by them and cannot help being influenced by them regardless of their characteristics. Walsh and Jorgensen (2020, p. 126) explain DAT as follows:

> The theory asserts that humans, like chameleons, take on the hues and colors of their environments, blending in and conforming with natural ease. Most Americans probably like baseball, hot dogs, apple pie, and Chevrolets, as a Chevrolet commercial used to remind us. But do we prefer these things over, say, soccer, bratwurst, strudel, and Volkswagens because the former are demonstrably superior to the latter or simply because we are Americans and not Germans? We view the world differentially according to the attitudes, beliefs, and expectations of the groups around which our lives revolve; it could hardly be otherwise, particularly during our formative years. Sutherland's basic premise is that delinquent behavior is learned just as readily as we learn to play the games, enjoy the food, and drive the cars that are integral parts of our cultural lives.

DAT is primarily a theory of peer influence, and the type of peer groups individuals have access to are contingent on the social context and the neighborhoods in which they reside. Delinquent peer groups convey their attitudes, values, and motivations to group members, and the various techniques of committing crimes. Sutherland argues that learning criminal conduct is a process of modeling the self after and identifying with, individuals we admire, respect, and value. By emphasizing only social learning, DAT wants to lead us away from the notion that criminal behavior results from biological or psychological abnormalities or is invented anew by each criminal. According to DAT, criminality is not the result of individual traits or learned from impersonal communication from movies, books, or magazines. Despite Sutherland's later rejection of individual differences, he earlier gave them some recognition by noting that they affect relationship patterns: "Individual differences among people in respect to personal characteristics or social situations cause crime only as they affect differential association or frequency and consistency of contacts with criminal patterns" (1939, p. 8). Sutherland thus admits that differential association *intervenes* between individual character traits at one end and criminal behavior at the other. This is precisely what biopsychosocial criminology maintains.

The Issue of Self-Selection

This leads to the issue of self-selection into delinquent and criminal groups. Numerous studies of relationship patterns have shown that individual traits sort people into different relationship patterns (Benedict, 2019; Schindler et al., 2021). Differential association may be a case of birds of a feather flocking together rather than innocents with snow-white feathers joining an antisocial flock and dirtying their feathers. One early critic of DAT asked: "What is there to be learned about simple lying, taking things that belong to another, fighting and sex play?" (Glueck, 1956, p. 94). Another critic wrote that Sutherland had an overly benign view of delinquents as "slum boys who become delinquent as nice friendly lads, available for indoctrination into the delinquent subcultures" (Kornhauser, 1978, p. 201). In this view, flocking together in delinquent groups doubtless facilitates and accentuates delinquent activities but does not "cause" them.

Reviews of relationship patterns typically find that delinquent behavior *precedes* delinquent gang membership and that association with other like-minded individuals (rGE) simply speeds up and enhances antisocial behavior among those predisposed to it rather than being a stimulator of uncharacteristic behavior among the innocent. Gottfredson (2006, p. 92) summarized several studies addressing this issue and notes: "The evidence is consistent with the proposition that much of the variance in peer effects on delinquency is attributable to the selection effect of like individuals associating together." TenEyck and Barnes (2015) found that once the effect of self-selection into different peer groups was accounted for, there was no significant direct influence of peer groups on delinquency. However, self-selection and peer group influences operate simultaneously, each accounting for a portion of the correlation between an individual's delinquency and the influence of the peer group (Rebellon, 2012).

However, it is undeniable that social organization largely dictates people's associations. Children associate and become friends with other children in the neighborhoods their parents provide for them. In socially disorganized neighborhoods, it is not unreasonable to posit that delinquent peers may cause delinquency among youths who are otherwise insulated from it as well as accelerate it among youths who are attracted to it. The self-selection notion is valid for children in better neighborhoods with equal access to both prosocial and antisocial peers to select from, but not for those who grow up in the urban slums where prosocial peers are rare. Even in those neighborhoods, Mark Warr (2002) distinguishes between two approaches to the influence of delinquent peers that youth may take—private acceptance and compliance—and notes that DAT has only private acceptance in mind and ignores the idea of mere compliance.

Compliance is publicly engaging in delinquent activity to be seen as a complying person within the subculture without privately accepting it or the values and attitudes underpinning it. Private acceptance refers to the public and private acceptance of attitudes, values, and delinquent behaviors. Once initiated in delinquency, such people may continue offending well into adulthood. Warr says DAT was formulated only with private acceptance in mind while ignoring the idea of compliance. We saw earlier in Anderson's (1999) ethnographic study of Black urban areas that "decent" families comply ("code-switch") with the ambiance set by "street" families so they may live relatively safely.

Social Learning Theory

Social learning is the process of acquiring cultural norms of behavior by imitating role models in a social context. All meaningful behavioral learning is thus social, and social learning theory (SLT) seeks to elucidate mechanisms by which this is accomplished. SLT is associated primarily with Ronald Akers and is an extension of DAT. Robert Burgess and Akers (1966) added the concepts of operant psychology to DAT and claimed it was differential reinforcement that either amplified or extinguished any behavior, including criminal behavior. Rather than focusing solely on differential association to explain a person's social behavior, SLT focuses on four principles: differential reinforcement, differential association, imitation, and definitions (as defined in DAT). Differential reinforcement is defined as, "the balance of anticipated or actual rewards and punishments that follow or are consequences of behavior" (Akers, 2011, pp. 66–67). Psychological principles are central to SLT, although Akers insists it is in the same sociological tradition as DAT and retains all the processes found in DAT in modified form. For some, the balance of anticipated or actual rewards and punishments processes moves them in prosocial directions, for others, it moves them in antisocial directions, but the balance can fluctuate over time.

Akers notes that law violation will happen when the following four things occur:

He or she differentially associates with others who commit, model, and support violations of social and legal norms (differential association).

The violative behavior is differentially reinforced over behavior in conformity to the norm (differential reinforcement).

He or she is more exposed to and observes more deviant models than conforming models (imitation).
His or her own learned definitions are favorable toward committing the deviant acts (excess of definitions) (Akers, 1998, p. 51).

The most important of these four principles is differential reinforcement, which is based on the principles of operant psychology; that is, the principle that future behavior is governed by its past consequences. When we behave in some meaningful fashion, consequences are generated in the form of feedback from others that we interpret as positive or negative. Behavior is either positively reinforced, in which case it is likely to be repeated, or positively punished and will likely not be repeated. The most effective reinforcements and punishments are social and derived primarily from one's intimate social groups as one receives various forms of praise or admonition from others whose opinions we respect and value.

The loot from a successful burglary, the euphoric feelings from getting away with it, and the status achieved among antisocial peers are examples of positive reinforcement. Negative reinforcement occurs when some aversive condition is avoided or removed such as removal of an unwanted reputation following when peers learn of one's acts of bravado. Both examples strengthen and amplify criminal behavior. Punishment may lead to the weakening or elimination of behavior and may also be positive or negative. Positive punishment is the application of something undesirable such as a prison term. Negative punishment is the removal of a pleasant stimulus such as the loss of "street cred" in the neighborhood. From the SLT's perspective, acquiring Sutherland's "definitions favorable" to antisocial behavior depends on an individual's history of reinforcement and punishment.

Each peer group member participates in the reinforcement/punishment process via the reciprocal effects each member has on their peers since it is them that hand out the cheers and boos. Of course, what is reinforcing for some may be punishing for others. For teens who value the approval of their parents and teachers, an arrest is experienced as punishment. For teens who value the approval of antisocial peers, such an outcome is a reinforcer since it marks them officially as "badass." The social context is an important component of SLT because most behavior occurs in the presence of others who provide both the social context and the available social reinforcements or punishments.

Discrimination is another important component of SLT. Discriminative stimuli are signals from others indicating behavior that will be rewarded or punished in a particular social context. Reinforcing or punishing stimuli *follow* a person's behavior, but discriminative stimuli occur *before* the behavior occurs. An example of a discriminative stimulus is a person approached in the street by a young girl crying, a police officer, an aggressive drunk, or the person's mother. The person's response will represent what he or she has previously learned about those people or others like them. In other words, discrimination involves distinguishing between stimuli that have been reinforced or punished in the past and similar stimuli you expect will result in the same response in future. An unlocked car with the keys in it, for example, is a discriminative stimulus that signals "immediate reward" for the criminal, but for the average person, it does not signal anything except a foolish driver.

The Neglect of Individual Differences

SLT adds to DAT by specifying how definitions favorable to law violation are learned by operant conditioning but neglects individual differences in the ease or difficulty with which persons learn. All social behavior, including crime, is socially learned, but as Fox (2017, p. 25) observes: "This begs the question: why are some individuals more likely to associate or model antisocial peers, or feel reinforcement and rewards for their antisocial behavior?" Some people find hell-raising exciting and reinforcing and are more susceptible to short-term rewards because they lack self-control. Others can better appreciate the long-term rewards of behaving well because they can self-regulate. While the former are much more likely to be found in poor neighborhoods, it is not all about the environment. Many people in poor neighborhoods reject criminal activity, and some in more affluent neighborhoods embrace it.

However, we want to know why some people are inclined to learn one thing and others to learn other things and what makes them succeed or fail in their learning endeavors. Cao (2004, p. 97) opines that SLT assumes "a passive and unintentional actor who lacks individuality and [is] better at explaining the transmission of criminal behavior than its origins." And, because of their "limited conception of human nature, learning theories generally also ignore the differential receptivity of individuals to criminal messages." Ruth Kornhauser likewise criticized learning theories as resting on the untenable assumptions that "man has no nature, socialization is perfectly successful, and cultural variability is unlimited" (1978, p. 34).

If there is no human nature and "socialization is perfectly successful," the subculture in which delinquent values and behavioral norms are transmitted is deviant, not the individuals who conform to them. But humans do have a nature, and some individuals have genetic variations in that nature (differences in self-control, IQ, fearlessness, empathy, and so forth) that render them more ready to engage in antisocial behavior than others because of their personalities and will find such behavior is reinforced in delinquent areas. As criminologist Gwynn Nettler (1984, p. 295) well put it: "Constitutions affect the impact of environment. What we learn and how well we learn it depends on constitution. The fire that melts the butter hardens the egg."

However, Akers denies that his theory ignores individual differences when he writes:

> An individual in a low crime group or category who is nevertheless more exposed to criminal associations, models, definitions, and reinforcement than someone in a high crime group or category will have a higher probability of committing criminal or deviant acts.
>
> *(1999, p. 482)*

This is an argument about different environments not about different individuals. It assumes automaton-like individuals enter environments at one end and emerge out the other end as criminal or non-criminal based only on exposure to different "associations, models, definitions, and reinforcement" and ignores the traits and characteristics they bring to the environment.

Policy Recommendations Derived from Social Learning Theories

Both DAT and SLT are concerned with the influence of role models in intimate peer groups, so providing prosocial role models for youths is the obvious suggestion. However, getting most parents to convince their children to attend a Saturday Bible study group rather than to hang out with their friends and party would be a Herculean task. Other less cerebral programs that bring youths together for prosocial purposes, such as sports leagues and community projects, might be high on the agenda of policymakers, but the lure of "the streets" and of the friends they have grown up with remains a powerful force retarding such efforts. Probation and parole departments recognize the importance of keeping convicted felons away from each other, making it a revocable offense to "associate with known felons." However, probation and parole officers know how hopeless this is for felons whose friendship network, and even their families, largely consists of felons. The good news is that most delinquents will desist with age, and the breakup of the friendship group by the incarceration, migration, death, or marriage of its members will break the grip of antisocial behavior for many of the remaining members (Moffitt, 2017).

Thus, unlike the top-down policies of crime prevention of programs such as PRWORA and MoT, the policies recommendations of DAT and SLT are bottom-up and strive to prevent crime or further crime by focusing on instilling prosocial attitudes and values before antisocial behavior is initiated or after it is. Social learning theories concentrate their efforts on explaining how individuals learn to commit crimes and delinquent acts, and thus policies derived from them must address how they learn and how they may unlearn such behavior and learn prosocial behavior. As Ronald Akers views such programs:

> The application of social learning theory is found in programs designed, directly or indirectly, to affect associations, reinforcement, definitions and attitudes, modeling and imitation, discriminative stimuli, and other learning and variables by which behavior is acquired and changed. The general prediction is that the greater the degree to which an intervention project is designed or otherwise reflects these social learning principles, the greater the effectiveness of the program in preventing, controlling, or countering delinquent or criminal behavior.
>
> *(2010, p. 89)*

The Provo Experiment

I will concentrate on the three programs Akers mentions that have been most prominent in the literature, beginning with the Provo (Utah) Experiment. According to Akers: "The Provo Experiment [which began in 1956] offered a semi-residential alternative to regular juvenile probation and to incarceration in a state training school for adjudicated delinquent boys" (2010, p. 90). All boys were adjudicated habitual delinquents and were candidates for the reformatory. They were assigned randomly to one of three groups: (1) regular community probation, (2) the semi-residential facility of Pinehills, and (3) a secure-custody state reformatory. The Pinehills program, which extended over five years, was designed to render its residents ambivalent about their delinquent behavior amenable to rehabilitation and to develop a pro-social peer culture within the facility (Empey & Rabow, 1961).

Akers notes that the Pinehills program proved successful initially, but faded over time: "The Pinehills boys did better than the state training school boys six months after release and even four years later. However, after four years the Pinehills boys did little better than the juveniles placed on community probation" (2010, p. 90). Robert Martinson had a less sanguine take on the Provo Project:

> If one judges the program not only by its "successful" boys but by all the boys who were subjected to it—those who succeeded and those who, not surprisingly, failed—the totals show no significant improvement in recidivism rates compared with boys on regular probation.
>
> *(1974, p. 39)*

Of course, Martinson is best known for asserting that nothing designed to rehabilitate delinquents and criminals works.

People change their voluntary behavior only when they want to and only want to when they perceive such a change will be in their best interest. During their stay at Pinehills, it was in their best interest to change their "definitions favorable to law violation," because failure to do so could result in removal from the program and being sent to the reformatory. Once released from the sway of the Pinehills milieu, new prosocial definitions temporarily held sway, but boys reverted to their delinquent ways (probably helped on by peer pressure) as their memories of the program faded and their perceptions of their best interest were again rooted in antisocial behavior. Perhaps this is not surprising since the frequency, duration, priority, and intensity of exposure to antisocial definitions was much greater than their limited exposure to prosocial definitions at Pinehills.

The Teaching-Family Model

The Teaching-Family Model is another program that Akers highlights. This model was shaped by a prototype treatment program called Achievement Place which began in 1967. According to Kingsley (2006, p. 483):

> The Teaching-Family Model is based on a set of clearly stated criteria: (1) A married couple with training and certification by the Teaching Family Association, (2) No more than 8 youths in an accredited home, (3) a system of self-governance by the clients, (4) a behavior modification system.

The theoretical underpinning of the model is thus the operant psychology principles stressed by Akers' SLT. That is, residents operate a system of peer-oriented self-government under the assumption that lessons stick better when applied by peers. Parent teachers helped the process by attempting to shape the behavior of their charges by applying the principles of differential reinforcement. This was done in a "token economy" by which tokens that could be redeemed for valued items were given for good behavior and taken away for bad behavior. The Teaching-Family Model is a well-funded and well-developed program that provides preservice and in-service workshops and consulting services to families, both community-based and home-based, and Teaching-Family Association members pay frequent visits to "observe, provide on-site coaching, conduct information-data reviews, etc. with new site staff …. On-site visits were augmented by regular communications between visits" (Fixsen & Blase, 2019, p. 198).

As for treatment outcomes, Akers (2010, p. 203) observes

> Teaching-family homes did better on measures of school performance, evaluations by consumers (e.g., youths, parents, teachers, court workers, case workers) were more positive for teaching-family homes, but no difference was found for delinquent behavior outcomes either at discharge or up to three years later.

This is not to say, of course, that the children who did better on the positive evaluations are the same ones who committed later delinquency. I could find only one study that reported positive findings concerning delinquent behavior. In a small sample of 140 (102 boys) who had been in a Teaching-Family program and 52 (22 boys) control subjects, Kingsley (2006) found that although the Teaching-Family group was more delinquent pre-treatment, in one year post-treatment 27% of the Teaching-Family group had reoffended versus 47% of the control group.

The Seattle Social Development Project

How about a program aimed at providing at-risk children with prosocial norms and values *before* they are exposed to antisocial norms? The Seattle Social Development Project (SSDP), now known as The Raising Healthy Children (RHC) program, is modeled on DAT and SLT learning principles. The SSDP/RHC is a multicomponent intervention program serving low-SES children in high-crime areas. The program was designed to provide children with competency skills, strong attachment bonds to families and schools, and commitment to prosocial values to set them on a positive developmental trajectory during the first through sixth grade. But how well do these programs function to reduce antisocial behavior and other risky behaviors later in life?

In 1996, when participants were 21 years old, Hawkins et al. (2005) interviewed 605 of them and divided them into a full-intervention group (n = 144), a late-intervention group (n = 256), and a control group (n = 205). Although most variables under the umbrella of positive adjustment to school and emotional and mental health showed statistically significant different results between the full-intervention and control groups, but not between the late-intervention and control groups. However, as for delinquency and crime:

> No significant effects were found for either intervention group for committing any crime in the past year, having been arrested in the past year, using a variety of substances, using substances at a level that interfered with one's life or everyday activities, or having a court charge in the past year.
>
> *(p. 29)*

However, they reported that official records show that by age 21 years, some members of the intervention groups were committing crimes, although they were significantly less likely to have done so (42%) than controls (53%). Small as this 11% difference is, it still represents many crimes never committed.

One finding of importance for the probability of less crime in the future in the above study was a significantly reduced likelihood of out-of-wedlock births by age 21 years (38%) for the SSDP intervention girls than for the control group (56%). A later study by Hawkins et al. (2008) following the same sample to the ages of 24 through 27 found no effects of the intervention for substance use and crime. Overall, the SSDP program had some broad effects on positive functioning in school and at work and on emotional and mental health for the full-intervention group but not for the late-intervention group, indicating that, as with MoT participants, earlier intervention, when a child's brain is more malleable, provides the biggest bang for the crime prevention buck.

10

SOCIAL AND SELF-CONTROL THEORIES

Control Theories Versus Social Learning Theories

Control theories are in many ways the opposites of social learning theories. According to Pratt, Gau, and Franklin (2010), scholars from the social control and social traditions vehemently disagree on many issues relating to crime and criminals. Much of the disagreement appears ideological because criminologists who favor control theories tend to identify as conservatives and moderates, and criminologists favoring the social learning tradition identify themselves as liberals and radicals (Cooper, Walsh, & Ellis, 2010). Both traditions emphasize learning but disagree about what is to be learned. Social learning theories maintain that people have to learn to be antisocial. In contrast, control theories argue that people have to learn to be prosocial, which alerts us that they have very different views of human nature.

Social learning theories assume that criminal behavior requires a process of learning for it to emerge, which carries the *implicit* idea that people are good unless they learn to be otherwise. Control theories are *explicit* that selfish motives are natural, and we must learn to curb them. Social learning theories thus assume that crime is learned by good people living in bad environments and ask: "What causes crime?" Control theorists believe that the real question is "What makes a well-ordered society." They don't ask why some people behave antisocially, but why most people act prosocially most of the time. They also argue that people behave well if their ties to prosocial others are strong, but they may revert to predatory self-interest if they are not. After all, children hit, kick, bite, steal, and

DOI: 10.4324/9781003642268-13

scream, whenever the mood strikes them and do not have to learn not to do these things because in the absence of proper socialization, these things "come naturally."

There are two forms of behavioral control—social control and self-control. Durkheim's anomie theory and Shaw and McKay's human ecology theory may be viewed as social control theories because they point to circumstances (anomie or social disorganization) that weaken the social control of individuals' behavior. Social disorganization theory is more about social control, and Durkheim's anomie is more about self-control. Durkheim was adamant that people need constraints and obligations to give their lives meaning and structure, and to prevent them from reverting to self-interest: "The more weakened the groups to which he belongs, the less he depends on them, the more he consequently depends only on himself and recognizes no other rules of conduct than what are founded on his private interests" (1951, p. 209).

Social Control

For a peaceful social existence, all societies have created mechanisms designed to minimize nonconformity and deviance that we may collectively call social control. Social control may be direct, formal, and coercive, as exemplified by uniformed state symbols. Social control may also be indirect and informal, which is preferable because it leads to prosocial behavior regardless of the presence or absence of external coercion such as the possibility of arrest and imprisonment. Obeying society's rules of proper conduct because we believe the rules are right and just, not because we fear formal sanctions, means we have our own internalized police officer and judge in the form of a conscience.

We begin with Travis Hirschi's (1969) social bond theory. Hirschi saw the institutions of society as "good" and humans, in the absence of proper training, as "bad." Nettler (1984, p. 313) put the control argument colorfully: "If we grow up 'naturally,' without cultivation, like weeds, we grow up like weeds—rank." Development psychologists are virtually unanimous in their support of social control theories over social learning theories, noting that young children exhibit impulsive and aggressive behavior that diminishes in time with proper socialization (Eme, 2015). A 2-year-old's aggressive behavior may raise a chuckle, but if they don't learn to control it, at 22, it is no laughing matter. Nettler's "weediness" is the natural outcome for children who are not properly socialized. A longitudinal study of children's behavior from 2 to 12 years of age found that the frequency of hitting, biting, and kicking peaked at 27 months and declined by about 66% by age 12 (Tremblay & LeMarquand, 2001).

As Tremblay (2008, p. 2619) sums up the literature on this issue: "By monitoring the development of physical aggression from infancy onwards, recent longitudinal studies show that human infants spontaneously use physical aggression and that humans learn not to physically aggress rather than learn to aggress." Toddlers are too young to have learned antisocial definitions and are not associating with deviant peer toddlers, so their aggressive and impulsive behavior must be innate. From this perspective, criminals are simply toddlers who have failed to learn impulse control.

Social bonding/control theory is about the role of social relationships that bind people to the social order. This is the classical view of human nature that maintains that antisocial behavior will emerge automatically if controls are lacking; it needs no special motivating factors since humans are assumed to be naturally self-centered. The classical assumption of self-interested persons seeking pleasure and trying to avoid pain is foundational to the theory, but the theory attempts to account for why some people pursue their self-interest in legitimate ways and others do not. Prosocial socialization practices produce individuals capable of reining in their natural impulses and poor socialization practices do not. Hirschi formulated his theory with some foundational facts about the "typical" criminal and found him to be a young male who grew up in a fatherless home in an urban slum, has a history of difficulty in school, and is unemployed and deduced from this that those most likely to commit crimes lack the four elements of the social bond that form the foundation of prosocial behavior: attachment, commitment, involvement, and belief.

Attachment is the emotional component of conformity and refers to the emotional bonds between the individual and key social institutions, particularly the family. Attachment to prosocial others, particularly to parents, provides the foundation for all other social bonds because it leads us to feel valued, respected, and admired and to value the favorable judgments of those who made us feel that way. Much of our behavior is an attempt to gain favorable judgments from people and groups we care about. Lack of attachment to parents and lack of respect for their wishes easily spill over into a lack of attachment and respect for others in the social world. Much of the controlling power of others outside the family lies in the threat of reporting misbehavior to parents. If the child has little respect for parents, the control exercised by others has little effect: "If a person feels no emotional attachment to a person or institution, the rules tend to be denied legitimacy" (Hirschi, 1969, p. 127). Of course, people can be emotionally attached to deviant parents and peers and thus their deviant behavior can be viewed as conforming to deviant expectations. This is the sort of criticism followers of social learning theories might express. However, Hirschi expressly refers to attachment to prosocial others as a way to explain prosocial behavior and not to all attachments that may lead to other behaviors (Pratt, Gau, & Franklin, 2010). Additionally, attachment to antisocial others does not produce the other elements of the social bond: commitment, involvement, and a prosocial belief system.

Commitment is the ration component of conformity and refers to a lifestyle in which one has invested considerable time and energy in the pursuit of a lawful career. People who invest heavily in a conventional career have a valuable stake in conformity and are not likely to risk it by engaging in antisocial behavior. School dropouts and unemployed adults do not have a strong investment in conventional behavior and thus risk less by committing crimes. Acquiring a stake in conformity requires a disciplined application to tasks that children do not necessarily relish but complete them to gain approval from their parents and teachers. Attachment is thus the essential foundation for commitment to a prosocial lifestyle.

Involvement is a direct consequence of commitment and is part of a conventional pattern of social existence. Involvement is a matter of time and energy constrictions placed on us by the demands of our lawful activities that reduce exposure to illegal opportunities. Conversely, idleness or noninvolvement in conventional activities increases the possibility of exposure to illegal activities. As Hirschi put it: "Idle hands are the devil's workshop" (1969, p. 187).

Belief is the moral component of social conformity and refers to the acceptance of the social norms regulating conduct. Persons lacking attachment, commitment, and involvement tend not to believe in conventional morality. A belief system shorn of morality is concerned only with narrow self-interest. Unlike DAT and SLT, control theory does not view a criminal belief system as motivating criminal behavior. Rather, criminals act according to their urges and then justify or rationalize their behavior with statements such as "Do unto others as they would do unto you—only do it first," or "If I don't do it, others will." Control theorists aver that behavior gives birth to the belief rather than the belief giving birth to the behavior. Thus, crime is not motivated by the absence of social bonds; their absence merely represents social deficiencies that result in a reduction of the perceived potential costs of committing crime.

Self-Control

With Michael Gottfredson, Hirschi moved from explaining antisocial behavior in terms of social control toward explaining it in terms of self-control. Self-control is defined as the "extent to which [different people] are vulnerable to the temptations of the moment" (Gottfredson & Hirschi, 1990, p. 87). Self-control theory maintains that crime results from unrestrained natural human impulses to enhance pleasure and avoid pain. These impulses often lead to crimes when the opportunity arises, which Gottfredson and Hirschi (1990) define as "acts of force or fraud undertaken in pursuit of self-interest" (p. 15). Most crimes and analogous behaviors (e.g., heavy drinking, using illegal drugs, and casual sex) are spontaneous acts requiring little skill or motivation and earn the individual immediate and minimal short-term satisfaction.

People with low self-control lack patience, persistence, and diligence, and are oriented to the present rather than to the future, and crime affords them quick and easy ways to obtain money, sex, revenge, etc. Their low self-control leads them to take risks that they find exciting, and their extreme self-centeredness allows them to take what they want without experiencing pangs of guilt for causing the suffering of others (Gottfredson & Hirschi, 1990, pp. 89–90).

The classic self-control experiment is the "marshmallow test." In this simple experiment, 600 preschoolers were told that they could eat a marshmallow placed before them immediately or wait 15 minutes and be rewarded with an additional marshmallow. Follow-up studies of some of these children in their adolescence found several robust correlations between delay time before succumbing to temptation (only one-third waited the full 15 minutes) and outcomes associated with SES such as SAT verbal ($r = 0.42$) and quantitative ($r = 0.57$) scores, "thinks and plans ahead" ($r = 0.36$) and "uses and respond to reason" ($r = 0.43$) (Shoda, Mischel, & Peake, 1990). Casey et al. (2011) brain-scanned 26 of the original participants in their mid-40s and showed that self-control levels remained stable. High delayers more strongly activated regions in the prefrontal cortex than the more impulsive low delayers, and low delayers were more active in the reward-processing ventral striatum. This study shows that individuals engage the interacting neurocognitive systems involved in approach and avoidance behavior—the systems of self-control—when confronted with temptation. Among low delayers, the approach system is stronger, and among the high delayers, the avoidance system is more vigilant. Another longitudinal study correlated delay levels of 1,000 children between the ages of 3 and 11 with life outcomes at 32. Among these outcomes were substance abuse, health status, criminal conviction, giving birth out-of-wedlock, financial problems, and adult SES. Controlling for childhood SES and IQ, all outcomes were far more positive for those who demonstrated the ability to delay gratification as children than those who did not (Moffitt et al., 2011).

Self-control theory maintains that low self-control is established by incompetent parenting during early childhood, and tends to persist throughout life. It also avers that children *do not* learn low self-control, but rather they learn prosocial self-control; low self-control is the default outcome that occurs in the absence of proper socialization. Brannigan (1997, p. 425) notes that: "In the absence of interaction designed to promote empathy, identification, delayed gratification, a long-time horizon, and prosocial values, the infant appears to exhibit older evolutionary scripts of adaptation which favor immediate gratification and egoism." To produce self-control in offspring requires parental warmth, nurturance, vigilance, and willingness to practice "tough love." Effective parenting requires consistent and fair discipline when a child misbehaves. Overly harsh or overly permissive discipline, and inconsistent or erratic discipline, are unlikely to inculcate self-control in children. Factors that may result in low self-control include parental criminality (criminals are not very successful socializing agents), family size (the larger the family, the more difficult it is to monitor children's behavior), single-parent families (two parents are generally better than one), and working mothers (who negatively impact the development of self-control if no positive substitute monitors are provided and children are left to their own devices) (Gottfredson & Hirschi, 1990).

Gottfredson and Hirschi argue that children acquire or fail to acquire self-control during the first decade of life, after which the attained level of control remains stable across the life course. Subsequent experiences, situations, and circumstances have little independent effect on the probability of offending. Because low self-control is a stable component of a criminal personality, most criminals typically fail in anything that requires long-term commitment, such as school, employment, or marriage, because such commitments get in the way of immediate satisfaction of their desires. Self-control for prosocial behavior is imperative, but self-control is not a motivator of behavior; it is a brake, not an accelerator.

By itself, low self-control is not sufficient to account for offending. Because Gottfredson and Hirschi consider it a stable attribute of individuals across the life course, variation in criminal behavior cannot be explained by variation in their self-control. What explains variation in criminal behavior among low self-control individuals is variation in the *opportunities* to commit it. A criminal opportunity is "a situation that presents itself to someone with low self-control by which he or she can immediately satisfy needs with minimal mental or physical effort" (Gottfredson & Hirschi, 1990, pp. 12–13). Self-control theory is similar to routine activities theory: Crime results from people with low self-control (a motivated offender) meeting a criminal opportunity (a suitable target lacking a capable guardian). The difference is that low self-control theory emphasizes the motivated offender and ignores the target and guardian, whereas routine activities theory does the opposite. Gottfredson and Hirschi illustrate what they mean by the intersection of low self-control and opportunity by describing typical criminal incidents not as the culmination of foresight and planning but as situational opportunities witnessed by someone ready to take advantage of them.

Because of Gottfredson and Hirschi's emphasis on parenting in instilling self-control in their children, we may wonder why the elements of the social bond are absent in self-control theory. Both social control and self-control theories assume a natural inclination to pursue selfish interests with little effort and without regard for others, and both maintain that what distinguishes law-abiding people from criminals are the controls that prevent the former from acting on their natural impulses. Hirschi (2004, p. 543) addressed this concern by noting that, like self-control, "differences in social control are stable, that social control and self-control are the same thing." He welds the two theories together in two sentences: "Self-control is the set of inhibitions one carries with one wherever one goes. Their character may be initially described by going to the elements of the bond identified by social control theory: attachment, commitment, involvement, and belief" (pp. 543–544). Hirschi is saying that self-control and the social control exercised by others in the family, school, and workplace mutually affect one another constantly across the life course and that self-control and social control theories are now integrated.

If we combine both theories and treat them as one, as Hirschi now does, more criminologists checked it in the Cooper, Walsh, and Ellis (2010) survey as the theory that best explains serious criminal behavior than any other. Matt DeLisi (2011, p. 103) calls self-control theory the "T-Rex of criminology," stating that "in terms of empirical tests of its theoretical ideas, citations, [and] influence on the field, self-control theory is 'peerless.'" DeLisi also asserts that self-control is primarily, but not completely, a brain-based disorder and that Gottfredson and Hirschi were wrong in saying that parenting is the sole cause of self-control.

Child Effects and Genetics

Gottfredson and Hirschi's theory has thus been criticized for attributing variation in self-control solely to variation in parental behavior and for ignoring child effects. The child development literature is unequivocal in its assertion that socialization is a two-way street in which parental behavior is shaped by the evocative behavior (evocative rGE) of the child just as much as the child's behavior is shaped by his or her parents (Kuo et al., 2021). Children bring variable levels of self-control with them to the socialization process rather than socialization alone producing those variable levels. Lilly, Cullen, and Ball (2007, p. 110) point this out: "Research suggests that parents may affect levels of self-control less by their parenting styles and more by genetic transmission." This is supported by many studies that have found a strong genetic and neurobiological component to low self-control (Javakhishvili & Vazsonyi, 2022; Wright & Beaver, 2012). A meta-analysis of 31 twin studies found the heritability of self-control to be 0.60 (Willems et al., 2019). The primary gene product underlying self-control has been consistently found to be serotonin and/or its regulation (Boisvert et al., 2018).

This does not mean that parenting is irrelevant; loving and conscientious parenting means more than anything else for the healthy development of prosocial children. It only means that a more sophisticated level of understanding of self-control requires genetically informed samples and the assessment of the influences of children's evocative behavior on parenting behavior. For instance, Belsky and Beaver (2011) looked at a variety of plasticity alleles of genes in the dopaminergic and serotonergic systems associated with antisocial behavior and low self-control and found significant interactions between parenting quality and self-control among 1,588 youths (754 males and 832 females). They found that males raised in homes with strong parenting quality showed moderate to excellent self-control depending on their genetic risk. Male children with a genetic tendency for low self-control may not display the tendency if effectively parented, and children with a genetic propensity for high self-control may not display good self-control if they are inadequately socialized—nurture is just as important as nature. This effect was not seen for females, which they explain by writing: "Perhaps females are simply more easily socialized, so parenting affects the self-regulation of all girls to the same extent irrespective of their genetic make-up" (p. 624). Studies of gender differences in self-control have, without exception, shown that females have higher levels of self-control than males regardless of methods used, culture, race/ethnicity, or age of subjects (Chapple & Johnson, 2007).

Policy Recommendations of Control Theories

Policy recommendations derived from Hirschi's combined theory of social and self-control rest on the core assumption of parental socialization practices within the family: "Stability lies at the heart of the concept of self-control, and justifies our emphasis on early childhood socialization" (Gottfredson & Hirschi, 1990, pp. 58–59). The importance stressed by Gottfredson and Hirschi on nurturance and attachment to parents strongly supports the idea of early family interventions designed to cultivate them. Given that they emphasize the importance of strong and stable two-parent homes, it suggests that they would support programs such as the Out-of-Wedlock Birth Reduction Bonus provision of PRWORA addressed in Chapter 1 that had the effect of reducing nonmarital births and welfare rolls while increasing the income of low-SES families. Indeed, Gottfredson and Hirschi (1997, p. 33) have remarked that *the* policy recommendation deducible from self-control theory is reducing nonmarital births: "Delaying pregnancy among unmarried girls would probably do more to affect the long-term crime rates than all the criminal justice programs combined."

We could go further in our efforts to support stable, resilient families. Almost all wealthy modern nations provide families with children cash family allowances and paid maternal leave, but there has been some movement in certain European countries away from universal provision to targeted intervention only for unstable families (Devaney et al., 2021). Many of the most generous programs found in Europe do not exist in the United States, which indicates that politics and ideology dictate the direction of criminal justice policy more than criminological theory. This is the case even within "social welfare" states in Europe (Hidalgo et al., 2018). However, it is difficult to determine if such programs translate into delinquency and crime prevention throughout a person's childhood, adolescent, and adult lives.

Alex Piquero's (2010, p. 80) evaluation of Gottfredson and Hirschi's general theory (self-control theory) leads him to propose that it has both short-term and long-term policy strategies:

> Boiled down to its core, Gottfredson and Hirschi's general theory of crime really has two key policy prescriptions: a short-term strategy that makes criminal events less attractive to potential offenders by making them more difficult to commit successfully (increase certainty); and a longer-term strategy that focuses prevention and intervention efforts that improve child-rearing practices (which produce more self-control) in the first decade of life.

The Police Role in Social Control

Gottfredson and Hirschi's short-term strategy owes a debt to Cohen and Felson's (1979) routine activities theory (crime results when a motivated offender meets a suitable target lacking a capable guardian) addressed previously. Hirschi and Gottfredson (2001, p. 93) note that prevention is better than cure: "Efforts directed at offenders—treatment, deterrence, incapacitation—will be highly inefficient compared to programs that restrict access to [criminal opportunities]." The idea is to remove temptations from sight now rather than trying to get offenders to resist them directly in the future. Hirschi and Gottfredson highlight target hardening of suitable targets, but downplay the role of the police as capable guardians:

> Self-control theory leads to the conclusion that the formal criminal justice system can play only a minor role in the prevention and control of crime. Because potential offenders do not consider the long-term consequences of their acts, modification of these consequences will have little effect on their behavior. Because criminal acts are so quickly and easily accomplished, they are only rarely directly observed by agents of the criminal justice system. As a result, even large increases in the number of such agents would have minimal effect on the rates of most crimes.
>
> *(Hirschi & Gottfredson, 2001, 93)*

This is an odd position to take, especially in light of the de-policing observed following the death of George Floyd at the hands of the police in Minneapolis in 2020. As previously noted, the value of something is often best noticed by its absence, and when there is a reduction in proactive policing, crime surges (McNeeley, 2015). In 2020, the police cleared only 36.7% of violent crimes and 12.1% of property crimes, including only 54% of murders, which is the lowest clearance rate for homicide on record, and arrests plummeted by 24% (Walsh & Jorgensen, 2025). In contrast, homicide clearance rates have remained steady in Western Europe for many years, ranging from 98% in Finland to 80% in Sweden (Liem et al., 2019). New York's Broken Windows approach to policing became a key part of a proactive policing strategy that made New York City the safest big city in America. However, due to the anti-police rhetoric in evidence after Mr. Floyd's death and stop-and-frisk banned, New York saw the number of shooting victims in the city more than doubled from 923 in 2019 to 1,868 in 2020, and murder rose almost 45% from 2019 (Chapman, 2021). Rosenfeld and Lopez (2020) estimated that de-policing in the wake of the George Floyd incident caused the death of more than 700 people and led to the shooting of more than 2,800 others nationwide. Rosenfeld and Wallman (2019, p. 51) state: "Ample research findings have demonstrated the effectiveness of proactive policing practices, such as targeted patrol, in reducing crime rates." Mourtgos, Adams, and Nix (2022) also noted that the rapid loss of police officers in response to the anti-police rhetoric in 2020 resulted in higher homicide rates, particularly in communities of color.

Piquero remarked ten years before the decline in proactive policing that the idea that the police had minimal impact on crime is a strange notion:

> Gottfredson and Hirschi claim that the police have no effect on crime, there is ample evidence to suggest that in some contexts the police do have some effect on crime, but it should be remembered that what the police do on the street is the most important—that is, keeping offenders guessing, rotating crack-downs, and the like.
>
> *(2010, p. 80)*

Recall that self-control theory maintains that what explains variation in criminal behavior among low self-control individuals is variation in opportunities to commit it. It is undeniable that the police play a vital role in reducing those opportunities by their mere presence (Rosenfeld & Lopez, 2021).

Gottfredson and Hirschi maintain that low self-control is the default result of incompetent parenting during early childhood and that, once established, self-control tends to persist throughout life. This leads us to the second leg of Gottfredson and Hirschi's broad policy proposals: long-term strategies aimed at prevention and intervention strategies aimed at improving child-rearing practices to produce higher levels of self-control early in a child's life. Programs to improve self-control in adults are generally ineffective (Friese et al., 2017), which supports Hirschi and Gottfredson's claim that "differences [in self-control] observed at ages 8 to 10 tend to persist from then on" (2001, p. 90). The prognosis for improving self-control in young children is more positive because their brains are more malleable. It has been noted that: "Evidence for multiple system models comes from functional MRI (fMRI) studies showing that self-controlled choices were associated with lateral prefrontal areas of the brain, whereas more impulsive choices were associated with the ventral striatum and ventromedial prefrontal cortex" (Duckworth, Milkman, & Laibson, 2018, p. 104).

Programs for Improving Self-Control

Children (particularly adolescents) are naturally more motivated than adults to gain immediate rewards that activate the ventral striatum reward system, which is why we consistently see a large uptick in antisocial behavior in adolescents. Avoiding such rewards if they involve behavior harmful to self or other require the more reasoned higher-order sensory processing of the lateral prefrontal areas of pre-frontal cortex regions (Silverman, Jedd, & Luciana, 2015). Adolescents are increasingly more likely to exercise control of their impulses as they age into adulthood.

Bleidorn et al.'s (2022) meta-analysis of longitudinal studies containing 421,045 individuals found that all studies report a prosocial trajectory with age toward conscientiousness and agreeableness, major components of the self-control concept.

How successful are programs designed to improve childhood self-control? Although effect sizes are generally small to moderate (in the 0.20 to 0.60 range), Piquero, Jennings, and Farrington's meta-analysis of 34 studies found that:

> (1) self-control improvement programs improve a child's/adolescent's self-control, (2) these interventions also reduce delinquency, and (3) the positive effects generally hold across a number of different moderator variables and groupings as well as by outcome source (parent-, teacher-, direct observer-, self-, and clinical report). Unpacking these findings yields the overall conclusion that self-control is malleable, that self-control can be improved, and that reductions in delinquency follow from this self-control improvement.
>
> *(2010, pp. 828–829)*

A later meta-analysis of 41 self-control improvement studies conducted by Piquero et al. (2016) examined overall effect size estimates. They found that average, positive, and significant effect sizes were observed for improving self-control (0.32) and reducing delinquency (0.27), and concluded: "Early self-control improvement programs are an effective evidence-based strategy for improving self-control and reducing delinquency" (2016, p. 249). However, these effect sizes are on the low side (0.50 is considered moderate and 0.80 strong), and we cannot determine if these improvements held over the long term. Self-control is relatively easy in an experimental setting in which a correct choice may be inferred from an experimenter's response. However, in a natural setting, subjects (because they were candidates for self-control improvement in the first place) are likely to prioritize immediate gratification over long-term gains. To ascertain, if self-control gains survive beyond the experimental period, we would have to see meta-analyses of longitudinal studies lasting at least ten years post-treatment of much larger samples than is usually the case. However, the fact remains that the best mechanism for self-control development in children is rearing in a stable and loving two-parent family (Gottfredson, & Hirschi, 2016).

PART IV

Specific Syndromes Associated with Criminal Behavior and Prevention and Treatment Policies

11

ATTENTION-DEFICIT/HYPERACTIVITY DISORDER

Causes and Treatment

The Prevalence of ADHD

The following two chapters addressing attention-deficit/hyperactivity disorder (ADHD) and schizophrenia differ from previous chapters in which criminological theories were addressed first followed by prevention and treatment policies. Because ADHD and schizophrenia are well-defined neuropsychiatric conditions with known treatment modalities and not patterns of "antisociality" that people may drift in and out of, the putative causes of these conditions and their treatment modalities inform one another, they are addressed simultaneously rather than in separate sections. These modalities are not crime prevention policies per se, but rather treatment protocols that do, however, prevent delinquency and crime among the afflicted. Although people burdened with ADHD or schizophrenia are relatively few, they commit delinquent and criminal acts (and are victimized) at levels highly disproportionate to their numbers.

ADHD is the most commonly diagnosed childhood neuropsychiatric behavioral disorder and is usually diagnosed before age 12 (Retz et al., 2021). Most high-spirited children sometimes manifest ADHD-like symptoms such as inattention and impulsiveness, but do so relatively mildly and those symptoms do not cluster together as they do in ADHD children. The American Psychiatric Association defines ADHD in the DSM-5 (2013, pp. 59–60) as a behavioral disorder characterized by an impairing pattern of chronic inattention and/or hyperactivity-impulsivity occurring in most settings more frequently and severely than is typical for individuals at the same stage of development. ADHD is marked by motivational dysfunction

DOI: 10.4324/9781003642268-15

characterized by excessive impulsive tendencies, emotional dysregulation, and risk-taking behaviors across many different settings. It has a significant genetic correlation with schizophrenia (rg = 0.22) indicating that it shares some of the same alleles associated with it, most probably polymorphisms of the dopaminergic and serotonergic systems (Legge et al., 2021). Unlike individuals with schizophrenia, however, people with ADHD do not exhibit symptoms such as delusions and anhedonia, but rather knowingly, albeit impulsively, engage in antisocial behaviors such as substance abuse, gambling, unrestricted sexuality, and crime and delinquency.

Some medical professionals question the validity of the ADHD diagnosis for the lack of a clear biological (as opposed to behavioral) test for its presence such as a blood test or throat swab, but Faraone et al. (2021, p. 793) defend its validity:

> ADHD meets standard criteria for validity of a mental disorder. ... The disorder is considered valid because: 1) well-trained professionals in a variety of settings and cultures agree on its presence or absence using well-defined criteria and 2) the diagnosis is useful for predicting a) additional problems the patient may have (e.g., difficulties learning in school); b) future patient outcomes (e.g., risk for future drug abuse); c) response to treatment (e.g., medications and psychological treatments); and d) features that indicate a consistent set of causes for the disorder (e.g., findings from genetics or brain imaging).

There are three types of ADHD: (1) predominately inattentive type (unorganized, easily distracted, and forgetful), (2) predominantly hyperactive-impulsive type (constantly in motion, restless, and impulsive), and (3) combined type in which the symptoms of the first two types are equally in evidence. The combined type requires at least six of nine symptoms from each of the first two types for a combined type diagnosis. Most ADHD individuals evidence the criteria for the combined type, and because it is the most prevalent type, we concentrate on it. As with schizophrenia, the symptoms of ADHD vary widely in their severity and frequency of occurrence and thus should also be viewed as a spectrum disorder rather than a discreet category. It should be noted that not all children diagnosed with ADHD carry their symptoms into adulthood, and the severity of symptoms tends to get better over time for most adults (Sonuga-Barke et al., 2023).

Estimates of the prevalence of ADHD vary widely. The largest rates were found by Wong and Landes (2022) from data on American children aged 5 to 17 from the 2004 to 2018 National Health Interview Survey Sample Child Files (n = 120,129). They report a prevalence of ever being diagnosed with ADHD of 13.26% for males and 5.86% for females. Lower estimates, based on 154 studies from around the world, found ADHD to be prevalent in 5% to 7% of children (Polanczyk et al., 2014). Differences in prevalence rates across nations may be due to the assessment measures used, different diagnostic criteria and assigned symptom thresholds, or whether subjects were assessed by a mental health professional. Assessment by a mental health professional is preferable to inferences based on teachers, parents, or self-reports of ADHD-like symptoms and behavior. A male/female ratio of about 3:1 is typically reported. Males typically have significantly greater symptom severity and are comorbid for other antisocial conditions such as oppositional defiant disorder (ODD) and conduct disorder (CD) than females and females generally show better inhibitory control (Arnett et al., 2015).

ADHD and Delinquent and Criminal Behavior

Unnever, Cullen, and Pratt (2003) observe that ADHD has been neglected by criminologists who are reluctant to engage with anything with the whiff of biology. Individuals with ADHD have many other conditions that are associated with delinquency and crime such as substance abuse, few prosocial friends, and poor educational outcomes such as low grades, greater rates of suspension, and higher drop-out rates. Unnever, Cullen, and Pratt (2003) propose that the neurological and temperamental deficits underlying ADHD may underlie Gottfredson and Hirschi's (1990) concept of low self-control; the "powerhouse" theory of traditional criminology that DeLisi (2011, p. 103) labeled the "T-rex of criminology." Eme (2015, p. 446) takes DeLisi further: "If the brain-based disorder of low self-control is the T-Rex of criminology, then ADHD is the T-Rex of the brain-based disorder of low self-control." Of course, not all individuals with low self-control have ADHD.

The evidence linking ADHD to crime and delinquency is consistently found to be strong. Individuals with ADHD are invariably found to be overrepresented in juvenile detention centers, jails, and prisons worldwide (Rösler et al., 2004). Based on numerous studies, Eme (2012) reports that about 28% of juveniles entering the juvenile justice system have a diagnosis of ADHD, which is about four times more than expected from the ADHD prevalence rate in the United States. Eme considers this a conservative estimate since ADHD prevalence rate estimates from five other Western societies of juveniles entering their juvenile justice systems averaged 45%. Beaudry et al.'s (2021) review of 47 studies from 19 countries comprising 28,033 male and 4,754 female adolescents in juvenile detention centers with various kinds of mental disorders found that the prevalence rates of various mental disorders were greater for ADHD in both male (61.7%) and female (59%) adolescents than they are for any of the other mental disorder.

Adults with ADHD are also found to be greatly overrepresented in adult correctional facilities around the world. Gudjonsson et al.'s (2009) review of prevalence rates of ADHD among prison inmates in several countries found rates ranging from 24% to 67%, with their study showing that 62.5% of inmates were either fully ADHD symptomatic or in partial remission. A German study (Rösler et al., 2004) found that 45% of inmates had some form of ADHD compared to 9.4% of a control sample, which is almost five times greater. This study found that 85.5% of the inmates with ADHD were comorbid for alcohol and substance abuse or dependence. Knecht et al. (2015) found that inmates with ADHD significantly exceed the population prevalence of ADHD in 9 out of 10 countries and most were comorbid for substance abuse. A meta-analysis of 42 studies conducted in 15 countries found a prevalence rate of 25.5% for ADHD among incarcerated populations (Young et al, 2015). ADHD is not only a robust predictor of criminal behavior and incarceration, but it also impacts individuals' adaptation to imprisonment. A Scottish study found that inmates with ADHD have eight times more prison violations such as verbal and physical aggression, destruction of property, and self-injury than non-ADHD inmates (Young et al., 2009).

For assessing criminal convictions, data from the Scandinavian countries are peerless because Scandinavian researchers have access to huge national databases containing official records. For instance, Ångström et al. (2024) used the Swedish National Patient Register and the Swedish National Crime Register of individuals born between 1986 and 1997 (635,391 males and 600,548 females) to assess violent and nonviolent criminal convictions among ADHD patients and controls over seven years. There were 27,103 (4.3%) males and 15,960 (2.7%) females in the data with ADHD. The cumulative incidence for nonviolent criminal convictions was 54.2% for male ADHD subjects and 19.0% for non-ADHD males and for violent criminal convictions, it was 28.3% versus 5.5% for ADHD and non-ADHD males, respectively. Among ADHD females, the cumulative incidence of violent convictions was 11.5% versus 1.2% for non-ADHD females. For nonviolent criminal convictions, it was 30.6% for ADHD females and 7.7% for non-ADHD females. Lower socioeconomic status and substance abuse increased the relative risk for criminal convictions in both ADHD patients and controls.

ADHD/Conduct Disorder Comorbidity

The probability of delinquent/criminal acts for ADHD individuals rises if they are comorbid for CD and/or oppositional-defiant disorder (ODD).

CD has an onset at around five years of age and is defined as persistent serious antisocial acts such as assault, theft, fire setting, bullying, cruelty to animals, and vandalism. It is a neurological disorder with heritability estimates between 0.27 and 0.78 (Coolidge, Thede, & Young, 2000). ADHD/CD comorbidity is found to co-occur in about 50% of cases in most studies (Waschbusch et al., 2002), Lynam (1996, p. 209) notes that ADHD+CD is a "particularly virulent strain .... best described as fledgling psychopathy." DeLisi et al. (2014) compared ADHD+CD youths with youth with ADHD only, and with CD only on psychopathic personality traits and their association with delinquency among an institutionalized sample of 252 youths and found that youths with ADHD+CD were significantly more psychopathic than their ADHD-only peers, and much more so than peers with neither diagnosis. Childhood CD is a requirement for the psychiatric diagnosis of antisocial personality disorder (ASPD) in adulthood. Using data from the Pittsburgh ADHD Longitudinal Study, Sibley et al. (2011) developed similar contrasting groups finding that the ADHD+CD youth were at the highest risk for offending across all measures of severity, variety, and early age of delinquency initiation.

ODD is an earlier-appearing and less severe disorder than CD and is characterized by behaviors such as temper tantrums and lying. The odds of inheriting alleles for comorbid disorders are determined by genetic linkage studies and are quantified by log of the odds ratio (LOD) scores. The closer two or more alleles are together at a chromosomal locus the greater the odds they will be jointly transmitted. An LOD score of 3 is considered the minimal standard for linkage; i.e., the likelihood that two genes have not separated during meiosis. An LOD of 3 means the hypothesis that the genetic markers are linked is 1,000 times as likely as the null hypothesis that they are not. A study of 616 subjects found that the LOD score for ADHD+CD was 5.34, for ODD+CD it was 6.68, and for ODD+ADHD it was 14.19, indicating a strong genetic linkage for these conditions (Jain et al., 2007).

The combination of ADHD+CD in children strongly engages evocative rGE because children take this profile with them in all their social interactions. The antisocial behaviors associated with ADHD+CD invite negative reactions from parents, peers, and teachers, that further exacerbate the child's antisocial tendencies. Lynam (1996, p. 22) describes the trajectory from ADHD+CD to criminality stating that this comorbidity:

> [M]ay tax the skills of parents and lead to the adoption of coercive child rearing techniques, which in turn may enhance the risk of antisocial behavior. Entry into school may bring academic failure and increase the child's frustration, which may increase his or her level of aggressive

behavior. Finally, the peer rejection associated with hyperactivity may lead to increased social isolation and conflict with peers.

De la Paz et al. (2023) looked at the "genetic load" for ADHD and evocative rGE effects for ADHD (but not ADHD+CD) in a sample of 803 youths. Evocative effects were higher for youth with higher genetic loads, which also significantly predicted more ADHD symptoms. These elevated symptoms, in turn, significantly predicted lower levels of parental involvement and higher levels of poor parental supervision and inconsistent discipline. Such parental reactions are almost guaranteed to increase their offspring's future antisocial activities.

Causes and Treatment of ADHD

ADHD causality is heterogeneous, encompassing genetic, neurobiological, developmental, and environmental factors, and is thus an excellent candidate for biopsychosocial assessment. The consensus from a large number of twin studies indicates heritability estimates between 70% and 80% (Faraone & Larsson, 2019), making ADHD one of the neurodevelopmental disorders with very high heritability. A large population-based healthcare database from Germany composed of 286,653 nontwin sibling pairs and 12,486 twin pairs provided a heritability estimate for clinically diagnosed ADHD in males of 0.88 and 0.77 for females (Langner et al., 2013). Langner et al. (2013) also found an ADHD concordance rate of 75.2 for male MZ twins and 15.5 for male DZ twins and 46.7 and 9.7, respectively, for female MZ and DZ twins. The genes involved regulate neurotransmission, and: "Dopamine and norepinephrine are the key neurotransmitters that are implicated in the pathophysiology of this condition" (Mehta et al., 2019, p. 235). Molecular genetic studies have identified common DNA variants with genome-wide SNP heritability estimates ranging from 0.10 to 0.28 (Demontis et al., 2019). As we have seen, the large gap between quantitative behavioral genetic heritability estimates and SNP hereditability estimates is due to the polygenetic nature of conditions such as ADHD, with potentially thousands of coding and regulatory genes being involved that individually only have minute effect sizes.

Psychostimulant drugs are the mainstay of ADHD treatment because they act as dual dopamine (DA) and norepinephrine (NE) reuptake inhibitors, thus increasing their availability. Structurally, the hyperactivity, inattention, and impulsivity of people with ADHD mean that they have under-aroused brains. Attention and control require the coordination of cortical and subcortical functioning, and the structure for maintaining awareness of what is happening in the world. The reticular activating system (RAS) is located in the brainstem, regulates cortical activation, and determines the extent of this awareness (Berger et al., 2021). The ascending branch of the RAS is the brain's antenna by which stimuli from the outside world meet the inside world and send it on for processing. If a person's RAS excites cortical neurons less than it should, the cortex is suboptimally aroused and he or she requires greater levels of stimuli to achieve the same level of arousal that others have at lower stimuli levels. Under-arousal is consistently related to criminality (Kavish et al., 2019). As Ellis (2005, p. 292) remarks: "Suboptimal arousal manifests itself in lowered sensitivity to pain and in seeking elevated levels of sensory stimulation."

The electrical chatter of billions of neurons is measured by the electroencephalogram (EEG) which records the background patterns of brain waves that measure relative levels of a person's arousal. The frequency bands of these waves range from theta (deep REM sleep), delta (non-REM sleep), alpha (when eyes are closed and visual stimuli are limited), to beta (very alert and focused). ADHD children show a greater predominance of slow wave activity in the EEG power spectrum relative to fast wave activity (Kiiski et al., 2020). As Alim and Imtiaz (2023, p. 193) put it: "Most patients with ADHD have a common brain-wave pattern that consists of an abundance of slow (delta or theta) brain waves and a shortage of fast (beta) brain waves." Much of the problem lies in the poor regulation of the discharge of NE by the locus coeruleus, a vital part of the RAS (Aston-Jones & Cohen, 2005). This implies that drug-based treatment of ADHD should involve both DA and NE neurostimulants.

The most frequently prescribed drugs for ADHD are methylphenidate-based stimulants such as Ritalin and the nonstimulant atomoxetine (Perugi, De Rosa, & Barbuti, 2022). Individuals with ADHD have been shown to have lower levels of the DA metabolite homovanillic acid in cerebral spinal fluid, indicating low DA brain activity (Dalley & Roiser, 2012). Stimulant drugs increase the availability of synaptic DA by occupying DA transporters so that they cannot be retaken into their vesicles, thus increasing DA availability in the PFC and subcortical areas. Atomoxetine is an NE reuptake inhibitor that increases NE activity and facilitates dopamine activity in the frontal lobes. Nonstimulant drugs are less effective at controlling symptoms than stimulants, which have direct effects on both dopamine and NE transporters but have the advantage of not being available to non-ADHD individuals who obtain them to get high. Both stimulant and nonstimulant drugs have been shown to increase cortical attention and facilitation with stimulant medication working better for some people and nonstimulants for others in reducing symptoms (Perugi, De Rosa, & Barbuti, 2022). These drugs have a calming or normalizing effect on suboptimally aroused individuals by raising the activity of the brain's sensory mechanisms to normal levels, thus relieving boredom because the brain is now more attentive to features of the environment that it could not previously capture.

Because ADHD is a disorder of self-regulation, biopsychosocial theories of ADHD highlight the balance between dopamine and serotonin transmission, which are at the core of the behavioral activating (or approach) system (BAS) and behavioral inhibition system (BIS) of reinforcement sensitivity theory, plays a causal role (Walsh, 2019). Depletion of serotonin in the orbitofrontal cortex results in deficits in emotion regulation, and inhibition and selective serotonin reuptake inhibitors are an effective part of the ADHD treatment armamentarium (Pourhamzeh et al., 2022). The DA receptor D4 (DRD4), the DA transporter (DAT1), and the serotonin transporter (5-HTT) are the usual suspects. The association of the DRD4-7R allele with ADHD is the most replicated in molecular genetic studies of ADHD (Bobb et al., 2006). Carrasco et al.'s (2006) G*x*E study found that neither the DRD4-7R nor the DAT1-10R polymorphisms had a statistically significant effect on ADHD symptoms alone. However, individuals who possessed both polymorphisms were significantly more likely to be diagnosed with ADHD (an odds ratio of 12.7) than subjects possessing neither or only one of these alleles.

The ventral striatum (VS) plays an important role in reward processing, which is more salient for people with ADHD relative to non-ADHD individuals. The orbitofrontal cortex has also been a major focus since it is strongly innervated by the VS when processing rewards. Consistent with inattentive and impulsive characteristics of ADHD, Tomasi and Volkow (2012) found that resting-state connectivity was enhanced in reward-related networks in ADHA subjects but decreased in attention-related networks relative to non-ADHD controls. Ma et al. (2016) found increased reward signaling within the superior frontal gyrus (which constitutes about one-third of the frontal lobes) and the VS relative to controls. They also found hyperconnectivity between VS and motor control regions in the ADHD group. Connectivity was associated with performance improvement in controls on reward-related tasks but not in the ADHD group, which suggests inefficient connectivity and deficient cognitive control in ADHD subjects. Ma et al. (2016, p. 225) concluded: "Adolescents with ADHD show increased neural sensitivity to rewards and its interactions with interference control in VS and motor regions, respectively. The findings support theoretical models of altered reward-cognitive control integration in individuals with ADHD."

Kasparek, Theiner, and Filova (2015) reviewed patterns of morphological and functional brain changes in children and adults with ADHD and noted that they point to disorders of many areas of the brain, and to changes in brain structure and function from childhood to adulthood. Most clearly, they show an improvement in the caudate nucleus, which is part of the dorsal striatum, an area highly innervated by DA neurons. Because dendritic plasticity is modulated by the dopaminergic system, Kasparek, Theiner, and Filova conclude that treatment with methylphenidate may be behind the observed improvement of brain changes observed in neuroimaging studies: "Changes in neuronal plasticity may be behind persisting brain changes in ADHD. Current treatment approaches seem to improve these neuroplastic processes, and, therefore, may have a positive effect on the neuropathology of ADHD" (2015, p. 931).

ADHD medication significantly reduces criminal offending. For instance, a Swedish cohort study of 25,656 ADHD patients found a 33% reduction in criminality among ADHD-medicated men and a 40% reduction for medicated women (Lichtenstein et al., 2012), and a Danish national study of 4,231 individuals with childhood ADHD found that adult crime rates were 30%–40% lower during periods in which they were taking ADHD medication than when they were not (Mohr-Jensen et al., 2019).

Environmental Factors

A heritability of 0.80 for ADHD leaves causal space for environmental effects, albeit not for the same effects criminologists typically examine. Sonuga-Barke et al. (2023) identified nine significant associations between environmental factors and ADHD, most of which were prenatal or perinatal factors. Studies purporting to identify environmental risk factors for ADHD find small effects. However, these studies tend to rely on self-reports to assess ADHD rather than clinical diagnoses and rarely look to genetics (Froehlich et al., 2011). For instance, meta-analyses covering over three million people have found prenatal exposure to maternal smoking is associated with about a 50% increase in the incidence of ADHD. But as Faraone et al. (2021, p. 795) note:

> Although this association has also been seen in large population studies, it disappears after adjusting for family history of ADHD, which indicates that the association between maternal smoking during pregnancy and ADHD is due to familial or genetic factors that increase the risk for both smoking and ADHD.

This highlights the importance of investigating gene-environment interactions if we are to gain a better understanding of any behavior.

Dinkler et al. (2017) looked at both genetic and environmental factors in a Swedish twin study of ADHD and child maltreatment (emotional abuse/

neglect, physical neglect, physical abuse, and/or sexual abuse). Among 18,192 nine-year-old MZ and DZ twins, there were 374 cases of reported maltreatment. It was found that maltreated children had significantly more neurodevelopmental disorders and that ADHD had a small association with maltreatment. Most of the covariance of child maltreatment with neurodevelopmental disorders was explained by common genetic effects. Cecil and Nigg (2022, p. 516) note:

> The existence of passive correlation between genetic and environmental risk (rGE) makes it difficult to disentangle the causal role of genes and environments based purely on observational studies. This means that what looks like an environmental effect could be a genetic one. However, rGE can also be compatible with causal effects, in that environment can mediate genetic effects.

Nonpharmacological Treatment of ADHD

Although medications for ADHD are highly effective, noncompliance and its sale to non-ADHD people are problems, and cardiovascular problems are an issue with some patients on methylphenidate because it increases heart rate and blood pressure (Theiner et al., 2015). Even when these problems are not in evidence, it is recommended that pharmacological treatment be augmented with other treatments. As Retz et al. (2021, p. 241) remark:

> Multimodal interventions are recommended for treatment of ADHD, addressing psychological, behavioral and educational needs by combining pharmacological and non-pharmacological treatment. The rationale behind multimodal treatment is that ADHD medication will reduce symptom severity of ADHD, thus increasing engagement in and benefit from subsequent non-pharmacological interventions. Non-pharmacological interventions usually comprise psychoeducation and cognitive behavioral therapy (CBT), with learning of strategies to manage ADHD symptoms; interventions requiring sustained attention and working memory.

One such treatment is repetitive transcranial magnetic stimulation (rTMS) therapy. RTMS is a noninvasive technique in which patients have a magnetic stimulator placed on their heads, most typically directed to the right dorsolateral prefrontal cortex, that sends a series of magnetic pulses to the brain. These pulses depolarize neurons repetitively, making targeted neurons more excitable and attentive to stimuli. RTMS changes how the brain circuits are arranged during stimulation, and the goal is to permanently alter synaptic pathways so that patients will be more responsive to environmental cues without medication. Theiner et al. (2015, p. 337) explain how rTMS works:

> The complete mechanism of changes remains unclear, but it is believed that rTMS affects gene expression, synaptic plasticity, dopamine release, and release of endogenous opioids. The ability of rTMS to affect not only the particular area it is aimed at but also the whole functional site is crucial as it is able to modulate function in more distant parts of the brain.

A typical treatment period is 5 days a week (30-minute sessions) for 4 to 6 weeks, but it can be shorter or longer depending on an individual's response to treatment (Niederhofer, 2008).

The neuropsychological effects of consistent cardiovascular exercise in enhancing multiple facets of physical, mental, and social well-being are well known. Exercise increases the release of DA and other neurochemicals that are deficient in ADHD individuals. As Den Heijer et al. (2017, p. 22) point out in their review of the literature: "Regular physical exercise may, therefore, be especially beneficial for children with ADHD, because cardio exercise increases specific catecholamines and proteins/enzymes that are typically reduced in ADHD (e.g., dopamine, tyrosine hydroxylase and brain-derived neurotrophic factor)." A systematic review and meta-analysis of studies conducted between 1980 and 2017 of nonpharmacological interventions of ADHD patients and controls contrasted the effects of neurofeedback (NF), cognitive behavioral therapy (CBT), cognitive training (CT), and physical exercise (PE). Although all had positive effects on ADHD symptoms, PE demonstrated the highest average effect size in improving ADHD symptomology (d = .93), followed by CBT (d = .70), NF (d = .61), and CT (d = .45) (Lambez et al., 2020).

12

SCHIZOPHRENIA

Causes and Treatment

The Prevalence of Schizophrenia

Mental disorders of all kinds take a heavy toll on individuals, families, communities, and the legal system. In the United States, in 1955, there were 339 people per 100,000 in state mental hospitals but in 2001, there were only 20 per 100,000 (Lamb, Weinberger, & Gross, 2004). This 94% decrease in the mental health hospital population is the result of a combination of the development of antipsychotic drugs, concerns about the ethics of involuntary hospitalization, and the deinstitutionalization movement (Muesger et al., 2013). Only the most severely impaired are hospitalized long-term today, leaving jails and prisons as surrogate mental hospitals to absorb most of the mentally disordered population when they get into legal difficulties. In 2016, upwards of 41% of males and 69% of females in prison in the United States had a history of some form of mental disorder (Maruschak, Bronson, & Alper, 2021), and about 25% of people in jails have been diagnosed with a mental disorder (Grosholz & Semenza, 2021).

Nothing highlights the difficulty of understanding the complexity of the human condition like schizophrenia. Schizophrenia is a chronic neurodevelopmental disorder and is the most widespread of the psychotic disorders and lifetime prevalence estimates range from 0.48% to 0.75% (Moreno-Küstner, Martin, & Pastor, 2018). The disorder affects males and females equally, but it has the most common age of onset for males between 15 and 25 years, and between 25 and 35 years for females (Maruschak, Bronson, & Alper, 2021). It appears that females have

DOI: 10.4324/9781003642268-16

some protection from schizophrenia during their peak reproductive years due to the antidopaminergic effects (dopamine is strongly implicated in schizophrenia) of estrogen (Johnstone et al., 2022). The earlier the onset of the disease the more severe the impairment, and like other mental disorders that emerge during adolescence, probably partially reflect aberrations in the maturational changes that normally take place in the brain during this period (Paus, Keshavan, & Giedd, 2008).

Despite more than a century of research and the mountains of empirical data generated, there is no specifically confirmed cause of schizophrenia. The causes of this devastating condition are highly heterogeneous and involve many biological and environmental factors, with some playing a major role in some individuals and only a minor role in others. Furthermore, some of these factors may only be correlates acting as markers for unidentified factors (Wahbeh & Avramopoulos, 2021). The Diagnostic and Statistical Manual of Mental Disorders (DSM-5) changed the name for this disorder from schizophrenia to "schizophrenia spectrum disorder" in 2013 to emphasize that symptoms and their severity lie on continua. However, almost all subsequent studies of the condition have continued to use the term "schizophrenia" with the understanding that it is a given that it is a spectrum disorder. Some schizophrenics are rigid, unresponsive, slow-moving, and sometimes immobile (catatonic); some are unkempt, illogical, and frenetic (hebephrenic/disorganized); and some are hostile and distrusting (paranoid).

Schizophrenia Criminal Behavior

Before deinstitutionalization, the relationship between schizophrenia and criminal behavior was not readily apparent. With deinstitutionalization and the return of the mentally ill to their communities came their greater visibility and vulnerability to arrest. There is some reluctance to affirm the link between crime and schizophrenia due to the fear of further stigmatizing an already stigmatized group but the evidence cannot be dismissed. Researchers in Denmark looked at over 300,000 individuals with a history of psychiatric hospitalization (90% schizophrenic) followed to age 43 and found that they were 3 to 11 times more likely to have criminal convictions than people with no history of psychiatric illness (Hodkins et al., 1996). A Swedish study reported that people with psychosis are about four times more likely to have a criminal record than members of the general population (Tuninger et al., 2001). A meta-analysis of 20 studies found the odds ratios for violence among persons with schizophrenia compared to controls were up to 7 for men and 29 for women. In five studies that compared schizophrenic persons to the general population, the pooled odds ratio for homicide was 19.5 (Fazel et al., 2009a). Whiting et al.'s (2022) meta-analysis of 24 studies from 15 countries over 40 years comparing schizophrenic and nonschizophrenic subjects found a pooled odds ratio of 4.5 for violent crime among males and one of 10.2 for women. The higher odds ratios for women reflect the low rates of violence among women in general rather than symptoms having greater effects on females with schizophrenia. The pooled odds ratio of committing a homicide was strong at 17.7, which is close to that found by Fazel et al. (2009a).

The most consistent findings from structural brain imaging studies of highly aggressive schizophrenia patients with histories of violence are reduced volumes in the orbitofrontal lobes and the anterior cingulate cortex (Fjellvang, Grøning, & Haukvik, 2018). These are areas important to affective regulation (the anterior cingulate cortex) or psychosis symptoms (the orbitofrontal lobes). Shaw et al.'s (2006) study of 1,594 homicide offenders reported that 5% of them were diagnosed schizophrenics. Even taking the high estimate of 0.75% for the prevalence of schizophrenia, this amounts to a rate 6.66 times greater than expected. Likewise, Baird et al. (2020) found that between 1997 and 2012, 6% of all homicides in England were committed by individuals with schizophrenia. Again, taking the high estimate of 0.75% for the prevalence of schizophrenia, this amounts to a rate eight times greater than expected. A study of Russian homicide offenders over 40 years found a lower percentage of homicide offenders (3.1%) had a diagnosis of schizophrenia, but that is still over four times the high-end schizophrenia prevalence rate (Golenkov et al., 2022).

Individuals with schizophrenia are at an increased risk for criminal behavior when they have comorbidities, such as substance abuse, and demographic factors such as living in poor urban neighborhoods, and childhood abuse and neglect. Fazel et al. (2009b) looked at 33 years of data for a sample of 8,003 people with schizophrenia and 80,025 controls. They showed an odds ratio of 8.9 for having at least one violent offense among people with schizophrenia compared with controls. They also found that 27.6% of those with schizophrenia who were comorbid for substance abuse had violent convictions versus 8.5% of schizophrenic patients without substance abuse history. Silverstein et al. (2015) note that this 8.9 odds ratio is similar to that in substance abuse individuals not suffering from schizophrenia, but also that the "risk for homicide is higher regardless of substance-abuse status (0.3% vs. 0.02% [15 times higher] in the general population)" (pp. 23–24).

The symptoms of schizophrenia thus have effects independent of comorbidities. Noting that children must learn *not* to be aggressive rather than *to be* aggressive, Sheilagh Hodgins (2017, p. 1022) remarks:

> Given that by age 2, children who are developing schizophrenia show motor abnormalities such as delays in walking and talking and specific

neurological soft signs, and in the subsequent years further motor deficiencies, neurological signs, receptive language deficits and lower than average IQ, it may be that for some of them the challenge of learning not-to-be-aggressive is too great.

The evidence that persons with schizophrenia are at higher risk for committing crimes than persons in general is consistent and robust. However, compared with the general population, victimization rates for people with severe mental disorders are also greater. For example, de Vries et al.'s (2019) meta-analysis of 27 studies found that the mentally ill were between four and six times more likely to be victims of a crime than people in general. They put the increased risk down to mentally disordered people presenting as easy targets lacking a guardianship network and showing behavioral symptoms that invite negative responses from others.

Genetics and Neurobiology of Schizophrenia

Schizophrenia is a multidetermined condition that has spawned many different causal models, none of which is necessary and sufficient to account for the syndrome (Walsh & Yun, 2013). The current best estimate of the heritability of schizophrenia is around 80% (Owen, Sawa, & Mortensen, 2016) of which GWAS polymorphism studies explain around 24% of the genetic liability (Legge et al., 2021). Legge et al. (2021, p. 2175) emphasize the polygenic nature of schizophrenia:

> GWAS demonstrated the polygenic nature of psychiatric disorders and how hundreds or thousands of variants contribute to liability to schizophrenia. Rare variant studies in schizophrenia have also made important achievements, including identification of overlap of implicated genes and gene sets with other neurodevelopmental disorders. This pleiotropy further adds to the existing complex picture emerging out of these studies.

However, while genes are implicated, they do not have the causal power that heritability studies might lead us to believe. Concordance rates between MZ twins illustrate this. For example, based on six national twin register studies, Torrey and Yolken (2019) showed that the schizophrenia concordance rate in MZ twins was only 28% and only 6% for dizygotic twins, and Saunders (2020) notes that average concordance rates of 30%–40% for MZ and 5%–10% for DZ twins have been reported. The MZ concordance rate shows a fairly robust genetic effect. However, we should expect much higher concordance rates because MZ twins share 100% of their genes and typically 100% of their common rearing environment. Because we do not, other factors may play a bigger part than genes. Epigenetic processes may provide part of the answer for the much lower-than-expected MZ concordance rates for schizophrenia as well as various other outcomes. A study of phenotypic discordance for a number of these outcomes (e.g., homosexual identity) among MZ twins found that as twins got older, they diverged epigenetically, with 50-year-old twin pairs averaging four times the epigenetic differences than 3-year-old twin pairs, indicating that epigenetic alterations occur and accumulate throughout life (Fraga et al., 2005). *In vivo* and postmortem studies of brain tissue have demonstrated that several genes associated with schizophrenia are particularly susceptible to epigenetic modification (Gavin & Sharma, 2010).

Functional cognitive deficits are the major symptoms of schizophrenia, and thus, these deficits must involve dysregulation of multiple neurotransmitters. Persons with schizophrenia show abnormalities of PFC functioning due to a disturbance of the signal-to-noise (S/N) ratio during information processing. Signaling is the inter-neuronal communication of meaningful information; noise is the random firing of neurons such as occurs during REM sleep. If the S/N ratio is beyond the normal range, communication between brain regions is haphazard, leading to aberrant responses. DA signaling in the PFC is a critical factor in modulating the S/N ratio and how persons interpret perceptions. As noted in Chapter 3, variation in DA signaling is mediated by catechol-O-methyltransferase (COMT), an enzyme that plays a crucial role in DA degradation. Differences in methylation patterns between MZ twins who are discordant for schizophrenia are evident in the COMT and dopamine D2 receptor genes (Rutten & Mill, 2009).

The most prevalent drug treatments for schizophrenia are DA antagonists, but they fail to work in about one-third of cases, even though these cases receive as much DA blockage as those for whom the drug works (Abi-Dargham et al., 2022). This suggests that other neurotransmitters are involved in the aberrant S/N ratio, including glutamate, the brain's principal excitatory transmitter, and gamma-aminobutyric acid (GABA), the principal inhibitory transmitter. These neurotransmitters work in unison to control the brain's level of excitation. Glutaminergic functioning became a candidate after it was found that phencyclidine (PCP) caused schizophrenia-like symptoms by inhibiting the glutamate receptor N-methyl-D-aspartate (NMDA) (Keshavan, Nasrallah & Tandon, 2011). Up to 90% of people with schizophrenia smoke as opposed to about 22% of the general population, which may be seen as an effort to self-medicate because nicotine increases glutamate release and increases dopamine in the dorsolateral PFC where dopamine is depleted in schizophrenic patients due to treatment with dopamine antagonists (Hunt et al., 2018).

Because glutamate is the most common of all neurotransmitters and plays a pivotal role in neural communication, and because NMDA receptors play a key role in the development of neural pathways and in pruning neural connections, glutamate plays an important part in the explanation of schizophrenia (Javitt et al., 2008). Guàrdia et al. (2021) maintain that the *hypo*-functioning of either glutamate or NMDA receptors in the PFC is a putative cause of psychotic symptoms, as is the *hyper*-functioning of the cortical serotonin 5-HT2A receptor. Abi-Dargham et al. (2022, p. 200) point out: "NMDA receptors in the synaptic membrane maintain and strengthen relevant connections. These combined effects gate out 'noise,' sharpening the 'signal.'"

Egerton et al. (2017) examined GABA, glutamate, and dopamine levels in patients at ultra-high risk for psychosis using magnetic resonance spectroscopy (a technique that compares the chemical composition of normal brain tissue with abnormal tissue) and an MRI-based technique for measuring tissue perfusion. Significant differences in GABA levels in the prefrontal cortex in ultra-high-risk patients and DA levels in the midbrain and basal ganglia circuits were found in schizophrenic patients. There were also significant correlations between hippocampal glutamate levels and striatal dopamine, which supports the notion that dysregulation of GABA and glutamate systems precede DA dysfunction. In line with these findings, Marsman et al. (2014) found a strong negative correction ($r = -0.91$) in medial prefrontal PFC GABA/creatine ratios in patients with schizophrenia symptoms controlling for age and sex. Creatine is an amino acid whose main function is to facilitate the recycling of adenosine triphosphate (ATP), the energy source that drives processes in living cells. GABA's inhibitory role reduces stress, increases concentration, and has a guardian role in preventing random neuronal firing. Stress increases creatine levels, which increases intercellular energy transfer and the possibility of random firing. A decreased GABA/creatine ratio increases cortical excitability in people with schizophrenia (Draper et al., 2014).

Swathy and Banerjee (2017, p. 721) assert that: "Impairments of neurotransmitter systems due to differential methylation of genes of dopaminergic, serotonergic and glutamatergic systems can result in SCZ [schizophrenic] condition." Postmortem studies of schizophrenic patients' brains reveal a large number of areas showing signs of either hyper- or hypomethylation compared with brain areas among normal healthy controls indicating that genes coding for various neurotransmitters are either hypo- or hyperactive (Trépanier et al., 2016). Many gene methylations appear to occur early in life and are developmentally conserved. Postmortem studies of fetal brains compared with adult brains show that if an allele evidenced high levels of methylation prenatally, it also tended to be similar in adults (Hannon et al., 2016).

Schizophrenia may be a condition of both brain function (malfunctioning genes and their neurotransmitter products) and brain structure (its architecture). The structure of the intraneural connections in the brains of schizophrenic patients between regions controlling mood regulation and executive functioning may be subpar. Reviewing several diffusion tensor imaging studies that focus on the white matter tracts between the amygdala and the frontal lobes, Dabiri et al. (2022, p. 9) note: "The uncinate fasciculus is of particular interest since it connects the mood region (amygdala) with the executive function regions (the medial-and orbitofrontal cortices). Reduced fractional anisotropy is seen in patients with schizophrenia suggesting diminished white matter structural integrity."

Schizophrenia and the Two-Hit Model of Neurodevelopment

The causes of schizophrenia may have their effect *in utero* during vital periods of neurogenesis. Neuroscientists have developed a neurodevelopmental "two-hit" model that unites genetics, epigenetics, immunology, and two temporally distinct critical periods of brain development in a comprehensive attempt to show how these many factors combine to produce the symptoms associated with schizophrenia. The first hit is a priming hit thought to disrupt neurogenesis prenatal, and the second hit involves neuroplasticity processes occurring in adolescence (van der Meer et al., 2022). Fatemi and Folsom (2009, p. 528) note:

> According to this model, early developmental insults may lead to dysfunction of specific neural networks that would account for premorbid signs and symptoms observed in individuals that later develop schizophrenia. At adolescence, excessive elimination of synapses and loss of plasticity may account for the emergence of symptoms.

Poor premorbid psychosocial functioning may be present years before schizophrenic psychosis is evident, which suggests there is a priming first hit at an early stage of neurodevelopment, probably during embryogenesis. The transition from early premorbid features to overt psychosis around adolescence suggests a second hit that builds on the foundation laid down by the first. There are several environmental candidates for delivering the first hit. For instance, a 10% increase in the risk of developing schizophrenia was found among children born from January through March in the northern hemisphere, a time when many viral infections are present (Krause et al, 2010), and Mednick, Machon, and Huttunen (1988) have shown that the risk for schizophrenia increased by 50% for individuals whose mothers were exposed during the second trimester to a virulent type of influenza during the 1957 epidemic in Finland.

When the immune system detects a foreign substance in the host body, it mobilizes a class of proteins called cytokines that carry signals from cell to cell near the location of the antigen that can alter cell functioning initiating an immune response that triggers inflammation. If a woman contracts an infectious disease or ingests teratogenic substances while pregnant, her immune system releases cytokines that enter fetal circulation. Cytokines play a role in the proliferation, differentiation, and survival of neurons, and they influence neurotransmission by modulating neuronal and glial cell functioning. As Depino (2006, p. 7777) explains, "cytokines released by the maternal immune system (and/or the placental or fetal immune system) in response to infection may be responsible for the interaction between maternal infection during pregnancy, altered neuronal development, and mental diseases." As Carnac (2022, p. 14) notes about the pathway: "High levels of cytokines in the developing fetus could affect neurodevelopment because cytokines bind to receptors on target cells, resulting in signal transduction pathways that alter gene expression in those target cells." Chronic environmental stress is also known to cause persistent low-grade inflammation.

Mechanisms involved in the second hit are more speculative. One theory posits that infections acquired during gestation are associated with neuro-inflammatory processes that lie dormant (or semi-dormant in cases where premorbid symptoms are in evidence) until puberty when immune surveillance is weakened (Muller & Schwarz, 2006). The immune system can keep the latent problem in abeyance until puberty when the thymus gland undergoes major reductions in tissue volume and function (Kinney et al., 2010). The thymus gland is responsible for the maintenance of the immune response. It increases rapidly from infancy to puberty, slowly building up the body's stock of T-cells (thymus lymphocytes—white blood cells), vital to immunity. After reaching its maximum size at puberty, the thymus decreases by about 3% each year to become almost indistinguishable from surrounding tissue in old age (Haynes et al., 2000).

Holttinen, Pirkola, and Kaltiala (2023, p. 104) note that "Schizophrenia spectrum disorders are rare up to the age of 13 years but show a marked increase in prevalence between ages 15–17, with the peak age of onset between 15 and 30 years." Synaptic pruning occurs with a vengeance during adolescence and is a normal part of brain maturation refining neuronal connectivity and function. This exaggerated synaptic pruning appears to be the best candidate for the second hit. When synaptic pruning goes beyond normal limits, it results in gray matter loss observed in the brains of persons with schizophrenia (Rosenthal et al., 2011). In this view, aberrant immune system chemistry initiated by the first hit combines with excessive synaptic pruning during adolescence and the reduction in thymus structure and function to produce the symptoms of schizophrenia. This combination either initiates or contributes to the dysregulation of the neurotransmitter systems that cause the aberrant S/N ratio of schizophrenia. According to Kinney et al. (2010, p. 555), the neurodevelopmental theory of abnormal immune system response "may help explain roles of prenatal hazards, post-pubertal onset, stress, genes, climate, infections, and brain dysfunction."

The synaptic pruning model has received support from Sekar et al. (2016) who analyzed SNPs from 28,799 schizophrenia cases and 35,986 controls from 40 cohorts in 22 countries searching for clues about the process that leads to abnormal synaptic pruning and brain tissue loss in schizophrenia. They zeroed in on the gene complement component 4 (C4), which consists of proteins that work with the immune system by marking infectious agents for destruction. C4 has another role in the maturing brain; tagging synaptic connections for pruning during the adolescent maturation of neuronal circuits. Certain alleles of the C4 gene expressed in neurons are associated with the risk of schizophrenia in proportion to their level of C4 expression, which is significantly greater in schizophrenic patients. Sekar et al. (2016, p. 183) concluded:

> The possibility that neuron-microglia interactions via the complement cascade contribute to schizophrenia pathogenesis – for example, that schizophrenia arises or intensifies from excessive or inappropriate synaptic pruning during adolescence and early adulthood – would offer a potential mechanism for these longstanding observations about age of onset and synapse loss.

Microglia are microglial cells that serve as defense mechanisms in the brain that constantly scavenge the brain for infectious agents and damaged or superfluous neurons and synapses, and clear cellular debris (Chamera et al., 2020).

In line with the neurodevelopmental model, Dennis van der Meer et al. (2022) compared the timing of expression of 345 putative risk genes in 743 schizophrenic patients with an equal number of sex- and age-matched healthy controls. They identified 183 genes that significantly upregulated prenatally and downregulated postnatally and 162 genes with the opposite pattern. These genes were associated with neurotransmission and the immune system. They calculated two set-specific polygenic risk scores and found an interaction between the scores in which higher prenatal polygenic risk was only significantly associated with schizophrenic patients at higher levels of postnatal polygenic risk. They concluded:

> Our results are thereby in accordance with the two-hit hypothesis of schizophrenia, that deviant brain maturation exacerbates earlier insults

> to the system to bring about the disorder. We provide genetics-based evidence of this hypothesis, captured by an interaction term between the set-specific polygenic scores; while the´hits´ are generally assumed to be environmental due to the temporal dimension, they may also be partly genetic, considering that genes exert their effects at specific times depending on when they are expressed. The amount of expression, and its impact on molecular processes downstream, can thereby be moderated both by environmental influences and genetic variation.
>
> *(2022, p. 4)*

Treatment for Schizophrenia

As is the case with almost all chronic medical conditions, schizophrenia cannot be cured. Chronic conditions are managed by focusing on the symptoms and prescribing medications to ease them. Pharmacological treatment is the mainstay of schizophrenia management, with DA antagonists being the most often administered drugs. DA antagonist drugs work by alleviating positive symptoms such as delusions, hallucinations, and movement disorders in the brains of most schizophrenic people by blockading D2 and D3 receptors, but they do not help the negative symptoms such as anhedonia, asociality, and taking care of basic needs. The effectiveness of different drugs on positive is directly related to how well they block DA. Purper-Ouakil et al. (2011, p. r72) explain how these medications work: "Therapeutic effects of DA stimulation is thought to involve a weakening of inappropriate network connections (*i.e.,* producing a decrease of 'noise') whereas enhanced NE [norepinephrine] transmission may function by strengthening appropriate connections (*i.e.,* producing an increase of 'signal')."

Treatment targeting the dopaminergic system alone is not sufficient as we have seen that they do not work for about one-third of patients and have minimal effects on negative symptoms (e.g., anhedonia, depression, and anxiety). Because glutamate is the most abundant neurotransmitter, medications targeting NMDA receptors have been developed, particularly for the negative symptoms of schizophrenia. Because of the heterogeneous nature of schizophrenia causality, Yang and Tsai (2017, p. 8) report that there are many new medications undergoing development and clinical trials:

> Advances in pharmacogenomics (the study of the genetic determinants of drug response) generate optimism about applying these strategies in treating schizophrenia. Over a hundred compounds, which encompass a broad range of targets in schizophrenia, are currently in various stages of drug development.

Almost all people with schizophrenia have difficulty getting their basic needs met, leading them to rely heavily on family members, disability payments, and psychosocial counseling for support.

Psychosocial treatments augment, not replace, pharmacological treatment and are aimed mostly at education addressing the nature of the disease and its management and psychosocial adjustment to it. Most individuals with schizophrenia can lead relatively normal lives while on their medication as long as they are not comorbid for substance abuse or antisocial personality disorder. Unfortunately, many patients frequently refuse medication or stop taking them for a variety of reasons. For instance, they may have experienced adverse side effects, may not perceive their need for medication because they deny being mentally ill, or are paranoid about the treatment provider's motives. Patients who are noncompliant with their medication regimens greatly increase their risk of relapse and getting themselves into more legal trouble.

This is where psychosocial therapies can play their part in educating patients and family members about the effectiveness of their treatment and the importance of patients taking their medication. Educating family members about the condition and developing a collaborative relationship between them and the treatment team can significantly reduce the burden on them while simultaneously helping patients cope with the challenges of their condition. These family education groups may be single- or multiple-family groups lasting up to two years and are designed to reduce stress and improve communication between family members and patients. Mueser et al. (2013, p. 473) note that: "Research on longer-term family programs (≥5 sessions) has shown significant effects in the moderate-to-small range on reducing relapses and hospitalizations, and small effects in other areas such as improved psychosocial functioning." They conclude their review of research on multiple psychosocial programs for patients with schizophrenia with these words of optimism:

> Substantial progress has been made in establishing empirically supported psychosocial interventions for schizophrenia. These interventions have been shown to improve a broad range of outcomes related to different dimensions of psychosocial functioning (e.g., work, social relationships, independent living skills), psychopathology (e.g., psychotic symptoms, relapses, and hospitalizations), and associated impairments (e.g., cognitive functioning). Promising practices may supplement or even enhance these evidence-based treatments, with the ultimate goal of helping individuals with schizophrenia achieve their highest quality of life possible and recover from this illness.
>
> *(p. 487)*

13

SUBSTANCE ABUSE DISORDERS AND CRIMINAL BEHAVIOR

Alcohol Abuse and Crime

We humans have an inordinate fondness for mind-altering substances; we gulp, sniff, inhale, and inject with a gusto that suggests sobriety is a difficult state for us to tolerate. We drink to be sociable, loosen our tongues, feel good, sedate ourselves, and anesthetize the pains of life. Alcohol allows us to reinvent ourselves as superior beings; the worried become carefree and confident, the timid courageous, and the wallflower flirtatious. No wonder Ben Franklin once remarked: "Beer is proof positive that God loves us and wants us to be happy." But we pay a huge price since alcohol is our greatest drug of abuse. Citing data from the Centers for Disease Control and Prevention, Trangenstein et al. (2018, p. 2234) note: "Every day, there are 43 homicides in the United States, and excessive drinking (e.g., binge drinking, heavy drinking) is responsible for 20 of them." Estimates are that one-third of all arrests in the United States are for alcohol-related offenses and about 75% of robberies and 80% of homicides involve a drunken offender and/or victim (Schmalleger, 2004). About 55% of intimate partner violence offenses involve alcohol, and they are more likely to result in injury or death when alcohol is involved than when it is not (Babcock & Iyican, 2022). The economic cost of alcohol abuse in the United States is estimated at a staggering $235 billion per year (Manthey et al., 2021).

Alcohol affects behavior by inhibiting the functioning of the higher brain centers. As more alcohol is ingested, behavior increasingly becomes less controlled by the PFC and more by the limbic system, resulting in the expression of raw primary emotions. This is why individuals prone to

DOI: 10.4324/9781003642268-17

aggression are more likely to commit impulsive violence under the influence of alcohol. Alcohol abusers who recognize its dangers may stop drinking in the face of social, marital, and occupational problems, but those who continue to drink despite these problems are probably alcoholics. Alcoholism is a chronic condition marked by progressive incapacity to control drinking despite psychological, social, and physiological disruptions. It is a state of altered cellular physiology caused by the repetitive consumption of alcohol that manifests itself in physical disturbances (withdrawal symptoms) when alcohol use is suspended. Although only about 14% of frequent alcohol users descend into the hell of addiction (Bierut et al, 2010), nonalcoholics who abuse alcohol constitute the majority of legal problems because they are the majority of drinkers. The acute effects of alcohol on violence are much greater than the chronic effects; that is, the immediate effects of impaired judgment caused by heavy drinking rather than the results of long-term effects on the physiology of alcoholic individuals.

The Genetics of Alcoholism

Family, adoptee, and twin studies lead to the conclusion that vulnerability to alcoholism is strongly related to genetics. If millions can drink every day without it seriously affecting their lives, it means that those who cannot must have some congenital liability. From 13 twin and 5 adoption studies, the mean estimate of the heritability of alcoholism was 0.49 with a tight 95% confidence interval of 0.47–0.54, and a nonshared environmental estimate of 0.39 (Verhulst, Neale, & Kendler, 2015). A bewildering number of genes regulating neurotransmitters and enzymes are implicated in alcoholism. For instance, a meta-analysis of 2,343 lines of evidence from peer-reviewed journals identified 316 alcohol addiction-related genes and 13 addiction-related molecular pathways to alcohol addiction (Li, Mao, & Wei, 2008). Thus,

> Genetic vulnerability to alcoholism is likely to be due to numerous genes of small to modest effects on many neurotransmitter systems (e.g., opioid, serotonin, dopamine, GABA, glutamate, and cannabinoid) and signal transduction pathways within the mesolimbic dopamine reward pathways and interacting stress response systems."
>
> *(Enoch, 2006, p. 194)*

These same polymorphisms also affect traits marking vulnerability to criminality (Sontate et al., 2021). This does not mean that alcoholism and criminality are synonymous. It does mean that there are so many genetic, neurobiological, and environmental similarities between them and one can be used to predict the other. For example, a large study of twins found that factors accompanying disorders such as antisocial personality disorder and conduct disorder also accounted for 71% of the genetic liability to alcoholism (Kendler et al., 2003).

There is an old saying among alcoholics: “One drink is one too many, but a hundred drinks are never enough.” This informs us that a single drink activates DA release, but one drink leads to a craving for more that no amount will satiate. One line of thought is that the craving brain is a reward-dominant brain because the craving for alcohol (or other drugs) is largely unopposed by serotonin (Yacubian et al., 2007). Alcohol initially increases serotonin but then rapidly decreases it, thereby allowing for the reduced impulse-control capacity of the PFC (Sontate et al., 2021). The craving brain concept is common to all craving behaviors (gambling, sex, drugs, etc.) not just to alcoholism, which is why individuals easily addicted are also ripe candidates for criminal behavior. But addiction is not only about impulsive craving. We all receive gratification from the natural pleasures such as eating, drinking, and sexual activity that natural selection has built into us that contribute to our survival and reproductive efforts. However, the euphoria obtained from evolutionarily novel pleasures (alcohol and drugs) hijacks the brain because they involve greater DA activity, thus usurping neural circuits that control responses to natural rewards. As Hyman (2007, p. 10) explains: “Unlike natural rewards, addictive drugs always signal ‘better than expected.’ Neural circuits ‘over-learn’ on an excessive and grossly distorted dopamine signal.” Once acquainted with alcohol, the nucleus accumbens will increase DA activity in anticipation of the substance, thus reinforcing repeated consumption.

Dopaminergic neurons transmit signals by phasic firing (short transient bursts) or tonic firing (low signaling for a longer period). Patterns of phasic/tonic firing are thought to determine the salience of a reward signal (Tsai et al., 2009). A reward that is “better than expected” results in increased DA firing and a reward “worse than expected” results in less firing. Natural rewards, such as food, drink, and sex, are “just as expected” and do not alter the normal rates of DA neuronal firing. It has been proposed that the transition from casual use of alcohol and other drugs to addiction reflects the shift from “better than expected” to “worse than expected” (Wand, 2008). There is much evidence that in alcoholics and drug addicts, dopamine mediates desire (“wanting”) more than hedonic pleasure (“liking”). An alcoholic or drug addict wants their drug of choice to avoid negative withdrawal pains rather than liking their drug of choice for the positive pleasure it formerly provided. Berridge and Robinson (2016, p. 672) note that the nucleus accumbens is more of a “wanting” system than a “liking” system that generates hedonic pleasure: “The [pleasure] hotspot constitutes only 10% of total nucleus accumbens volume: the remaining 90% of the nucleus accumbens lacks any ability to enhance 'liking', though still robustly causes intense 'wanting.'" Stewart (2019, p. 218) avers that: "This change in reinforcement mechanisms [from positive to negative] appears to parallel the remapping of striatal dopaminergic circuitry, wherein once-exaggerated responses to drug highs within this region of the brain are blunted in favor of heightened responses to drug habits."

Researchers divide alcoholics broadly into *Type I* and *Type II* alcoholics. As Crabbe (2002, p. 449) describes the types: "Type I alcoholism is characterized by mild abuse, minimal criminality, and passive-dependent personality variables, whereas Type II alcoholism is characterized by early onset, violence, and criminality, and is largely limited to males." According to Chen et al. (2011, pp. 752–753): "Type II alcoholics are male predominant, have high genetic diathesis, and exhibit alcohol problems at an early age. They use alcohol for its euphoric effects and are characterized by high novelty seeking and low harm-avoidance personality traits." Type II alcoholics start drinking at an early age, rapidly become addicted, and have many character and behavioral problems that precede their alcoholism. Type I alcoholics start drinking later than Type IIs and progress to alcoholism slowly. They typically have families and careers, and if they have character defects, they are the result of their alcohol abuse rather than congenital. McGue (1999) reported heritability estimates for Type II alcoholics of about 0.90 and about 0.40 for Type I alcoholics. A Swedish population study of 184,770 individuals (71% males) divided alcoholics into four groups and found a heritability of 0.60 for class 4 alcoholics (roughly analogous to Type II alcoholics) and for those analogous to Type I alcoholics, the heritability was 0.20. Among class 4 alcoholics, 67.8% had at least one criminal conviction, and among class 1 alcoholics, 33.8% did (Long et al., 2019).

Alcohol addiction is a form of alcohol-induced neural plasticity moving from liking to wanting. Although alcohol is ultimately a brain-numbing depressant, at low dosage it is a stimulant. It also reduces anxiety and fear by increasing gamma-aminobutyric acid (GABA) levels and enhancing binding to its receptors. GABA is the major inhibitory neurotransmitter; when it occupies a receptor, it reduces the neuron's electrical activity. The effect of alcohol-enhanced GABA expression is "reduced anxiety about the consequences of aggressive behavior" (Martin 2004, p. 143). It is this reduced anxiety that emboldens the drinker. Alcohol ingestion also inhibits the release of glutamate, the major excitatory neurotransmitter, which accounts for the inhibition of cognitive and motor skills and sedative effects of alcohol. Allostatic adjustments to GABA receptors in response to excessive activation involve reducing the number of functional GABA receptors. This results in the lessened ability of the GABAergic system to counteract the glutamatergic excitation of neurons, thus upsetting the normal fine balance between excitation and inhibition of the central nervous system. This is the reason that those who are seriously dependent on alcohol even after short abstinence can experience anxiety attacks, tremors, convulsions, insomnia, memory loss, and intense "wanting" (negative reinforcement), and this is why abstinence is so difficult to maintain.

Illicit Drugs and Crime

Alcohol is a legal and socially acceptable way of drugging oneself; illicit drugs are not. Drug abuse is strongly related to criminal behavior. Based on urinalysis, the Office of Drug Control Policy's Arrestee Drug Abuse Monitoring (ADAM) Program estimates that between 65% and 75% of the U.S. arrestee population had recently used one or more illicit drugs (Lattimore et al., 2014). These data clearly show that drug abuse is strongly associated with criminal behavior, but is the association a causal one? Similar explanations for criminal and drug-abusing behaviors are often offered, suggesting that neither one causes the other, but rather both are caused by common factors. As Gottfredson, Kearley, and Bushway (2017, p. 602) explain:

> The common cause explanation of the drug-crime relationship posits that drug use and crime do not have a direct causal link but instead are related by a number of common causes. These common causes include genetic or temperamental traits, antisocial personality disorder, parental alcoholism, and poor relations with parents.

While drug abuse does not usually initiate a criminal career, it increases the seriousness of one (Gottfredson, Kearley, and Bushway, 2017; Quinn & Sneed, 2008), and although the typical drug addict is not driven to a crime by drugs, chronic drug abuse, and criminality are part of a broader propensity of some individuals to engage in a variety of antisocial behaviors. Several studies have shown that traits characterizing antisocial individuals such as ADHD/CD comorbidity, impulsiveness, and high scores on the Hare Psychopathy Checklist-Revised also characterize drug addicts (Fishbein, 2003; McDermott et al., 2000). The reciprocal nature of the drugs/crime connection is explained by Menard, Mihalic, and Huizinga (2001, p. 295):

> Initiation of substance abuse is preceded by initiation of crime for most individuals (and therefore cannot be a cause of crime). At a later stage of involvement, however, serious illicit drug use appears to contribute to continuity in serious crime, and serious crime contributes to continuity in serious illicit drug use.

Much of the criminal behavior surrounding drug addiction, however, is not a function of the pharmacological nature of the drugs themselves as it is in alcohol, but rather of the behaviors engaged in by addicts to secure resources to feed their habits, such as by drug dealing, prostitution, burglary, and robbery.

The Genetics and Neurobiology of Drug Addiction

Understanding how drugs (including alcohol) alter brain chemistry provides criminologists with a better understanding of both why addiction is so difficult to beat and of the importance of gene-environment interactions. As is the case with alcoholism, multiple genes, enzymes, and transcription factors are involved in drug addiction, with over 100 genes known to be changed with repeated cocaine exposure (Simon & Kreek, 2016). There are three models of the pathway from use to addiction, with all three having in common the role played by DA signaling, and all point to weak executive functioning (low self-control) which implicates the roles of the PFC and the serotonergic system (Ahmed, Graupner, & Gutkin, 2009). As Popescu et al. (2021, p. 2) inform us: "Mounting evidence places the dopaminergic-mesolimbic system as the leading system in the development of addiction, due to its role in encoding motivation and reward."

We couch our discussion primarily in terms of cocaine addiction because it has the largest average heritability coefficient (0.67) of all commonly abused substances (Bevilacqua & Goldman, 2009). Cocaine is highly attractive to its users because it produces euphoria, increases self-esteem and sexual appetites, and enhances cognitive and physical activity. Many people use cocaine recreationally, but it is estimated that 20%–40% of people who do so become addicted (Vsevolozhskaya & Anthony, 2016). The bare outline of what cocaine does is that it releases DA in the pleasure centers and then blocks its reuptake into the presynaptic knob. This blockage leaves signaling at DA receptors for much longer than the milliseconds it resides there in response to natural rewards. When DA stays in the synaptic gap and is not taken back up for repackaging, it is eventually broken down by enzymes leading to the depletion of the neurons' supply, leaving the abuser unable to feel little pleasure from natural rewards and eventually from cocaine itself due to allostatic processes changing the brain's hedonic set point (Walsh, Johnson, & Bolen, 2012). Addict's brains become changed by complex gene transcription factors and epigenetic processes that sustain extra dendritic branches on neurons in the nucleus accumbens and PFC, resulting in increased drug-seeking behavior (Nestler & Lüscher, 2019).

Psychosocial Stress and Addiction

There are many biological pathways to addiction, but we must realize that they all interact with environmental experiences captured by the plastic brain. Psychosocial stress is strongly related to both the onset of alcohol/drug dependence and relapse. Childhood stressors such as harsh and inconsistent parenting, rejection, and physical, sexual, and emotional abuse have all been associated with increased vulnerability to addiction and relapse (Enoch, 2006). As Nestler & Lüscher (2019, p. 56) remark:

> Recent work for example has shown that early life stress causes lifelong changes in steady-state expression levels of numerous genes in mesocorticolimbic brain regions as well as primes or desensitizes many other genes for altered expression in response to subsequent stress in adulthood.

When we note where substance abuse and addiction are most prevalent, we find that they are in the same stress-filled neighborhoods where child abuse, neglect, and violent crime are also most prevalent. When a family member becomes addicted, it leads to further family stress and increases the likelihood that others in the family will succumb to addiction.

The body's response to stress is regulated by the hypothalamic-pituitary-adrenal (HPA) axis. Alcohol and drugs can directly activate the HPA axis resulting in the release of hormones such as cortisol that act on the mesolimbic DA system mediating the rewards associated with alcohol and illicit drugs (Clay & Parker, 2018). Drugs of abuse can stimulate the HPA axis to increase the perception of reward and at the same time function as self-medications to alleviate stress. People living in stressful environments may become locked into a vicious cycle of HPA axis drug-induced activation (boosting the pleasure "liking") leading to "wanting" to alleviate negative effects (fear and anxiety) that result from HPA axis activation, which again activates the HPA axis and keeps the whole process recycling. Such a vicious circle: "results in gross impairment of the normal stress response and other signaling mechanisms in the brain results in a state of anxiety and internal stress" (Wand, 2008, p. 119). Stress hormones also significantly impair the executive function of the PFC, and:

> Chronic exposure to stress and drug abuse both lead to down-regulation deficit of the brain reward system. In the case of drug abuse, as a direct result of the over-activation of the brain reward system, driven by the positive reinforcement that characterises the binge/intoxication stage.
>
> *(Ruisoto & Contador, 2019, p. 64)*

No one wants to be an alcoholic or drug addict, but if they are, they "want" their drug of choice more than "like" it. For those who decide they want to change their life around, motivation to achieve and maintain sobriety is crucial to reaching long-term success, but many potholes in the road must be navigated. As Parker et al. (2021, p. 162) opine: "The most prevalent de-motivator, or challenge, identified by participants was the looming external temptation to relapse." These relapse temptations include socioeconomic stressors, depression, meeting a former drinking or drug-abusing friend, or such simple triggers as walking past a bar, being at a party, looking at a syringe, or just observing a "Just say no!" poster.

Treatment: Alcohol Addiction

Because addiction is a brain chemistry problem, pharmacological treatment stabilizes brain chemistry and renders addicts more receptive to psychosocial counseling. However, despite the cascade of research on the neuroscience of addiction, the National Institute on Drug Abuse (NIDA, 2016, p. 5) notes the failure to translate the evidence into treatment interventions resulting in a "bench-to-bedside gap." It is estimated that less than 1% of eligible jail or prison inmates receive medication for either alcohol or drug abuse (Bronson et al., 2017). This state of affairs leaves us with a host of psychosocial interventions until correctional treatment staff, including physicians, catch up. Of course, there are other arguments for not using pharmaceutical treatment in correctional settings such as their costs, ethical concerns about coerced drug treatment, adverse side effects, substituting one drug for another, and the idea that they treat only symptoms. But drugs for all chronic disease conditions treat only symptoms, and have side effects, and it is realized that radical lifestyle changes must accompany drug treatment for all such conditions. Proponents of pharmacological treatment thus emphasize that it is not a magic bullet and that it augments, not replaces, traditional psychosocial treatment methods.

There are several approved medications for alcoholism, none of which are mood-altering, habit-forming, or develop tolerance, thus gainsaying the objection that pharmacological treatment is mere drug substitution. However, they all have adverse side effects and must be monitored by physicians knowledgeable about addiction. A survey of 589 board-certified addiction physicians determined that oral naltrexone, injectable long-acting naltrexone, and disulfiram were the most common drugs prescribed (Ehrie et al., 2020). Naltrexone is an opioid receptor antagonist that binds to receptor sites that alcohol (and other drugs) target. It blocks pathways to the nucleus accumbens reducing the amount of DA released and thus the reinforcing effects of alcohol and other drugs. A Swedish study of 125,556 first-time treatment subjects for alcohol disorders found that naltrexone combined with disulfiram was more successful in lowering the risk of alcohol-related hospitalization than other drug combinations or no medication (Heikkinen et al., 2021).

Disulfiram is an aversive therapy that works by quickly producing nausea and headaches when alcohol is ingested. It inhibits the enzyme acetaldehyde dehydrogenase that metabolizes alcohol resulting in an over-accumulation of acetaldehyde (ADH), which is normally further broken down and excreted in the urine. Disulfiram retards this breakdown for several days thus maintaining high levels of ADH in the body (a multiday hangover). The unpleasant feelings accompanying alcohol ingestion felt while ADH is retained at high levels in the body act as a negative reinforcer. However, like other conditioned responses, the effects are reduced over time as the drug is no longer taken. A meta-analysis of 22 studies found a higher success rate for subjects receiving disulfiram compared to controls (Skinner et al., 2014).

Alcoholics Anonymous (AA) is a nonmedical model for alcohol abuse and is the most accessed model in the world for achieving abstinence from alcohol and increasing abusers' quality of life (Kelly, 2017). AA is a nonprofessional, peer support, 12-step no-nonsense organization that meets in informal groups to discuss the problems of alcohol informally. Each member of AA has a fellow alcoholic sponsor they can call for support when urges to abandon abstinence intrude. It is not considered treatment, but rather as a lifetime process of personal transformation. It is thought to work by facilitating positive changes within the social networks of its members, boosting their recovery motivation, coping skills, and psychological well-being (Kelly, 2017). Kelly, Humphreys, and Ferri's (2020) meta-analysis of 27 studies which included 10,565 subjects concluded:

> The current review demonstrates that Alcoholics Anonymous/Twelve-Step Facilitation (AA/TSF) is superior to other well-established treatments when it comes to increasing abstinence and is at least as

> effective as other well-established treatments for other alcohol-related outcomes such as drinking consequences, drinking intensity, and addiction severity.

There are other self-help programs such as Rational Recovery and Secular Sobriety for those who object to what they may consider the "spiritual" nature of AA.

Treatment: Drug Addiction

The pharmacological treatment of drug addiction is similar to that of alcohol addiction. Naltrexone is a treatment that claims success in curbing both alcohol and drug addiction. A study of federal probationers with drug addictions found that about one-third of probationers who received naltrexone plus counseling relapsed, as opposed to two-thirds of those who received only counseling (Kleber, 2003). A drug called Vivitrol is a slow-release version of naltrexone. It releases the drug into the bloodstream slowly over days, and controlled clinical trials have shown it to be effective not only in preventing drug abuse relapse but also in diminishing the craving for drugs. "Vivitrol is the first non-narcotic, non-addictive, extended-release medication approved for the treatment of opioid dependence—marking an important turning point in our approach to treatment" (Volkow, 2010, np). Bratina et al. (2020, p. 45) report that both prison staff and inmates have positive views of Vivitrol treatment,

> staff and clients extolled Vivitrol because of the need for monthly, not daily, injections and how the drug would negate any effects of other drug use. Both staff and clients described Vivitrol as a relapse prevention medication, while drugs like Suboxone [the brand name of a buprenorphine/naloxone combination medication], are harm reduction medications.

Other drugs used to treat addiction include methadone and buprenorphine, which are agonists while naloxone is an antagonist. Agonist turns receptors on, and antagonists turn them off.

An agonist binds to a receptor and activates a similar response to natural brain chemicals, whereas an antagonist binds to the receptor and prevents a brain response. Methadone is a synthetic agonist that does not produce euphoria, eliminates withdrawal symptoms, and relieves drug cravings by activating the same receptors that drugs of abuse activate. Although it occupies and activates the same opioid receptors, it does so more slowly than other opioids. Buprenorphine is a partial opioid agonist that binds to the same opioid receptors but activates them less strongly than methadone but has the same effects. Buprenorphine is often preferred over methadone as a treatment option because it can be delivered via a six-month subdermal implant or a once-monthly injection, thus eliminating the necessity of daily medication.

Evans et al. (2019) conducted a randomized trial of male inmates who received either buprenorphine or methadone treatment and were compared with inmates who received neither five years after release for rearrests. There was no difference between the buprenorphine and methadone groups in the proportion arrested (approximately 55%) during the five years but members of both groups were less likely to be arrested relative to group members receiving neither. The methadone group did better versus the no-treatment group (OR = 0.50) as did the buprenorphine group (OR = 0.39). Similarly, Evans, Wilson, and Friedmann (2022) compared inmates of two jails who did (n = 197) and did not (n = 272) receive buprenorphine treatment for one-year post-release recidivism. They found that fewer individuals from the jail where buprenorphine treatment was provided recidivated less often than those from the jail that did not (48.2% vs. 62.5%; p = 0.001).

Cocaine addiction presents a bigger treatment problem than opioid drugs and is a bigger social problem. Brandt et al. (2021) report that in 2017, 52% of all fatal drug overdoses in the United States involved cocaine. Cocaine acts as a reuptake inhibitor of dopamine, serotonin, and norepinephrine, resulting in stronger and prolonged signaling. Prolonged cocaine usage causes brain circuitry changes that progressively sensitize the dopaminergic system and lead to recurrent and intense cocaine wanting. Developing pharmacological treatments for cocaine abuse is challenging because cocaine has effects that involve many different neurotransmitters and thus drugs must have more than one molecular target (Kampman, 2019). Topiramate, a drug used to control seizures and to prevent migraine headaches, shows some promise. Topiramate is a GABA agonist and a glutamate antagonist and it has effects on both GABA and glutamate neurotransmission by facilitating increased levels of GABA while inhibiting glutamate transmission.

Kampman (2019, p. 6) recommends augmenting topiramate with long-acting stimulants as agonist replacements: "Combinations of topiramate and long-acting stimulants take advantage of two separate mechanisms of action and thus far seem to offer benefits over stimulants or topiramate alone." Tardelli et al. (2023, p. 5) note how prescribed stimulants work to reduce cocaine craving: "In fact, amphetamine maintenance attenuates cocaine abuse behaviors by reducing its effects on nucleus accumbens dopamine levels and preventing cocaine-induced rewarding and reinforcing effects." However, progress has been painfully slow in bringing the focus down to a treatment regimen that we can be confident about, and there is a bewildering number of drugs that have been tried with mixed results. For instance, Lassi et al. (2022) list three drugs as "promising" for reducing cocaine craving in the short-term, and eleven in the long-term. There are many problems with studies attempting to develop medications for cocaine addiction. Patients must be monitored closely with slow titration rates to achieve correct target dose levels, the side effects can be unpleasant, and retention rates in studies are low and follow-up rates even more so.

As for nonpharmaceutical treatment, the Delaware Multistage Program implemented in prison settings, and transitioning into the community offers hopeful findings (Stohr, 2020). In the first stage, offenders spend 12 months in a prison-based therapeutic community (TC) called Key; in Phase 2, they spend six months in a prerelease TC called Crest; and in Phase 3, they receive an additional six months of counseling while on parole or in work release (Key-Crest). Comparing drug use and arrest outcomes for offenders completing all phases 18 months after release from prison and a comparison group of offenders who did not participate in any of the phases, 76% of Key-Crest members remained drug-free and 71% remained arrest-free, compared with only 19% and 30%, respectively, of the control group. Inciardi, Martin, and Butzin (2004) followed this same group for five years after release from prison. As expected, the greater the time lapse between treatments, the greater the relapse rate. Over the five years, it was found that 71% of drug abusers who went through all phases of Key-Crest treatment had relapsed and 52% had been rearrested. However, the contrast with the comparison group still makes the Key-Crest program results impressive because among the control subjects, 95% had relapsed and 77% had been rearrested. This study shows how difficult it is to battle addiction even after a long period of extensive psychosocial treatment.

Cocaine Anonymous (CA) is a 12-step program modeled on AA and aims for complete abstinence. As the CA website defines its mandate:

> Cocaine Anonymous is a Fellowship of men and women who share their experience, strength and hope with each other that they may solve their common problem and help others recover from their addiction. The only requirement for membership is a desire to stop using cocaine and all other mind-altering substances.

In a comprehensive review of 428 studies, only 10 studies with a combined total of 1,071 subjects were deemed high enough quality for meta-analysis (Bøg et al., 2017). Even these studies were difficult to compare given the heterogeneity of designs and other concerns. For this reason, Bøg et al. did not report an overall effect size but cautiously concluded: "The evidence from comparing 12-step with an add-on treatment against psychosocial intervention with an (identical) add-on treatment for the outcome of drug use were cautiously in favour of 12-step at 6 months follow-up" (p. 54).

Drug Policy: Harm Reduction

The current war on drugs, like the war on alcohol during Prohibition, causes more crime and harm than it prevents. For this reason, most Western countries have abandoned their drug wars in favor of pragmatic harm reduction policies; that is, a set of practical strategies aimed solely at minimizing overall harm. Although the United States is a world leader in legalizing medical and recreational cannabis, it is among only a handful of countries that reject harm reduction policies for more serious drugs (Dolan, Larney, & Wodak, 2007). Harm reduction programs involve syringe exchange programs, drug substitution programs, and safe injection facilities without mandating (although encouraging) that addicts seek treatment and the legalization of drug usage. Such practices may upset the moral sensibilities of some people, but they offer practical solutions if the goal is to reduce the overall social harm of drugs. The International Harm Reduction Association (IHRA, 2010, np) defines harm reduction:

> Harm reduction refers to policies, programmes and practices that aim to reduce the harms associated with the use of psychoactive drugs in people unable or unwilling to stop. The defining features are the focus on the prevention of harm, rather than on the prevention of drug use itself, and they focus on people who continue to use drugs.

The goal of the IHRA is not to reduce drug consumption, although it applauds efforts to do so, but rather to weigh the risks and harms caused by criminalizing drugs against the risks and harms associated with legalizing them. It focuses on minimizing the costly negative health and behavioral effects of substance abuse that exist when drugs are obtained illicitly such as deaths from overdoses and the transmission of infectious diseases such as HIV, hepatitis C virus, and tuberculosis. While the IHRA decries the presence of these dangerous substances, it also knows that Pandora's box has been opened and there is no closing it. Harm reduction aims to legalize drugs so that criminal elements no longer control the market, as was the case with alcohol after Prohibition was lifted. Such programs in other countries make formerly illegal substances legally obtainable from licensed physicians (often free of charge), thus reducing addicts' need to engage in crime to feed their habits. Prisons in the United States are overflowing with drug offenders, so legalizing drugs should not only reduce crime but save the taxpayer billions in criminal justice costs. How successful have harm reduction programs been in countries that have adopted them? According to Wodak (2007, p. 61): "No country which has started harm reduction programs has ever regretted that decision and then reversed their commitment." Harm reduction policies are not perfect and involve trade-offs rather than solutions, but if policies must be evidence-based, then the evidence doesn't get much better than that.

14

THE MICROENVIRONMENT

Teratogens and Diet

Neural Development and Teratogens

Neurogenesis is an incredibly complex process that begins about three weeks after conception by forming the neural tube. From a single precursor cell (the zygote), about 250,000 neurons are produced every minute from immature cells called neuroblasts (Toga, Thompson, & Sowell, 2006). This is a critically vital period in brain development because, the: "*In utero* environment critically affects the brain development, thereby modifying neurobehavior of the offspring after birth" (Hwang, Ku, & Hashimoto-Torii, 2019, p. 138). Neuroblasts sprout axons with antennae that reach out to make synaptic connections with other neurons in the correct alignment, orientation, and layering to form various areas of the brain, differentiating according to what structures they are to be part of and what functions to perform. Cells must migrate from their birthplace to their eventual home, and it is during this migratory phase of maturation the brain is most vulnerable to perturbations (Volpe, 2019).

New brain cells must recognize the correct path and make the right connections to perform their allotted functions guided by glial cell scaffolds and molecular messengers. Once migration and connection are accomplished, the paring back process of their number begins with only about half surviving. The winners are the cells that secured a supply of a class of chemicals known as neurotrophins, whose function is to stimulate and guide neurogenesis. These molecules are susceptible to confusion by alien molecules in the *in-utero* environment which may become so great that neurons may be sent to the wrong neighborhood or instructed to

DOI: 10.4324/9781003642268-18

self-destruct. These alien molecules are known collectively as teratogens, which are exogenous substances that can disrupt the development of an embryo/fetus and result in some form of neurological impairment. The most common of these teratogenic molecules is associated with alcohol introduced to the embryo/fetus by its mother's drinking while pregnant.

Alcohol, Drugs, and Tobacco

Fetal Alcohol Spectrum Disorder (FASD) refers to the range of physical, neurological, cognitive, socioemotional, and behavioral impairments that result from the exposure of an embryo/fetus to alcohol. The phrase "alcohol spectrum disorder" (FASD) emphasizes the continuous nature of the effects of prenatal alcohol exposure, which may be mild or result in fetal alcohol syndrome (FAS) at the severe end of the spectrum. The negative effects on the developing embryo/fetus depend on the dose, duration, and pattern of alcohol consumption (particularly binge drinking), and individual genetic susceptibility. Alcohol consumed by a pregnant woman easily crosses the placenta and increases fetal alcohol concentrations to levels equivalent to those in the mother within 2 hours of her ingestion (Subramoney et al., 2018). FAS can result in several physical abnormalities, but neuroscientists are concerned with its effects on the migration and hook-up of neurons in brain areas such as the frontal lobes, amygdala, hippocampus, hypothalamus, and the serotonergic system. Fetal alcohol exposure changes the expressions of many genes that are associated with neuronal migration and interferes with the myelination process (Kawasawa, 2017) and is the foremost preventable cause of cognitive impairment in the world (Roozen et al., 2016).

The prevalence of FASD in the United States is around 1% of live births and for full-blown FAS about 0.33 per 1,000 live births (Manning & Hoyme, 2007). It is found in all ethnic and racial groups, but African American children are 5 times more likely and American Indian/Alaska Native children are 16 times more likely to exhibit FAS than White children; Asian American children have the lowest rate (Sokol, Delaney-Black, & Nordstrom, 2003). Large SES differences are also found. From a review of the literature, by the National Institute of Alcohol Abuse and Alcoholism, it has been shown that the FAS rate in the middle class is 0.26 per 1,000 and the lowest SES class is about 3.4 per 1,000 (May & Gossage, 2001).

The traits and behaviors associated with FAS include low IQ, hyperactivity, impulsiveness, attention-deficit/hyperactivity disorder (ADHD), poor social, emotional, and moral development, and a highly elevated probability of alcoholism (May et al., 2021). Each item in this cumulative list of deficits is linked to high levels of antisocial behavior and criminal offending independent of FAS, and FAS individuals are almost always saddled with them all. It has been claimed that: "Juveniles with FASD are 19 times more likely to be incarcerated, and a long-term study documented 60% of the FASD participants over the age of 12 had criminal histories" (Brown et al., 2014, p. 2). A review of 30 studies of children of alcoholic parents found that all studies showed a significant relationship between children having alcoholic parents and their own delinquent and criminal behavior (Ellis & Walsh, 2000). This points to passive rGE mechanisms in which alcoholic parents provide offspring with a suite of genes conducive to alcoholism and antisocial behavior and an environment (e.g., modeling, poverty, poor parenting, and abuse-neglect) that are conducive to the development of offspring alcoholism.

Cocaine is another teratogen. It is estimated that as many as 375,000 infants are born each year have been exposed to cocaine *in utero*, and that in some inner-city hospitals, as many as half of pregnant women test positive for it (Mayes et al., 1995). As with alcohol, cocaine readily crosses the placenta and directly affects neuronal maturation during embryo/fetal development during critical periods. A study of neonates born in inner-city hospitals in four large American cities who were and who were not exposed to cocaine *in utero* found that cocaine exposure results in serious central and peripheral nervous system symptoms (Bauer et al., 2005). Cocaine-exposed infants were 42 times more likely to have a diagnosis of hepatitis and 15 times more likely to have a diagnosis of syphilis than controls. This reflects their mothers' risky antisocial lifestyles and lack of responsibility. Only 10.1% of the mothers of cocaine-exposed infants were married. In terms of the antisocial behavior of the offspring of these women, Richardson et al. (2019) found that prenatal cocaine exposure was significantly associated with ever being arrested and with a diagnosis of conduct disorder (odds ratios of 3 and 2, respectively) independent of covariates.

Yet another common teratogenic risk is maternal smoking. Maternal smoking has its primary risk in fetal intermittent hypoxia, which is the intermittent reduction of oxygen available to the fetus due to vasoconstriction that may lead to cell death. Cohort studies (e.g., Brennan, Grekin, & Sarnoff, 1999) consistently find that maternal smoking during pregnancy predicts criminal behavior in fetal-exposed offspring independent of other risk factors. A review of several such studies found odds ratios ranging between 1.5 and 4.0 for fetal tobacco-exposed individuals versus nonexposed individuals for various forms of antisocial behavior across diverse contexts and independent of other factors such as maternal SES and IQ (Wakschlag et al., 2002). A Swedish cohort study of over 500,000 subjects revealed that maternal smoking during pregnancy was predictive of offspring having a criminal conviction (D'Onofrio et al., 2010). The association between maternal smoking and offspring offending is small but consistent.

Lead Exposure

Exposure to noxious substances in the environment outside the womb, such as lead, over which the mother has no control, has negative effects on children's brains, manifested most clearly in the reduction of IQ. The IQ decrement per unit increase in µg/dL (micrograms per deciliter of blood) of lead is an average of one-half point (Koller et al., 2004). The main modern source of lead exposure is lead dust from lead-based paint in older houses in the poorest urban neighborhoods. Toxic levels of lead (>40 µg/dL) distort enzymes, interfere with the development of the endogenous opiate system, disrupt the dopamine system, and reduce serotonin and MAOA levels (Wright et al., 2008). An fMRI study found that brain gray matter was inversely correlated with mean childhood lead concentrations in mostly Black young adults participating in the longitudinal Cincinnati Lead Study (Cecil et al., 2008). The mean blood lead concentration of the sample was 13.3 µg/dL, which is well below toxic levels but far above the average of 1.5 µg/dL for the general population in 2006 (Bellinger, 2008). The gray matter lost was small (about 1.2%) but mostly concentrated in vital behavior-moderating areas responsible for executive functioning and mood regulation such as the frontal lobes and the anterior cingulate cortex.

Another sample from the Cincinnati Lead Study examined the relationship between childhood blood lead and verified criminal arrests. The mean number of arrests for the males in the sample who were ever arrested was 5.2. The main finding was that after adjusting for relevant covariates, for every 5 µg/dL lead increase, there was an increase in the probability of arrest for a violent crime of about 50% (Wright et al., 2008). Reuben et al.'s (2019) longitudinal study of 579 New Zealand lead-exposed children found that higher childhood blood lead levels were associated with more psychopathology across the life course. Controlling for several covariates, each 5 µg/dL increase in childhood blood lead level was significantly associated with an increase in neuroticism, which is positively related to antisocial behavior, and decreases in agreeableness and conscientiousness, which are negatively related to antisocial behavior. Several other studies have found weak to moderate effects of lead exposure on crime (Sampson & Winter, 2018).

Lead competes with calcium for absorption, if children do not receive adequate dietary calcium, it absorbs lead. This is important because blood lead levels are associated with a calcium absorption gene called the vitamin

D receptor (VDR) gene (Chakraborty et al., 2008). A polymorphism (the Fok1 enzyme) of the VDR renders calcium absorption more efficient for its carriers, which is beneficial in the presence of adequate dietary calcium, but not in its absence. This polymorphism is more prevalent among Blacks than among Whites or Asians (Chakraborty et al., 2008), which creates a G*x*E in which African Americans will absorb more lead than similarly exposed members of other racial groups.

Diet: Breastfeeding

The old cliché that we are what we eat may be oversold, but there is more than a grain of truth there. The brain is at work 24/7, and it requires a lot of fuel obtained from our food, and the quality of that food makes a difference in how well our brains work. To the extent that this is true, we expect diet to affect behavior, including antisocial behavior. High-quality food containing vital vitamins, minerals, antioxidants, and polyunsaturated fatty acids nourishes the brain and makes it run smoothly while foods high in refined sugars, saturated fats, and carbohydrates make it sluggish. Because of the convenience and low cost of processed foods, a "junk food" diet is widely consumed in low SES communities where most delinquents and criminals reside. Most people living in those communities likely have eaten mostly processed junk foods all their lives. However, this only establishes a correlation between diet and antisocial behavior; can there be something causal between diet and behavior? The suggestion that delinquent and criminal behavior may be to some limited extent causally related to dietary deficiencies may not be taken seriously by most criminologists. Yet there is a body of literature that suggests that it is. Nutrition is most important for optimal infant brain development when it is most plastic.

The first food newborn infants may ingest is their mother's breast milk. Pediatricians Lawrence and Lawrence (2011, p. 267) gush over the many benefits of breastfeeding for mothers and infants: "Over the past 50 to 60 years, human milk has been described and recognized as the best first food for human infants; breast is best! Human milk provides substantial nutritional, cognitive, emotional, and immunologic benefits for the infant." Newborn's innate immune systems cannot mount a fully effective response to all antigens in their environment. Fortunately, newborns receive a 100% safe vaccine in the form of colostrum; mom's high-octane milk expressed from about the fourth to the eighth day of breastfeeding. After a few days of ingesting this superfood, the infant gets 10–14 days of transitional milk; a blend of colostrum and thinner breast milk. Transitional milk is eventually replaced by regular breast milk, which contains many chemical compounds important for brain development. This natural formula contains elements that support the baby's immune system such as just the right amounts of proteins and polyunsaturated fatty acids, among other nutrients not found in the right amounts (either too much or too little) in cow's milk, and is little improved upon by commercial milk formulas (Lawrence & Lawrence, 2011). Breast milk transfers many of the mother's developed antibodies to the nursing infant, and since mothers and their babies are typically exposed to the same antigens, infants gain further protection (Petherick, 2010).

The cognitive effects of breastfeeding are typically assessed via IQ scores. A South Korean study (Kim et al., 2017) of children aged between 8 and 11 found that those who were ever-breastfed scored significantly higher on learning skills such as speaking, reading, writing, spelling, and mathematics compared to children who were never breastfed after controlling for various gestational and SES variables. A Spanish cohort study (Julvez et al., 2014) assessed children's IQ scores at age 4 and found that children who never breastfed had a mean IQ of 98 and that children who were breastfed longer than six months had a mean of 108. After adjusting for SES, maternal education, smoking, and infant birth weight, the 10-point advantage diminished to a 7.5-point advantage. Unfortunately, such studies rarely have access to mothers' IQs. Because of the positive relationship between mothers' IQ and the probability of prolonged breastfeeding, the relationship may be a genetic effect on children's IQ rather than a breastfeeding effect.

Kramer et al. (2008) controlled for this concern with a randomized experimental design in a study of 13,889 Belarusian breastfeeding mothers. A random half of them were given incentives to prolong breastfeeding, while the other half were not. When the children were assessed 6 years later, it was found that the children breastfed for more than six months had a mean IQ almost six points higher than the control group children. The experimental research design allowed researchers to measure breastfeeding effects on IQ without concerns about biasing confounds. Similarly, a study of 3,000 British and New Zealand children born in the early 1970s and IQ tested in the 1990s found that subjects who were breastfed scored on average 6 to 7 points higher on IQ tests than nonbreastfed subjects (Caspi et al., 2007). This was true for 90% of breastfed subjects who had at least one copy of the C (cytosine) base variant of the fatty acid desaturase (FADS2) gene that codes for an enzyme that converts fatty acids into two polyunsaturated acids that accumulate in the infant brain in the early months after birth. There was no IQ increase for breastfed children homozygous for the G (guanine) allele of the FADS2 gene. This G*x*E interaction showed no difference in the average scores of C versus G individuals who were not breastfed (the allele made no difference alone) and that breastfeeding made no difference for individuals homogeneous for the G allele.

However, there is another confound which cannot be directly observed. Breastfeeding might exert its effects through physical and emotional contact between mother and infant (Wallenborn et al., 2021). The tactile stimulation and mother/infant gaze are significantly elevated during breastfeeding and positively influence the child's emotional development. Breastfeeding combines the panoply of sight, sound, smell, touch, and the tangible evidence in the mother's arms that affirms her womanhood and stimulates the release of oxytocin (the "cuddle chemical"), which intensifies the warm feeling that is released in a felicitous feedback loop. Oxytocin is also conveyed to infants through breast milk and skin contact (UvnäsMoberg et al., 2020). Lactating mothers show significantly fewer stress responses to infant stimuli, as determined by skin conductance and cardiac response measures, than nonlactating mothers, and the oxytocin-generated sense of emotional warmness motivates a significantly greater desire to pick up their infants in response to infant-presented stimuli (Hiller, 2004).

Breastfeeding and the tactile stimulation accompanying it, is an experience-expected feature of brain development since it was the only way of feeding hominin/hominid infants during the vast majority of our evolution. As an experience-expected feature, the failure of the infant to experience it may be seen as the deprivation of important brain development input. However, regardless of whether it is the nutritional or emotional aspects of breastfeeding or a combination of both that confers developmental benefits, there are still benefits. Unfortunately, the literature consistently shows a marked downward gradient in the rates of breastfeeding as maternal IQ and SES fall. Children of lower-SES women are thus more likely to be deprived of important experience-expected input. A random sample of 10,519 California mothers found that the odds of breastfeeding in the highest income category were 3.65 times the odds of women in the lowest income category (Heck et al., 2006). The Department of Health and Human Service's National Immunization Program survey (2004) revealed that 29.3% of Black infants were breastfeeding at six months versus 43.2% of White, and 53.7% of Asian infants.

Diet and the Gut Microbiome

Extended breastfeeding places infants on a positive trajectory, but their diet in later years may also impact their behavior. Research in criminology has established links between nutrition and criminal behavior. For instance, Zaalberg et al. (2010) note:

> In the last three decades, evidence seems to be mounting that dietary status and (deviant) behavior are associated. Ecological data and correlational studies, for instance, suggested associations between dietary habits such as fish consumption on the one hand, and psychiatric disorders, developmental disorders, and aggression and criminal behavior.
>
> *(p. 117)*

Zaalberg et al. used a randomized double-blind, placebo-controlled design to test the effects of nutritional supplements on aggression, rule-breaking, and psychopathology among young Dutch prisoners. The treatment group received the full range of recommended vitamins, minerals, and essential fatty acids, and the number of staff-reported incidents of prisoner rule-breaking in the treatment group was reduced by 34% as opposed to a 14% *increase* in the placebo control group.

Similarly, Gesch et al. (2002) conducted a double-blind, placebo-controlled, randomized study of nutritional supplements with 231 young British adult prisoners, comparing disciplinary offenses before and during supplementation. The dietary supplementation was daily vitamin, mineral, and essential fatty acid capsules. Randomization ensured that the treatment and placebo groups were equivalent in average rates of disciplinary incidents before dietary supplementation. Based on prison disciplinary reports, the treatment groups achieved a 35.1% reduction in reports compared to the placebo group's 6.7% reduction. The greatest reduction occurred for the most serious incidents (including violence), with the treatment group showing a 37% reduction in reports over their baseline reports ($p = 0.005$); the placebo group showed a nonsignificant 10.1% reduction over baseline. Because a randomized design was employed, the difference between the two groups had to be attributed only to the dietary supplementation. On the other hand, Cortie et al. (2020) did not find a significant difference in behavioral infraction among Australian prisoners between the treatment group (who received omega-3 fatty acids and multivitamin supplements) and the placebo group.

Using data from the Early Childhood Longitudinal Study Birth Cohort, Jackson (2016) explored the link between poor nutritional quality and childhood antisocial behavior among 238 MZ and 738 same-sex DZ twins. He employed seven parent-rated questions and six teacher-rated questions as indicators of childhood antisocial behavior and diet was constructed by summing scores on six dietary components. Because twins were studied, we expect a great similarity in their diets, but a sizeable number differed in their dietary habits, yielding a small but statistically amount of nonshared source of variance in antisocial behavior. Genes ($h^2 = 0.83$) accounted for the highest proportion of variance in antisocial behavior. Jackson (2016, p. 19) concluded:

> the results of the current study give even more reason to believe that the link between poor nutrition and behavioral problems may actually be causal, as results were robust to both shared environmental and genetic factors. Ultimately, the findings imply that interventions aimed at preventing and/or minimizing antisocial behavior will likely prove more successful if they a) are implemented during earlier stages of the life course and b) take nutritional factors into account.

A growing body of evidence has revealed that the gut microbiome may have important effects on mental health and behavior, and may be the mediator between diet and antisocial behavior. The gut microbiome is the community of trillions of microorganisms in the gastrointestinal tract and their associated genetic material, and it is responsible for digestion, metabolic energy, making essential vitamins, and performing certain immune defense functions (Tcherni-Buzzeo, 2023). It has been noted that the gut microbiome has 100 times more genes than the human genome (Leung & Weiss, 2023). Wilson et al. (2020, p. 726) observe that: "The development of the gut microbiome begins at birth and in healthy individuals is largely completed within 3 years, but can be modified by environmental factors, particularly diet composition and volume, and antibiotic therapy."

Gato et al. (2018, p. 1193) note:

> The metabolic role of the human gut microbiome has been well studied and researchers are intrigued by the presence of a link between behavior and gut microbiota. This link has been deemed the gut-brain Axis (GBA) that includes a set of pathways which facilitate bidirectional interactions between the brain and gut microbiota.

For example, it is thought that 95% of the precursors of circulating serotonin, dopamine, and norepinephrine are produced by our gut microbiota (Arteaga-Henríquez et al., 2020). Many studies have shown that gut microbes play essential roles in neurodevelopment via the vagal nerve (a long nerve that connects the brain to the autonomic nervous system), and in cytokine and neurotransmitter production. Suboptimal gut microbial colonization may thus be detrimental to some neurodevelopmental outcomes (see Aatsinki et al., 2019 and Leung & Weiss, 2023 for reviews).

Gao et al. (2019) conducted resting-state fMRI scans of 39 1-year-old infants who provided fecal samples for the identification and quantification of gut bacterial taxa. They found that higher levels of microbiome diversity are statistically significantly related to weaker thalamus-amygdala connectivity and other brain areas involved in processing and responding to threat and early learning composite scores assessed at age 2 years. Microbiota populations change with dietary intake and thus provide clues as to how diet changes in the Dutch prisoners studied by Zaalberg et al. (2010) led to behavioral changes. Tcherni-Buzzeo (2023, p. 22) concludes her review of microbiome/neurobiology/criminal behavior research by noting:

> Though much research is still needed to better understand the mechanisms of influence, integrating the gut microbiome as an important factor in biosocial criminological research could improve crime prevention and recidivism reduction efforts and enrich more traditional criminological theories. The research reviewed here suggests that even small changes in the diet, with the help of pro- and prebiotics, have the potential to affect behavior in a positive way.

Delinquents and criminals are notorious for their poor diets, but Wilson et al. (2020, p. 738) note that there is "irrefutable evidence from around the world that the human microbiome can be modified by dietary change in children and adults." Foods that help to create a healthy gut microbiome are prebiotics and probiotics. Prebiotics are foods such as fruits, vegetables, legumes, and grains that are nondigestible substances, and probiotics are fermented foods such as sauerkraut, buttermilk, and yogurt with live cultures that aid digestion. Diets high in fast foods, sugar, and processed foods help to create an unhealthy gut microbiome.

Policy and Treatment Protocols

Literature reviews reveal only a small number of randomized-controlled treatment studies of FASD subjects, but Ordenewitz et al. (2021, p. 59) note that there is

> some evidence indicating that children and adolescents with FASD benefit from trainings of functional neurological deficits. Especially the combination of parent and children sessions appears to be a promising approach. Particularly, training of self-regulation skills and social interaction abilities seems to have a long-term as well as a transferring effect on attention and behavior.

However, these therapies have low success rates, especially in severe cases. Certain medical treatments are emerging, but FASD medication protocols are in their infancy. Because of this: "The experts recommended that clinicians first use nonpharmacological interventions, including functional behavior analysis, behavioral management, and environmental modifications, before pharmacotherapy" (Mela et al., 2020, p. e5). However, several drugs influencing dopamine, serotonin, and norepinephrine receptors such as central nervous system stimulants, some antipsychotics, selective serotonin reuptake inhibitors (SSRIs), and antioxidants have shown potential in managing FASD comorbid symptoms such as aggression, intellectual disabilities, and depression depending on what cluster of traits is presented (Andreu-Fernández et al., 2024).

Google Scholar searches reveal no treatment modalities specific to fetal cocaine-exposed or tobacco-exposed individuals. Presumably, the same psychosocial and pharmacological interventions used to address specific psychological and behavioral symptoms in FASD are used for cocaine exposure. Because prevention is better than cure, it may fall on primary care physicians to assess and address maternal addiction problems on a pregnant woman's first visit and then refer her to agencies that specialize in providing treatment for addiction and information on the dangers to her embryo/fetus of continuing her substance abuse. Unfortunately, those most in need of this information and this treatment are those who are least likely to take advantage of it or to understand it. These are the women most in need of the services of the Nurse-Family Partnership Program addressed in Chapter 16.

While the effects of alcohol, drugs, and tobacco occur in the womb, the effects of lead may be experienced throughout the childhood years for those living in pre-1978 housing. Many states and municipalities are engaged in lead abatement activities designed to eliminate lead-based paint hazards and soil contaminated by leaded gasoline before it was banned in 1996. Oxidative stress is the prime candidate for the molecular mechanism responsible for lead's negative impact. Oxidative stress is an imbalance between free radicals (oxygen-containing molecules with unpaired electrons that allow free radicals to react with other molecules) and antioxidants, molecules that help the body fight off harmful free radicals (Killian et al., 2020). Since we have noted that lead competes with calcium, it is not surprising that a diet high in milk and other dairy products has been shown to reduce lead toxicity of the sensory nervous system in lead workers (Gomes et al., 2017). Mouse studies have shown that optimized antioxidant (calcium, iron, and zinc) and micronutrient-rich (particularly vitamin C) milk formula effectively reduces lead poisoning (Zhang et al., 2013). It thus behooves us to optimize childhood diets, which can be done by assuring nutritious meals for all schoolchildren without access to such diets at home.

Perhaps the greater use of breastfeeding among higher-IQ and high-SES mothers is because they are financially able to do so. A major barrier to breastfeeding, and thus to the emotional bonding of mothers and infants as well, is the need to work. If breastfeeding rates are to increase, paid maternity leave is required in the United States, but as Widiss (2021, p. 2176) notes:

> The United States is the only developed country that fails to guarantee paid time off work to new parents. Just 21% of American workers—and just 9% of the lowest quartile of earners—receive paid parental or family leave from their employers.

The Family and Medical Leave Act (FMLA) of 1993 provides for only 12 weeks of unpaid leave and applies only to companies with over 50 employees. Most American new mothers use some combination of vacation time, short-term disability, sick leave, vacation time, or personal days off (Widiss, 2021).

Chai et al. (2018) studied how extending paid maternity leave affects breastfeeding duration among 992,419 newborns in 38 low-income and middle-income countries between 1996 and 2014. They found that extending the duration of legislated paid maternity leave appears to promote breastfeeding practices in those countries that provided such legislation compared with control nations that did not. Specifically, a one-month increase in paid maternity leave was associated with a 7.4% increase in the prevalence of early initiation of breastfeeding, a 5.9% increase in exclusive breastfeeding, and a 2.2% – month increase in breastfeeding duration. Paid maternity leave thus goes a long way to increase the probability of an experience-expected practice that pays many benefits in terms of optimal parent-child bonding and children's physical and psychological well-being.

While it is obvious that we cannot expect to control the diets of offenders in the community, we can control the diets of institutionalized offenders. The diets provided for institutionalized offenders are notoriously poor consisting mostly of processed foods high in carbohydrates and low in vital nutrients. Policy interventions focusing on providing all schoolchildren and institutionalized offenders with meals high in omega-3 supplementation, calcium, and vitamins, particularly vitamin C, may pay dividends for little cost. The reductions in offending provided by such interventions may be small, but any reduction is welcome. However, it should be recognized that there is no direct relationship between micronutrients and behavior and that there are many inflated claims regarding the dietary benefits of positively changing behavior.

PART V

Traditional and Biopsychosocial Approaches to Assessment and Treatment

15

CORRECTIONAL ASSESSMENT AND TREATMENT PROGRAMMING

The Rehabilitative Goal

The correctional system (jails, prisons, and probation/parole departments) has four major policy goals or, if you like, punishment justifications: deterrence, incapacitation, retribution, and rehabilitation (Stohr & Walsh, 2025). Here we only address the goal of rehabilitation, which means to restore or return to constructive or healthy activity. However, many (perhaps most) offenders have never experienced anything close to constructive or healthy activity. Correctional treatment or programming attempts to provide some of the things missing from the lives of offenders, but it obviously cannot supply the warmth and nurture so critical to healthy brain development during the early years of life or the deep sense of attachment and commitment to family, school, and other social institutions that issue from such experiences. Nonetheless, programming and treatment can provide valuable things such as education and job training, and may even change the destructive thinking patterns that infect criminal minds.

Habitual offenders tend to perceive the world in a fatalistic fashion, believing that there is little that they can do to change the circumstances of their lives. To illustrate criminal thinking ("stinkin' thinkin'"), Boyd Sharp (2006, p. 3) cited a cartoon in which one of the characters named Calvin said:

> I have concluded that nothing bad I do is my fault. ...I'm a helpless victim of countless bad influences. An unwholesome culture panders

DOI: 10.4324/9781003642268-20

to my undeveloped values and it pushes me into misbehavior. I take no responsibility for my behavior. I'm an innocent pawn of society.

Criminals think like Calvin—in the context of a society where many prefer to claim victimhood rather than personal responsibility ("McDonald's made me fat." "The Marlboro man made me smoke."). Many criminological theories contribute to this by locating the causes of crime on external factors rather than allowing criminals the dignity of owning responsibility for their behavioral choices.

Rehabilitative efforts should be viewed with the realization that they are ultimately intended to promote public safety. Rehabilitation is not about mollycoddling criminals because whatever helps offenders not to re-offend helps the community. The main concern of corrections is to reduce the risk offenders pose to society, not to improve their lives, but if offenders can improve their lives and become convinced of the value of walking the straight and narrow, the risk of community members being victimized is reduced proportionately. As Warren Burger, a former Supreme Court Chief Justice, opined: "To put people behind walls and bars and do little or nothing to change them is to win a battle but lose a war. It is wrong. It is expensive. It is stupid" (in West, 1991, p. 2). However, keep in mind that the vast majority of money assigned to correctional agencies is understandably spent on surveillance and control functions with only a pittance assigned to treatment programs.

The zeal for rehabilitation reached the pinnacle of its popularity during the 1950s through the 1970s, when the so-called medical model of criminal behavior prevailed. The medical model viewed crime as a moral sickness requiring treatment, and prisoners were to remain in custody under indeterminate sentences until "cured." Under this system classification systems, group and individual counseling, and therapeutic milieus were added to the usual rehabilitative fare of labor, basic education, and vocational training. However, the rehabilitative goal fell apart with Robert Martinson's (1974) article "What Works? Questions and Answers About Prison Reform," in which he concluded that "with few and isolated exceptions the rehabilitation efforts that have been reported so far have no appreciable effects on recidivism" (p. 25).

Unfortunately, the rhetorical question "What works?" got translated into a definitive "Nothing works." If we demand 100% success, then of course "nothing works." A program designed to change people's lives is not a dishwasher that either works or does not. Nothing works for anybody all of the time, but some things work for some people some of the time. We need to know what works for whom and under what conditions. It is safe to conclude, however, that recidivism is a lot more common than rehabilitation. For instance, a study of 404,638 prisoners released in 2005 from 30 state prisons found that 68% were arrested within three years after release and 77% within five years. These offenders were responsible for around 1,173,000 new arrests between 2005 and 2010 (Dunrose, Cooper, & Snyder, 2014). We cannot know from such raw data if there was a difference in rearrests between treated and untreated offenders, or if treated, the type or dosage of such treatment.

The problem with the rehabilitative programs Martinson (1974) surveyed is that they were rarely evidence-based, often sought to change behaviors unrelated to crime, were not intensive enough, and used staff who were not adequately trained to implement them. Few programs were based on even minimal empirical evidence as to their efficacy or on assessment of offender risk and needs and were often faddish "Let's try it and see what happens" programs. These programs included almost everything from acupuncture to Zen meditation and were offered in a one-size-fits-all fashion. One probation department insisted that male offenders should "get in touch" with their feminine side by having them dress in female clothes, and another required "poetry therapy" (Latessa, Cullen, & Gendreau, 2002).

Post-Martinson, Gendreau and Ross (1987, p 395) reviewed several evaluations of treatment programs and concluded: "It is downright ridiculous to say that 'Nothing works.' ... Much is going on to indicate that offender rehabilitation has been, can be, and will be achieved." Lipsey and Cullen (2007) reviewed numerous studies of a variety of correctional intervention programs conducted from 1990 to 2006 and concluded that treatment works moderately well in reducing recidivism, and Cullen and Gendreau (2000) maintain that a recidivism reduction in the 10% to 20% range is not an unrealistic expectation. A "success rate" is determined by the difference in recidivism between a treatment group and a control group. A review of studies from prison, jail, probation, and parole settings by Pearson et al. (2002) found that overall, 55.7% of the subjects in treatment groups were not rearrested compared with 43.3% of control group subjects who were not. One can look at such studies from a glass-half-full or a glass-half-empty perspective, with optimism cautiously growing in proportion to how long treatment effects last.

The best kind of treatment for offenders appears to be offense-specific programs. Gannon et al. (2019) conducted a meta-analysis of 70 studies that included 55,604 offenders in specialized programs who had committed sexual, domestic violence, and general violent offenses. It was found after a 5.5-year follow-up found that reductions in offense-specific recidivism were 32.6% for those in sexual offense programs, 36.0% in domestic violence programs, and 24.3% in general violence programs. Gannon and her colleagues maintain that treatment programs must be specialized and center on specific offenses and the best results are obtained when a clinical psychologist is in charge. They also note that many correctional systems are moving away from using psychologists for financial reasons and toward manual-based groups run by staff with little or no formal clinical training. The reported recidivism rates are encouraging, particularly given the long follow-up period. Of course, successes and failures include offenders who would not re-offend even if they did not receive treatment and those who would regardless of how much treatment they received. So perhaps treatment should be offender-specific as well as offense-specific.

Assessment and Prediction

Physicians know that medical treatment must be specific to the patient and thus undertake a thorough assessment of patients before deciding on a treatment protocol. Correctional staff must likewise assess offenders if their efforts are to be appropriately guided. Assessment is making informed judgments about something or someone based on relevant criteria. In corrections, assessment consists of formally evaluating offenders' deficiencies and the risks they pose to the community. Correctional workers use well-researched and tested instruments that document the skills, attitudes, beliefs, strengths, weaknesses, needs, deficiencies, and many other things that have led to an offender's criminal behavior and that may help or hinder rehabilitative efforts. The various instruments involved allow prison treatment specialists and probation and parole officers to develop realistic plans and strategies to help offenders become productive members of society.

Making predictions about a human's future behavior is difficult, but the best way to predict anyone's behavior is what they have done in the past; as William Shakespeare wrote: "Whereof what's past is prologue." However, the correctional system aims to change a person's criminal behavior, so predictions based only on previous behavior are inadequate in isolation; we need to be forward- as well as backward-looking. We may base predictions based on expert diagnosis and evaluation, such as a psychologist or psychiatrist might make, although such judgments have been found inferior to actuarial predictions. The actuarial method of making predictions is based on statistical algorithms of people similarly situated, averaged over many thousands of previous cases to take as much subjectivity out of the process as possible. Like any paper and pencil tests fed into a computer program, these methods are prone to error, but as Gottfredson and Moriarty (2006, p. 180) note, actuarial methods are an improvement over clinical judgments because "in virtually all decision-making situations ... actuarially developed predictions outperform human judgments."

For instance, a meta-analysis by Hanson and Morton-Bourgon (2009) looked at the accuracy of recidivism risk assessments for sex offenders in 118 prediction studies comparing predictions made by statistical actuarial methods versus unstructured clinical judgment and structured professional judgment. The effect sizes (d) for sex offense recidivism for unstructured clinical judgment, structured professional judgment, and statistical actuarial methods were 0.42, 0.46, and 0.67, respectively. For the prediction of violent offense recidivism, they were 0.22, 0.31, and 0.51, respectively, and in predicting recidivism of any kind, the respective effect sizes were 0.11, 0.26, and 0.52. Even actuarial methods thus produce only moderately accurate predictions since a strong effect size is considered to be 0.80 or higher. However, correctional assessment tools only contain psychosocial data and thus fail to incorporate the bio of the biopsychosocial whole.

Evidence-Based Practice and the Risk-Need-Responsivity Framework

The movement to an optimistic "What works?" orientation from "Nothing works" pessimism denotes the movement toward employing evidence-based practice (EBP) in corrections. EBP employs peer-reviewed research based on the best available data to guide policy and treatment decisions so that offender rehabilitation efforts can be improved. That is, to reduce offender recidivism, corrections agencies should implement practices consistently shown by rigorous empirical research to be effective. These efforts are taking place under the risk-need-responsivity (RNR) framework. In a nutshell, the risk principle predicts the probability of reoffending, the need principle addresses what should be done to prevent it, and the responsivity principle how treatment should be provided. The risk principle maintains that corrections personnel should prioritize supervision and treatment resources for higher-risk offenders. The need principle avers that they should target interventions to criminogenic needs. The responsivity principle maintains that if offenders are to respond to treatment in meaningful ways, treatment personnel should be responsive to different offender temperaments, cognitive abilities, learning styles, motivation for change, and development stages, and be aware that they must be treated with respect and dignity (Andrews & Bonta, 2014).

The RNR model is the premier treatment model in corrections in the United States and worldwide (Taxman & Smith, 2021). The risk factors are divided into dynamic and static categories. Static factors are factors that cannot change, such as age, gender, criminal history, age at first arrest, developmental history, and family background. While these static factors are useful for identifying an offender's recidivism risk, the important factors for treatment goals for reducing recidivism are dynamic. These factors must be prioritized if they are to have a positive impact on reducing recidivism. Risk factors associated with recidivism that can be changed are referred to as criminogenic needs. The need principle may refer to certain prosocial needs that offenders lack and may be driving their criminal conduct. For instance, long-term unemployment is a major predictor of offending, and if offenders' educational deficiencies impair their ability to secure and retain employment, education is a criminogenic need. If an offender's educational level does not affect his or her ability to secure and retain employment education is not a criminogenic need. The need principle may also refer to what offenders habitually do or think needs to be changed, such as the abuse of alcohol or drugs, antisocial associates, anger/hostility issues, poor social skills and attitudes toward work or school, poor family dynamics, low self-control, and criminal thinking patterns. The responsivity principle refers to how well individuals in treatment respond to the type of treatment they are exposed to, and the potential for a positive outcome. The idea is to treat as many criminogenic needs as possible. The crux of these principles is that treatment must be tailored to individual offenders' risks and needs and delivered in an atmosphere of acceptance, care, and respect.

Risk and needs assessment scales have been developed for the RNR model. There is a variety of risk and needs assessment tools based on the RNR model, with the Level of Service/Case Management Inventory (LS/CMI) being among the most widely used and researched offender assessment instruments (Labrecque et al., 2018) and arguably has the best predictive record (Ghasemi et al., 2021). The LS/CMI is a 42-item checklist that assesses criminogenic risks and needs in eight domains most often linked to reoffending. These domains are education and employment, family and marital, leisure and recreation, friends and companions, alcohol or drug problems, criminal attitudes or orientation, and antisocial behavioral patterns.

As well as this actuarial instrument performs relative to clinal-based assessments, tools are only as good as the workers using them, and workers are not immune from scoring them according to their ideologic propensities. For instance, Wu and Walsh (2007) found that liberal and conservative probation officers scored subjective items on sentencing guidelines significantly differently. Likewise, Miller and Maloney (2013) found that workers trained in the LS/CMI found that although it was filled out when required, decisions were not always based on it. They noted that

> about half of the tool-using subgroup were "substantive" compliers who completed tools carefully and honestly and tended to use them for decision making. The remaining tool users were "formal" in their

compliance: filling out the tools, but often making decisions that did not correspond with tool results, and in some cases even manipulating the information included in them.

(p. 716)

No instrument predicting human behavior comes anywhere near perfection, but as long as an instrument consistently performs significantly better than chance in its predictions, it is useful. However, tools can always be improved and correctional workers must be required to abide by them.

Anger Management Treatment

We have previously looked at individuals— attention-deficit/hyperactivity disorder (ADHD) individuals, people with schizophrenia, and substance abusers—who pose significant problems for the criminal justice system. We add individuals with anger problems and sex offenders in this chapter. A central component of many treatment programs in corrections is anger management, particularly in violent and sex offender treatment programs. Excessive anger leads to all sorts of negative consequences, including ruined relationships, problems at work, and criminal actions that result in incarceration, all of which produce yet more anger. Anger management programs consist of several cognitive behavioral techniques by which someone with problems controlling their anger can learn the causes and consequences of unreasonable anger and techniques to reduce it and avoid anger-inducing triggers.

Anger is often central to violent criminal behavior, and the frustrations resulting from being in custody or under correctional supervision in the community can lead to violence (Walsh, Wells, & Gann, 2020). As noted in Chapter 5, anger is a normal and often adaptive human emotion and is aroused when we feel offended or wronged; even Jesus got angry with the tradespeople and money changers in the Temple. The tendency to undo wrongdoing by retaliating is motivated by anger and is adaptive in that it warns those who have offended or wronged you that you are not to be treated that way. The problem, however, is not anger per se, but rather the inability of many criminals to manage it in adaptive ways. Anger is maladaptive if it leads to violence. Individuals who retaliate violently become excessively angry over minor real or imagined slights (being "dissed") or frustrated by goal blockage to the point of rage. This is partly the result of many people with anger management problems having IQs in the borderline intellectual disability range, low levels of literacy, and self-control issues that often lead to frustration and anger in many social situations (Hutchinson et al, 2017).

Anger management classes are typically taught in groups and designed to increase offenders' responsibility for ownership of their emotions and their reactions to them. Offenders often become frustrated and angry because they think that life is not fair to them ("I'm a victim of circumstances") and that the world owes them a living. This kind of destructive thinking must be challenged and replaced by individual responsibility. Anger management classes also teach such skills as rational thinking ("Did this person *really* mean to diss me?") to increase offender's ability to react to frustration and conflict in an assertive rather than an aggressive way and to develop effective communication skills (Jolliffe & Farrington, 2009). There is a growing consensus that properly conducted anger management programs reduce inmate violence and reduce violent recidivism for program completers versus control subjects by about 8% to 10% (Jolliffe & Farrington, 2009; Serin, Gobeil, & Preston, 2009). Although this seems like a small return on a corrections investment, even an 8% reduction in violent offenses prevents much needless suffering and millions of dollars in criminal justice and personal expenses.

Extensive research has shown that dysfunctions in serotoninergic transmission are associated with a tendency toward impulsive aggression and violence and a tendency to have a great deal of negative emotionality, including anger (see the discussion of the triple imbalance hypothesis of reactive violence in Chapter 4). Consequently, selective serotonin reuptake inhibitors (SSRIs), as regulators of the serotonin system, might reduce proneness to impulsive violence which is easily triggered in individuals prone to anger and cognitive distortions that render them highly sensitive to provocation. Angry impulsive aggression is different from premeditated aggression, which is planned and controlled for self-serving reasons; e.g., a premeditated murder or a robbery. Sertraline is the SSRI most often studied.

Sertraline blocks the serotonin transporter (5-HTT) into the presynaptic terminal, thus increasing serotonin levels at the synapse and decreasing serotonin turnover. In Romero-Martínez, Murciano-Martí, and Moya-Albiol's (2019) review of sertraline and anger studies, they note:

> Even though [the present study] includes empirical studies with different research designs (case studies, open clinical trials, and randomized controlled trials), the majority are unanimous in concluding that a large percentage of patients with high irritability responded satisfactorily to sertraline treatment, reducing their irritability and anger expression after several weeks of treatment.
>
> *(p. 11)*

They also concluded that dosage should be carefully titrated and that a small percentage of patients showed side effects, such as irritability after a few weeks of treatment, in which case the treatment should be discontinued or the dosage reduced. Of course, pharmacological treatment must always be augmented by psychosocial counseling that addresses ways of dealing positively with anger.

Butler et al. (2010) conducted a small pilot study with 34 repeat impulsive violent offenders who were administered 100 mg of sertraline each day for 12 weeks. They observed marked reductions from the baseline to a three-month follow-up. Impulsiveness was reduced by 35%, irritability by 45%, anger by 63%, assaultive behavior by 51%, verbal assault by 40%, and depression by 62%. Interestingly, and importantly, they reported that all offenders who completed the study requested a referral to their general practitioner to continue with the medication. Coccaro, Lee, and Kavoussi (2009) conducted a double-blind randomized, placebo-controlled trial of fluoxetine (another SSRI) with intermittent explosive disorder (IED) patients. IED involves frequent and sudden instances of impulsive, aggressive, violent behavior, or angry verbal outbursts that are far out of proportion to the situations that evoked them. They found that fluoxetine treatment was associated with full remission of aggression in 29% of patients and full or partial remission in 46%. The ideal situation, of course, would be a series of placebo double-blind randomized control trials to evaluate the effectiveness of SSRIs across a range of angry violent offenders. Of course, SSRIs are not a magic bullet. Anger-precipitated violence may be underlain by alcohol abuse or mental illness, in which case different treatment plans are required.

Sex Offender Treatment

Driven by sensationalized media accounts, the public harbors many misconceptions about sex offenders, viewing them as predatory dirty old men about whom we can do nothing except incapacitate them. Consequently, the system locks up some of them (the worst) under civil commitment orders after they have completed their prison terms, and are the only category of offenders who must register with the police—all 50 states have sex offender registration laws (Talbot et al., 2002). The term *sex offender* defines a broad category of offenders ranging from "flashers" to true sexual predators. But just as property offenders include everyone from petty shoplifters to career burglars, sex offenders are a heterogeneous group. About 98% of all sex offenders reside in the community on probation or parole (Walsh, Wells, & Gann, 2020), making the issue of sex offender treatment of the utmost importance.

Despite beliefs to the contrary, sex offenders are less likely to re-offend than any other type of offender. Looking at British crime statistics over many years, Mawby (2001) found that burglars are the most likely of all criminals to be reconvicted (76%) within two years of being released from prison, with sex offenders being the least likely (19%). Hanson and Bussiere's (1998) review of 61 studies of sex offender recidivism found an average rate of reconviction for sex crimes of 13.4% over a four- to five-year follow-up. Perhaps the most extensive recidivism study conducted to date was a study by the Bureau of Justice Statistics, whose researchers tracked 9,691 sex offenders and 272,111 non–sex offenders released from prisons in 15 states in 1994 at the same time (Langan, Schmitt, & Durose, 2003). Over a three-year follow-up, sex offenders had a lower rearrest rate (43%) than the non–sex offenders (68%). Rearrest rates included all types of crimes and technical violations, such as failing to register as a sex offender and missing appointments with their parole officers. Only 3.5% of the sex offenders were reconvicted of a new sex offense during the follow-up period. Because recidivism rates include only those offenses known to the police, all recidivism figures should be considered bare minimums.

State-of-the-art treatment of sex offenders must include a thorough assessment of psychosocial problem areas and deviant arousal patterns via plethysmography (PPG) and polygraph assessments (Marsh & Walsh, 1995). Sexual arousal patterns are assessed by the PPG, which is a mercury-filled rubber band placed around the penis that measures penile blood flow (the level of penile tumescence) when exposed to sexual images. Tumescence measures in response to deviant sexual images are compared with measures in response to nondeviant images. For example, if a man achieves a 10% erection when viewing nondeviant sexual images involving adults, but a 75% erection viewing sexual images of young boys, we know where his sexual tastes lie—the penis finds it difficult to lie. Of course, the PPG is not foolproof and can be manipulated (masturbation before testing to reduce arousal to images, for instance), although every effort is made to ensure it is not during testing.

Sex offender therapists agree that effective treatment is impossible until the full extent of the offender's sex offending history is acknowledged by them and known to treatment personnel (Walsh, Wells, & Gann, 2020). However, sex offenders are notorious for hiding their sexual offending histories, so a polygraph assessment is needed to assess this. Comparing self-reports before and after polygraph testing across two decades of research, it has been found that those who sexually offend children underreport the number of sex crimes they have committed for which they were neither arrested nor charged by about 500% and overreport their childhood sexual victimization (the "I'm a victim too" excuse) by about 250% (Hindman & Peters, 2000). If offenders fail the polygraph, they must retake it at their own expense until they pass. The polygraph, therefore, is a useful tool if the prerequisite of successful treatment is the complete acknowledgment of the extent of an offender's sex offending history.

Pharmacological Treatment

Unlike treatment for other problems in corrections, there is a great deal of interest in the pharmacological treatment of high-risk sex offenders, although cognitive behavioral therapy (CBT) remains the primary therapeutic approach. Many therapists and researchers have concluded that optimal treatment (following a thorough psychosocial and physiological assessment) combines pharmacological and psychotherapeutic approaches (Walsh, Wells, & Gann, 2020). The psychopharmacological approach to the treatment of high-risk sex offenders is premised on the fact that sex is a basic biological drive and that sex offenders' thoughts have excessive sexual content, which has been described as dysfunctional "sexual preoccupation" or "hypersexual cognition" (Winder et al., 2019). Consequently, the goal of this approach is to reduce a misdirected libido via testosterone-lowering drugs. Two types of antilibidinal medication may be used for high-risk sex offenders; SSRIs and antiandrogens, primarily cyproterone acetate (CPA) and medroxyprogesterone acetate (MPA) (Khan et al., 2015). SSRIs are the first option because they reduce libido, stabilize mood, and reduce impulsivity without serious side effects (Winder et al., 2019).

Both CPA and MPA are seen as temporary "chemical castrations" that allow offenders to concentrate on their psychosocial problems in therapy without distracting sexual fantasies and urges that may be evoked during therapy sessions by the telling of their offenses or hearing others describe theirs. CPA is a synthetic steroid that works by inhibiting the binding process of testosterone to its receptors. Turner, Basdekis-Jozsa, and Briken (2013, p. 571) succinctly describe how CPA works:

> CPA binds to the androgen receptors of, e.g., the testes or different brain areas such as the hypothalamus, the hippocampus, and the amygdala. By binding to androgen receptors, CPA competitively replaces testosterone and 5-a-dihydrotestosterone and thus inhibits their synthesis as well as their effect on sexuality and other body functions.

CPA is the primary antiandrogen medication used in European nations.

MPA is the primary antiandrogen agent used with sex offenders in the United States. MPA is a synthetic derivative of the steroid hormone progesterone (a precursor of testosterone) that works as an androgen agonist. It works to reduce free testosterone levels via multiple mechanisms.

It suppresses the activation of the hypothalamic-pituitary-adrenal and hypothalamic-pituitary-gonadal axes, activates a testosterone catabolizing enzyme, increases testosterone binding to testosterone-binding globulin, and reduces the cellular uptake of androgens by binding to androgen receptors (Holoyda & Kellaher, 2016). The extent to which these treatments reduce testosterone depends on the dosages administered.

Chemical castration is no longer allowed in California, Florida, Iowa, or Louisiana. (Hermawan & Hananto, 2022). Not all sex offenders should be treated with this drug, because there are sometimes serious side effects, including excessive weight gain, psychological malaise, migraine headaches, leg cramps, and elevated blood pressure. Additionally, treatment can be provided only by a medical doctor on a "voluntary" basis, although it has sometimes been required as the basis of granting probation or parole. Several reviews of the literature from Europe and America show that antiandrogen treatment results in low recidivism rates for repeat rapists and child molesters in the 2%–3% range (Maletzky & Field, 2003). A South Korean study found that chemical castration successfully reduced recidivism rates from 2% to 5% (Lee & Cho, 2013). A review of 11 meta-analyses covering 353 studies from 1943 to 2009 found that surgical castration had the strongest effect on lowering recidivism—although this is not an option in Western countries—followed by chemical castration (Kim, Benekos, & Merlo, 2016). Insight-oriented therapies such as psychoanalysis had essentially no effect, while CBT has significant effects, but much less so if not combined with antiandrogen medication.

16

BIOPSYCHOSOCIAL PREVENTION AND TREATMENT

The Crime Prevention Benefits of Fathers in the Home

The preceding chapters contain many biopsychosocial suggestions for improving crime prevention and treatment policies derived from traditional criminological theories. This chapter addresses crime prevention and treatment solely from the biopsychosocial perspective. This approach focuses primarily on identifying risk factors for children by seeking to improve environmental conditions to facilitate their healthy biological, psychological, and social development. It also focuses on suggestions for the individualized treatment of offenders based on biological risk factors as well as the usual psychosocial factors. This is analogous to the individualized approach to patient care in modern medicine.

The prenatal, perinatal, and early post-natal stages of brain development are crucial, and growing up in a poor and fatherless does not bode well for that process. Supporting the healthy development of young children is the best investment a society can make for crime prevention, with early intervention of paramount importance. As Rocque, Welsh, and Raine (2012, p. 311) point out:

> In terms of developmental crime prevention, research has suggested that the earlier the intervention, the better. The most important stages of development for cognitive growth appear to occur during pregnancy to the first 2 years of life, as PET scan technology has indicated impressive growth and maturation of cognitive functions during this period.

DOI: 10.4324/9781003642268-21

The earliest "intervention" for optimal brain development is growing up in a home in which both biological parents are present.

What are the benefits to children of having a biological father in the home in terms of enhancing optimal brain development and reducing antisocial behavior? Lisa van der Storm et al. (2021) note that parenting/child outcome studies focus solely on single mothers, but we saw in Chapter 1 that fewer than 5% of single-parent households are father-headed, so this is understandable. Not too long ago, American fathers neither sought nor assumed much active responsibility for child rearing, believing that the protective and provisioning roles were their areas of responsibility. However, parenting is becoming more equally shared between fathers and mothers in modern society. So, how does bipaternal parenting improve maternal-only parenting besides the obvious benefit of sharing the responsibility?

The deleterious impact on children raised in fatherless homes was noted in earlier chapters and it is safe to say that biopsychosocial criminologists would be in favor of the various provisions of the PRWORA (discussed in Chapter 1) aimed at preventing unwed motherhood and promoting marriage because of the positive effects on children of being raised by both biological parents. There is no doubt that, in general, having both biological parents involved in the process is preferable to single parenting, or one biological parent with a live-in partner or stepparent. A large study based on ten years of data from National Health Interview Surveys, Sullins (2021, p. 184) concludes: "This evidence strongly supports the claim that maximum child development occurs only in the persistent care of both of the child's own biological parents."

However, I do not want to give the impression that a father in the home is always preferable to single parenthood. Having a criminal, abusive, or substance-abusing man at home, particularly a live-in boyfriend, is highly undesirable, as decades of data from the National Incidence Study of Child Abuse and Neglect (NIS) have shown. The NIS is a congressionally mandated, periodic effort of the United States Department of Health and Human Services to determine the extent of child abuse and neglect in the United States. The fourth iteration of the study showed that an estimated 1,256,600 children in the United States were abused and/or neglected in the years 2005–2006. Looking at a nationally representative sample from the NIS data, Sedlak et al. (2010, p. 14) noted:

> Compared to children living with married biological parents, those whose single parent had a live-in partner had more than 8 times the rate of maltreatment overall, over 10 times the rate of abuse, and nearly 8 times the rate of neglect.

Bi-parental care is rare among animal species, and is not even found among chimpanzees and bonobos, our closest genetic relatives. Biparental care requires strong male-female bonding and evolutionary biologists tell us that natural selection for pair bonding will occur only when the help of a male positively influences the probability of offspring survival by procuring food for gestating and lactating mothers and defending mother and child against predation. Human neonates are helpless, and their ontogeny is very protracted and requires enormous parental investment relative to precocial species. In precocial species with ready access to food and with predation rates either so high or so low that male parental investment is unlikely to have any positive effect on offspring survival, pair bonding is not necessary, and therefore no evolutionary pressures would have been exerted for its selection (Quinlan & Quinlan 2007; Tumulty, Morales, & Summers 2014). Storey and Walsh (2011, p. 36) note: "Paternal care should only be selected if it promotes higher male reproductive success than not providing care." Nor will pair bonding be selected for when males cannot be reasonably sure that the child in whom he is investing time and resources is his because: "Parental investment theory suggests that males should be selected to recognize and differentially invest in their own offspring" (Storey & Walsh, 2011, p. 36).

Optimal socialization experiences for children virtually require the presence of a biological father. Prosocial socialization determines the development of self-regulation of emotion, thinking, and behavior and children's acquisition of their culture's moral standards, attitudes, and values. This leads to willing conformity and cooperation with the appropriate authority figures, good psychological adjustment, and fewer internalizing and externalizing problems (Cheung et al., 2018). This is problematic for the children of single mothers because in addition to the obvious financial burden, the responsibility of being the sole disciplinarian is an additional burden. Rebekah Coley (1998, p. 219) notes that the burdens on children are relational:

> Theoretical arguments claim that children in single-parent households have limited access to social relationships with nonmaternal adults and thus experience deficiencies in interpersonal resources compared to children residing with married parents. For example, children residing with only one parent are expected to have few opportunities for positive and warm interactions with adults and to lack adult, especially male, role models.

Mother Love and Father Love

These "warm interactions" are better known in popular parlance as love. Robert Wright notes the relational problem in fatherless homes: "Whenever marital institutions ...are allowed to dissolve, so that divorce and unwed motherhood are rampant, and many children no longer live with both natural parents, there will ensue a massive waste of the most precious evolutionary resource: Love" (1994, p. 104). Poet Robert Browning once wrote: "Motherhood: all love begins and ends there," which suggests that a mother's love is primordial and relatively unconditional and serves as the wellspring for all other forms of love. We can agree that it begins with she who nursed us at her breast, but it does not end there. It is doubtless the case that both father and mother love their children deeply, but the nature of mother and father love is subtly different. In general: "Mother love is selfless, sacrificial, and complete. A mother loves her child indiscriminately just because it is her child," and it is "both an extension and affirmation of herself" (Walsh, 2017, p. 81). Although most fathers undoubtedly feel the same way, Eric Eriksen opines that mother and father love is qualitatively different because their love is more "expectant and more instrumental" (Pruett, 1987, p. 49). Mothers and fathers differ in the way they parent their children, but both ways are required in that they complement and reinforce one another. The great philosopher of love, Erich Fromm, makes an observation similar to Eriksen:

> Mother loves her children because they are her children, and not because they are "good," obedient, or fulfill her wishes and commands. ...The nature of fatherly love is that he makes demands, establishes principles and laws, and that his love for the son depends on the obedience of the letter of these demands. He likes best the son who is most like him, who is most obedient, and is best fitted to become his successor as the inheritor of his possessions.
>
> *(1995, p. 42)*

Father love is thus seen as more rational and conditional than emotional and unconditional mother love. However, there is much overlap between mothers and fathers in these two strategies, which are "ideal types" that are simply more typical in most fathers and mothers. One style is not better than the other, they are just different and complementary, and both good mothers and fathers want their children to identify with them and adopt their values and standards of behavior. A father hopes that his son will become the kind of man he always wanted to be and that no matter how many princes court his daughter, he will always be king. Likewise, a mother hopes that her daughter will become the kind of woman she once aspired to be and that she will always be queen in her eyes.

Fathers are more likely to engage in childcare to the extent that they are in a strong intimate relationship with their wives (Comrie-Thomson et al., 2020). The long period of human infant dependency requires natural selection for strong mother-infant bonding which, in turn, demands selection pressure for male-female bonding: "The co-evolution of the family and the brain, building on the maternal/offspring attachments of our mammalian ancestors, involved profound adaptations in the hominid biology" (Papero et al., 2018, p. 22). Bonded males and females provide co-parental investment that increases the probability of their offspring surviving to reproductive age, thus passing on their genetic lineages. Marriage, viewed unromantically, is a reciprocal arrangement by which men and women subconsciously agree to cooperate in propagating each other's genes. Natural selection for intrafamilial attachments extended over millions of years during which many mechanisms for the intensification of mothering and male-female emotional bonding until they went to genetic fixation. Except for empathy, these mechanisms were not necessarily explicitly designed by natural selection to serve the function of maternal intensification or for mechanisms of male-female bonding. Nature is parsimonious in that it frequently retrofits mechanisms designed for one task to serve others. For the intensification of nurturance and attachment, neurological systems associated with feelings of joy and satisfaction were probably pressed into service.

There are important differences in what mothers and fathers encourage in their children. Fathers encourage children to take risks and face challenges, promote the independence and resilience needed when they leave the family home to start their own family, and set behavioral, work ethic, and relationship strengths for their children, especially influencing sons to understand the proper exercise of their masculinity. Mothers encourage these things too, but focus more on the emotionality of relationships, care, compassion, and how being nice leads to pleasant friendships and great marriages. Together, the socialization practices of mothers and fathers should lead to a healthy balance in children's lives since: "Mother love makes the child *capable* of love; father love takes that capability and cultivates it through the inculcation of the ideals of humanity and makes the child *worthy* of love" (Walsh, 2017, p. 83).

The Nurse-Family Partnership Program

What can be done to make the child "worthy" of love in the absence of a biological father? The Nurse-Family Partnership (NFP) program is designed to take up some of the slack. The NFP is a nonprofit organization that began in 1977 and now exists in 44 states and many other countries. The NFP is an intensive home-visiting program that connects first-time socioeconomically disadvantaged mothers, about 84% of whom are unmarried (Olds, 2006), with specially trained nurses who provide health services and behavioral advice regarding child development, including nurturing strategies, dietary advice, refraining from drugs, alcohol, and tobacco, and so on, during home visits that last from early pregnancy until the child's second birthday. Expectant mothers receive the support they need for a healthy pregnancy, and they often develop a close relationship with their assigned nurses who become trusted resources on whom mothers can rely. NFP is grounded in theories of human ecology, self-efficacy, and attachment theories, which "Together, these theories emphasize the importance of families' social context and individuals' beliefs, motivations, emotions, and internal representations of their experience in explaining the development of behavior" (Olds, 2006, p. 13).

Although not explicitly based on biopsychosocial principles, NFP practices accord with their emphasis on early nurturing for healthy brain development at a time when an infant's brain wiring is being organized. Biopsychosocial principles can explicate the biologically relevant processes by which NFP interventions work. The NFP was not designed explicitly to reduce further out-of-wedlock births but does so, as well as reducing reliance on welfare and reducing the incidence of child maltreatment (Eckenrode et al., 2017). The NFP website claims that for every dollar invested in the program for the highest-risk families, there is a saving of $5.70 in future welfare and criminal justice costs.

Studies assessing the NFP are uniformly positive, with effect sizes ranging from small to large, depending on what is measured. These studies are usually randomized trial experiments, with the treatment group receiving the most home visits versus control groups of either NFP participants who, for various reasons, had fewer home visits, or who received only standard prenatal clinical care. One early study (Olds et al., 1998) found that children in the NFP treatment group had fewer self-reported histories of running away, arrests, convictions, sentences to youth corrections, later initiation of sexual intercourse, fewer sex partners, and lower levels of substance abuse. Teachers also reported less disruptive school behavior in NFP children than in control children. However, a later study (Kitzman et al., 2019) found only one significant difference between NFP and control groups of 18-year-olds relating to antisocial behavior. NFP females had fewer arrests, but not males, although NFP subjects had several significant cognitively related advantages such as math and reading scores. As with

Moving to Opportunity studies discussed earlier, Eckenrode et al. (2010) showed positive treatment effects for girls but not boys.

In a meta-analysis of 37 studies from seven countries, Chen and Chan (2016) found that MFP programs significantly reduced self-reported and officially substantiated child maltreatment (effect size = 0.296). Overall, MFP programs reduce many of the problems associated with antisocial behavior such as poverty, educational achievement, and child maltreatment. It was noted, however, that the male children of mothers who participated in the MFP program, although gaining certain advantages, were still more involved in antisocial behavior than children who were not in the program but otherwise similarly situated except in one major way—they had a biological father in the home. Antisocial behavior is still higher among MFP children than among children from two-parent homes in similar neighborhoods, so while MFP programs are useful, they cannot replace the conditions found in homes where both biological parents are present. Perhaps the program should be extended until children are five years old, which covers the period in which synaptic growth and pruning organize young children's brains. But crime will always be with us no matter how macro-level programs may or may not work. We will thus always need programs to treat the criminally involved.

Biopsychosocial Criminology and Treatment

Because biopsychosocial criminology casts a wide net, it should be able to refine policies by a better understanding of how environmental risks translate into biological risks such as aberrant brain wiring, epigenetic modifications, allostatic load, and so forth. However, because it casts its net so widely, there are difficulties inherent in developing assessment tools capable of capturing all important factors relevant to treatment. Nevertheless, prominent crime prevention research scholar Matt Robinson, states:

> Since biosocial criminology meaningfully integrates perspective and theories from the biological and social sciences, the approach offers much hope in the area of crime prevention. At the very least, biosocial crime prevention should be far more effective than those strategies currently utilized.
>
> *(2009, p. 243)*

Robinson is joined by Lilly, Cullen, and Ball, who write: "Biosocial theories may have their greatest policy applications in terms of prevention and treatment programs" (2011, p. 376). Biopsychosocial criminologists are aware that biological, psychological, or social risk factors are important but realize that alone they cannot explain the etiology of criminal behavior and that prevention and treatment efforts require engaging them all. Mindful of how nurturing affects gene expression and brain development, biopsychosocial criminologists have advocated a wide array of nurturant strategies such as pre- and postnatal care for women, monitoring infants and children through their early developmental years, paid maternal leave, nutritional programs, and a whole host of other interventions. They are expensive but far less so than the war on poverty and the costs related to crime.

Treatment programs designed to reduce further offending affect criminality by reducing the number and severity of risk factors and increasing protective factors. Many risk factors of infancy and childhood, such as maternal prenatal substance use, low birth weight, nutritional deficits, maternal stress and depression, and poor parent-child attachment are addressed by macro-level programs such as the NFP program. Unfortunately, millions of at-risk individuals have not been exposed to them, and even if they had been, they bring with them individual risk factors resistant to pro-social socialization. In addition to biological risk factors, the vast majority of criminals marinated in violent and abusive environments that wired their brains to be adapted to such environments gave easy play to their risk alleles and conditioned their physiologies to fearlessness via high testosterone/cortisol ratios.

We have seen that traditional offender treatment programs show only small to modest effects. However, program results are typically analyzed for the total sample or subsamples based on demographic variables such as race or sex. Such analytical procedures may mask evidence of strong effects for some participants, weak or no effects, or perhaps even negative effects for others. Using individual genetic and neurobiological profiles could help to alleviate this problem. This is not unrealistic since it is an evolving component in medicine. Hassan et al. (2022) note the remarkable advances in personalized medicine:

> Personalized medicine is a practice of medicine that uses an individual's genetic profile to guide decisions made regarding the prevention, diagnosis, and treatment of disease. Personalized or precision medicine is an emerging medical practice based on a data-driven approach that considers relevant medical, genetic, behavioral, and environmental information about an individual to determine patient-specific therapy.
> *(p. 2)*

Personalized medicine is based on genomics and big data analytics using machine learning. Machine learning is a subset of artificial intelligence based on computers that learn to recognize patterns in the data fed to them without being programed for specific tasks. Computers progressively learn by exposure to new data and produce algorithms and statistical models to make predictions and decisions. Perhaps the day will come when we will see individualized treatment for antisocial behavior and thinking as routine in corrections.

We do not repeat discussions of pharmacological treatments for various offender types discussed in previous chapters here. As noted in the last chapter, treatment for criminal offenders should precede only after a thorough assessment of their risks for reoffending and their criminogenic needs. As previously noted, the premier assessment tool is the RNR model, but because of the strong sociological influence in criminology, it is entirely psychosocial and devoid of biological risk and needs factors. Despite having presumably been placed into treatment protocols based on RNR assessment, about 15% to 50% of individuals in correctional treatment programs do not complete them, derive less benefit from it if they do, or re-offend while in or after treatment (Vaske, 2017). This problem may be alleviated by knowing what biological factors offenders bring to the treatment process.

Physiological arousal level is the easiest of these factors to measure. Examining results from ten studies, Cornet et al. (2015) note that low levels of physiological arousal, such as a low resting heart rate and low cortisol levels, predict poor treatment outcomes. Knowledge of various aspects of offenders' biology (autonomic nervous system [ANS] arousal levels, testosterone/cortisol ratios, neurological deficits, and genetic profiles) as responsivity factors can help to determine who would benefit from what kinds of treatment and the dosage treatment level required. Some scholars may resist including biological risk factors in their treatment approach if they labor under the assumption that biological risk factors are static and distal. However, this assumption is erroneous since a cascade of research indicates that biological processes are dynamic and hardly distal since we take our biology with us into all situations. However, because our biology and the sum of our environmental experiences are inseparably intertwined, risk biomarkers can never be considered stand-alone factors, but rather as part of an expanded RNR model that integrates biopsychosocial-informed risk and needs factors that have been identified.

Danielle Boisvert (2021, p. 12) notes: "Developing risk assessment tools that integrate biological risk factors is an important next step in correctional rehabilitation, as it has the potential to increase the efficacies of risk prediction." She further (p. 13) claims that:

> Biopsychosocial risk assessments developed by interdisciplinary teams should enable practitioners to identify specific biological deficits, better assess individual risk levels, and more effectively match individuals

> to programs. This individualized approach may start by including neuropsychological and physiological tests and biosocially informed questionnaires to already developed risk assessments. In turn, more efficiently aligned treatment assignments based on an individual's biopsychosocial profile will likely facilitate improved behavior, thereby increasing the likelihood of desistance from crime.

Boisvert (2021, p. 12) also notes that the biosocial literature suggests including measures of biological indicators in risk assessments of offenders such as: "brain function and structure, neuropsychological deficits (e.g., executive functions), hormone levels (e.g., cortisol, testosterone), neurotransmitter levels (e.g., serotonin, dopamine), and autonomic nervous system functioning (e.g., heart rate, skin conductance), as well as genetics more broadly." Using the differential susceptibility hypothesis, such assessments would guide treatment providers to determine which programs would benefit which individuals and which would not, and what the "dosage" level should be rather than assuming that one-size-fits-all, as is typically the case (Vaske, 2017).

The expenses involved in the biological assessments mentioned are high relative to traditional paper-and-pencil assessment but much less than the cost of unsuccessfully treating criminals. We have seen that recidivism rates are unacceptably high and that Dunrose, Cooper, and Snyder's (2014) study of 404,638 released prisoners were responsible for around 1,173,000 arrests between 2005 and 2010. The cost of dealing with recidivism is enormous. We can either bear these costs and the cost of building additional prisons to incapacitate high-risk offenders or attempt biopsychosocial treatment methods. It could take decades to develop useful assessment instruments based on biopsychosocial insights just as it took decades to fine-tune the RNR.

To develop these tools, researchers from universities involved in biopsychosocial research could secure federal grants for pilot studies to develop preliminary tools and implement treatment based on them in two or three selected prisons. They could then conduct longitudinal recidivism experiments using propensity score matching techniques to remove self-selection effects, such as inmates self-selecting into treatment. The matched groups would consist of (1) those who received biopsychosocial treatment, (2) those who received traditional psychosocial treatment, and (3) those who received no treatment. After inmates are released, they could be tracked for up to five years to compare recidivism rates among the three groups. Following analyses of the results, assessment tools would be honed and the experiments repeated. Much valuable information will be gleaned from such experiments, but it will take decades to determine the efficacy of the assessment tools and treatment modalities.

Biopsychosocial Assessment Tools Currently Available

Certain biopsychosocial methods of assessment are currently available fairly cheaply. While direct measures of brain functioning via various brain-scanning measures are optimal, computerized neuropsychological assessments that correlate with them fairly strongly and have advantages of their own. For instance, the Go/No-Go task is a staple in cognitive research designed to measure the ability to control impulsive responses to "Go" and "No-Go" stimuli. Shi et al. (2019) showed that fewer errors in the Go/No-Go task and greater nucleus accumbens response predicted better adherence to extended-release naltrexone among opioid-dependent patients. Other neuropsychological assessments include the Cambridge Neuropsychological Test Automated Battery, which assesses various cognitive domains such as memory, attention, executive functions, learning, and problem-solving, and the Stroop task, which assesses the reaction time between automatic and controlled processing of congruent and incongruent information, which translates into the ability to control immediate impulses.

Given the strong evidence linking low autonomic arousal to criminal behavior, offenders' resting heart rates must be assessed. We are talking about low resting heart rates within normal boundaries, not at pathological levels, and it should be noted that a low resting heart rate can be due to excellent physical fitness or certain medication regimes. Resting heart rate is an easy measure to obtain. There are numerous devices on the market (Amazon.com lists a number of them ranging in price from $22 to $185) that accurately measure resting heart rate. Newsome and Cullen (2017, p. 1039) note that: "Many smartphones, which may already be issued to some correctional staff for work purposes, have the capability to capture heart rate and other physiological measures." The ratio of testosterone to cortisol measures (multiple saliva measures are required) also indexes ANS arousal at the endocrinological level.

A biopsychosocial model of offending was developed by de Ruigh et al. (2021) with 223 institutionally detained Dutch juveniles based on resting heart rate, ANS activity, and cortisol and testosterone measures. They developed three groups at low, medium, and high risk for reoffending based on these measures and various psychosocial measures. Recidivism rates 12 months after release were obtained via official files. The probability of reoffending for nonviolent and violent offenses in the low-risk group was 0.14 and 0.05, respectively. For the medium-risk group, the respective probabilities were 0.31 and 0.24; for the high-risk group, they were 0.43 and 0.30, respectively. The research team concluded: "This approach may be useful in the development of a biopsychosocial assessment tool and may eventually help clinicians to assign individuals to those subgroups and subsequently tailor intervention based on their re-offending risk" (p. 1).

Offender genotyping can be obtained via buccal swabs for about $10 each. The DNA swaps (and hormone samples) can be easily tested and analyzed in university laboratories. Gajos, Fagan, and Beaver (2016, p. 688) show how genetically informed programs can help to identify individual variability in program effectiveness:

> Using the diathesis-stress model along with the risk principle to help guide intervention efforts could shed light on why high-risk individuals benefit the most from interventions. These theoretical concepts could also be used to explain why low-risk individuals may not be as responsive to certain interventions.

As Bedoya and Portnoy (2023, p. 12) note:

> Understanding an individual's genetic make-up, including family history and genome sequencing, could aid in determining which medications are more likely to resolve psychiatric issues (including but not limited to antisocial tendencies), reducing the trial-and-error that typically occurs when starting a new medication.

The same logic applies to correctional assessment and treatment—different people respond differently to various treatments and we would like to know those who do or do not, and why they do or do not.

It is only necessary to test for risk or susceptibility genes, primarily of the serotonergic and dopaminergic systems. Recall that the differential sensitivity hypothesis avers that the same genetic characteristics ("dandelion or orchid") that make individuals vulnerable to adversity also make them more likely to benefit from nurturing support. In other words, genetically vulnerable individuals (orchids) in positive environments may outperform nongenetically vulnerable peers (dandelions) who are less affected by both bad and good environments. Brody et al. (2014) designed a randomized study of the differential sensitivity hypothesis based on DRD4 alleles among 502 youths in the Strong African American Families-Teen (SAAF–T) Program to test G*x*E prevention effects. SAAF–T is a five-session program designed for teens and their caregivers to build on the strengths of African American families to promote the positive development of teens and to promote nurturant parenting practices. The results showed a DRD4 × SAAF–T interaction in that over 22 months, male youths with at least one risk allele of DRD4-7R and not assigned to SAAF–T showed a significant increase in the frequency of substance use compared with youths who also carried at least one DRD4-7R but who were assigned to SAAF–T, or youths with six or fewer DRD4 repeats in either condition. Much the same results have been obtained using SAAF–T youths with at least one copy of the short allele of the 5-HTTLPR gene (Brody et al., 2009). Thus, youths who carried dopaminergic and serotonergic "risk" alleles were those most likely to benefit from the SAAF–T program.

Cognitive Behavioral Therapy

Cognitive behavioral therapy (CBT) is the most widely used counseling method in corrections, and meta-analyses of prison-based psychosocial treatment programs have found that CBT is the most effective treatment therapy (Doyle et al., 2019). Many biopsychosocial problems can be fruitfully addressed by CBT, which may be as just as effective as pharmaceutical approaches for certain conditions. For instance, meta-analyses of major depressive disorder have shown no statistically significant differences between CBT and pharmaceutical treatment with serotonin and norepinephrine reuptake inhibitors in efficacy and relapse rates (Ross et al., 2019). What reuptake inhibitors do in the brain, so does CBT. Cherkasova et al. (2020) conducted a study with two groups of attention-deficit/hyperactivity disorder (ADHD) patients, one with CBT + medication and the other with CBT only. Results showed greater improvements in the CBT + medication group for ADHD symptoms, organizational skills, and self-esteem but group differences diminished over follow-up time. The CBT alone group continued improving and the CBT + medication group maintained their gains. The lesson learned from such studies is that medications (selective serotonin reuptake inhibitors [SSRIs], stimulants, androgen agonists or antagonists, etc.) stabilize a person's biology so that nonmedication treatment such as CBT can stabilize a person's mind and thus his or her life. Additionally, just as a person's suitability and amenability to pharmacological treatment must be properly determined before proceeding, so must be a person's suitability and amenability to counseling.

McGuire et al. (2008) conducted a propensity score matching randomized controlled trial of 929 imprisoned British male offenders followed for 17 months after release. The groups consisted of those who did or did not participate in a 38-session CBT program each lasting 2 hours. Reconvictions during the 17 months were 42.1% for program completers, 81.6% for the comparison group, and 82.6% for those who started but did not complete the program. This is a highly significant finding, but there was no assessment before entry into the program to determine motivation and suitability. It could be the case that offenders who were unlikely to complete treatment were perhaps those with neurocognitive deficits such as concentration or executive function problems. Such people would have likely benefited by first entering a preparatory course such as the Cogmed training (a working memory improvement program) before entering programs designed to reduce criminal thinking, or perhaps they are people with callous and unemotional traits associated with psychopathy (Cornet et al, 2015), in which case an entirely different approach to their criminogenic risks and needs is required.

CBT aims at restructuring thought patterns, modifying feelings and behavior patterns that distort a person's perception of reality, and promoting new learning, and thus it involves brain synaptic changes. A meta-analysis of ten fMRI and PET scans by Porto et al. (2009) demonstrated the ability of CBT to modify dysfunctional neural activity related to a variety of anxiety disorders such as PTSD, obsessive compulsion disorder, and phobias, especially in conjunction with drug therapy. It does so by focusing patients away from pathological thoughts that hyperactivate the amygdala and insula and toward thoughts that lead to the regulation of negative emotions and fear extinction so that they reveal activation similar to healthy comparison subjects. Using fMRI, Mason et al. (2017) found increases in dorsolateral PFC connectivity with the amygdala following CBT treatment in patients suffering from psychosis. Vaske, Galyean, and Cullen (2011, p. 91) argue: "CBT may be effective in reducing problem behavior, including crime, because the intervention affects specific areas of the brain; thus, CBT → changes in cognition ↔ changes in brain functioning → changes in behavior." Thus, treatment interventions that successfully change cognitions reflect changes in brain functioning in regions involved in those cognitions. Cornet et al.'s (2014, p. 20) meta-analysis of 11 studies noted that they, "reveal evidence that specific neurobiological measures including hormones, brain activity, and heart rate variability, show some change in response to [CBT] intervention with some studies clearly linking neurobiological changes to behavioral improvement."

In short, while the use of biomarkers for offending is almost nonexistent in corrections at present, there are many neurophysiological, endocrinological, and genetic correlates of criminal behavior that are relatively easy to measure and could help treatment providers identify homogenous subgroups of offenders at different risk of re-offending. The time is well passed when we could ignore the part people's biology plays in their behavior. Certainly, the bench-to-practice time for implementing biopsychosocial assessment and treatment methods will be long and relatively expensive, but we cannot afford not to implement them if we are serious about tackling the crime problem.

REFERENCES

Aatsinki, A., Lahti, L., Uusitupa, H., Munukka, E., Keskitalo, A., Nolvi, S., O'Mahony, S., Pietilä, S., Elo, L., Eerola, E., & Karlsson, H. (2019). Gut microbiota composition is associated with temperament traits in infants. *Brain, Behavior, and Immunity, 80:* 849–858.

Abi-Dargham, A., Javitch, J., Slifstein, M., Anticevic, A., Calkins, M., Cho, Y., Fonteneau, C., Gil, R., Girgis, R., Gur, R. E., & Gur, R.C. (2022). Dopamine D1R receptor stimulation as a mechanistic pro-cognitive target for schizophrenia. *Schizophrenia Bulletin, 48:*199–210.

Abramson, L., Uzefovsky, F., Toccaceli, V., & Knafo-Noam, A. (2020). The genetic and environmental origins of emotional and cognitive empathy: Review and meta-analyses of twin studies. *Neuroscience & Biobehavioral Reviews, 114:* 113–133.

Agnew, R. (1992). Foundation for a general strain theory of crime and delinquency. *Criminology, 30:* 47–87.

Agnew, R. (2002). Experienced, vicarious, and anticipated strain: An exploratory study on physical victimization and delinquency. *Justice Quarterly, 19:* 603–632.

Agnew, R. (2005). *Why Do Criminals Offend? A General Theory of Crime and Delinquency.* Los Angeles: Roxbury.

Agnew, R. (2014). The role of the social environment in general strain theory. In Beaver, K., Barnes, J., & Boutwell, B. (eds.), *The nurture versus biosocial debate in criminology: On the origins of criminal behavior and criminality*, pp. 184–198. Thousand Oaks, CA: Sage.

Ahmed, S., Graupner, M., & Gutkin, B. (2009). Computational approaches to the neurobiology of drug addiction. *Pharmacopsychiatry, 42:* S144–S152.

Akers, R. (1998). *Social learning and social structure: A general theory of crime and deviance.* Boston, MA: Northeastern University Press.

Akers, R. (1999). Social learning and social structure: Reply to Sampson, Morash, and Krohn. *Theoretical Criminology, 3:* 477–493.

Akers, R. (2010). Nothing is as practical as a good theory: Social learning theory and the treatment and prevention of delinquency. In Barlow, H., & Decker,

S. (eds.), *Criminology and public policy: Putting theory to work*, pp. 84–105. Philadelphia, PA: Temple University Press.
Akers, R. (2011). *Social learning and social structure: A general theory of crime and deviance*. New Brunswick, NJ: Transaction Publishers.
Alim, A., & Imtiaz, M. (2023). Automatic identification of children with ADHD from EEG brain waves. *Signals 2023*, 4: 193–205.
Alsharif, A., Salleh, N., & Baharun, R. (2021). The neural correlates of emotion in decision-making. *International Journal of Academic Research in Business and Social Sciences*, *11:* 64–77.
American Psychiatric Association. (2013). *Diagnostic and Statistical Manual of MentalDisorders* (5th ed.). Arlington, VA: American Psychiatric Publishing.
Amodio, D., Devine, P., & Harmon-Jones, E. (2007). A dynamic model of guilt: Implications for motivation and self-regulation in the context of prejudice. *Psychological Science*, *18:* 524–530.
Anderson, E. (1999). *Code of the street: Decency, violence, and the moral life of the inner city*. New York: W.W. Norton.
Andresen, M., Curman, A., & Linning, S. (2017). The trajectories of crime at places: Understanding the patterns of disaggregated crime types. *Journal of Quantitative Criminology*, *33*: 427–449.
Andreu-Fernández, V., La Maida, N., Marquina, M., Mirahi, A., García-Algar, O., Pichini, S., & Minutillo, A. (2024). Novel interventions on comorbidities in patients with fetal alcohol spectrum disorder (FASD): An integrative review. *Biomedicines*, 12*:* 496.
Andrews, D., & Bonta, J. (2014). *The psychology of criminal conduct*. New York: Routledge.
Ångström, A., Andersson, A., Garcia-Argibay, M., Chang, Z., Lichtenstein, P., D'Onofrio, B., Tuvblad, C., Ghirardi, L., & Larsson, H. (2024). Criminal convictions in males and females diagnosed with attention deficit hyperactivity disorder: A Swedish national registry study. *JCPP Advances*, e12217.
Angus, D., Schutter, D., Terburg, D., van Honk, J., & Harmon-Jones, E. (2016). A review of social neuroscience research on anger and aggression. *Social Neuroscience*, 223–246.
Apps, M., Rushworth, M., & Chang, S. (2016). The anterior cingulate gyrus and social cognition: Tracking the motivation of others. *Neuron*, *90:* 692–707.
Arnett, A., Pennington, B., Willcutt, E., DeFries, J., & Olson, R. (2015). Sex differences in ADHD symptom severity. *Journal of Child Psychology and Psychiatry*, *56:* 632–639.
Arteaga-Henríquez, G., Rosales-Ortiz, S., Arias-Vásquez, A., Bitter, I., Ginsberg, Y., Ibañez-Jimenez, P., Kilencz, T., Lavebratt, C., Matura, S., Reif, A., & Rethelyi, J. (2020). Treating impulsivity with probiotics in adults (PROBIA): Study protocol of a multicenter, double-blind, randomized, placebo-controlled trial. *Trials*, *21:* 1–12.
Aston-Jones, G., & Cohen, J. (2005). An integrative theory of locus coeruleus-norepinephrine function: Adaptive gain and optimal performance. *Annual Review of Neuroscience*, *28:* 403–450.
Avinun, R., & Knafo, A. (2014). Parenting as a reaction evoked by children's genotype: A meta-analysis of children-as-twins studies. *Personality and Social Psychology Review*, *18:* 87–102.

Babbitt, C., Fedrigo, O., Pfefferle, A., Boyle, A., Horvath, J., Furey, T., & Wray, G. (2010). Both noncoding and protein-coding RNAs contribute to gene expression evolution in the primate brain. *Genome Biology and Evolution, 2:* 67–79.

Babcock, J., & Iyican, S. (2022). The proximal effect of alcohol on intimate partner violence: Comparing the antecedents of intoxicated and sober men's violent acts. *Journal of Interpersonal Violence, 23:* 372–389.

Baird, A., Webb, R., Hunt, I., Appleby, L., & Shaw, J. (2020). Homicide by men diagnosed with schizophrenia: National case–control study. *British Journal of Psychology open, 6:* e143.

Bailey, C. (1995). Workfare and involuntary servitude–What you wanted to know but were afraid to ask. *Boston College Third World Law Journal, 15*: 285–321.

Baker, L., Bezdjian, S., & Raine, A. (2006). Behavioral genetics: The science of antisocial behavior. *Law and contemporary problems, 69:* 7–46.

Bakermans-Kranenburg, M., & Van Ijzendoorn, M. (2007). Genetic vulnerability or differential susceptibility in child development: The case of attachment. *Journal of Child Psychology and Psychiatry, 48:* 1160–1173.

Bakermans-Kranenburg, M., & Van Ijzendoorn, M. (2015). The hidden efficacy of interventions: Genex environment experiments from a differential susceptibility perspective. *Annual Review of Psychology, 66:* 381–409.

Balasubramanian, V. (2021). Brain power. *Proceedings of the National Academy of Sciences, 118:* e2107022118.

Barkow, J. (1989). *Darwin, sex and status: Biological approaches to mind and culture.* Toronto: University of Toronto Press.

Barnes, J., & Boutwell, B. (2015). Biosocial criminology: The emergence of a new and diverse perspective. *Criminal justice studies, 28:* 1–5.

Bartels, M., & Hudziak, J. (2007). Genetically informative designs in the study of resilience in Developmental psychopathology. *Child and Adolescent Psychiatric Clinics of North America, 16:* 323–339.

Bauer, C., Langer, J., Shankaran, S., Bada, H., Lester, B., Wright, L., Krause-Steinrauf, H., Smeriglio, V., Finnegan, L., Maza, P., & Verter, J. (2005). Acute neonatal effects of cocaine exposure during pregnancy. *Archives of Pediatrics & Adolescent Medicine, 159:* 824–834.

Beach, W., & O'Driscoll, G., Jr. (2003). Explaining the factors of the index of economic freedom. In O'Driscoll, G. P., Jr., Holmes, K. P., & O'Grady, M. A. (eds.), *2003 Index of Economic Freedom.* Washington, DC: Heritage Foundation.

Beam, C., Pezzoli, P., Mendle, J., Burt, S., Neale, M., Boker, S., Keel, P., & Klump, K. (2022). How nonshared environmental factors come to correlate with heredity. *Development and Psychopathology, 34:* 321–333.

Beaudry, G., Yu, R., Långström, N., & Fazel, S. (2021). An updated systematic review and meta-regression analysis: Mental disorders among adolescents in juvenile detention and correctional facilities. *Journal of the American Academy of Child & Adolescent Psychiatry, 60:* 46–60.

Beaver, K. (2009). Molecular genetics and crime. In Walsh, A., & Beaver, K. (eds.), *Biosocial criminology: New directions in theory and research*, pp. 50–72. New York: Routledge.

Beaver, K., Barnes, J., & Boutwell, B. (2014). The 2-repeat allele of the MAOA gene confers an increased risk for shooting and stabbing behaviors. *Psychiatric Quarterly, 85:* 257–265.

Beaver, K., Wright, J., DeLisi, M., Walsh, A., Vaughn, M., Boisvert, D., & Vaske, J. (2007). A genex gene interaction between DRD2 and DRD4 is associated with conduct disorder and antisocial behavior in males. *Behavioral and Brain Functions*, *3:* 1–8.

Beaver, K., Wright, J., & Walsh, A. (2008). A gene-based evolutionary explanation for the association between criminal involvement and number of sex partners. *Social Biology*, *54:* 47–55.

Bedoya, A., & Portnoy, J. (2023). Biosocial criminology: History, theory, research evidence, and policy. *Victims & Offenders*, *18:* 1599–1629.

Bellinger, D. (2008). Neurological and behavioral consequences of childhood lead exposure. *PLoS Medicine*, *5:* 690–692.

Belsky, J., & Beaver, K. (2011). Cumulative-genetic plasticity, parenting and adolescent self-regulation. *Journal of Child Psychology and Psychiatry*, *52:* 619–626.

Belsky, J., Zhang, X., & Sayler, K. (2022). Differential susceptibility 2.0: Are the same children affected by different experiences and exposures? *Development and Psychopathology*, *34:* 1025–1033.

Benedict, R. (2019). *Patterns of culture*. New York: Routledge.

Bennett, W., DiIulio, J., & Walters, J. (1996). *Body count: Moral poverty – and how to win America's war against crime and drugs*. New York: Simon & Schuster.

Berger, C., Dück, A., Perin, F., Wunsch, K., Buchmann, J., Kölch, M., & Reis, O., Marx, I. (2021). Brain arousal as measured by EEG-assessment differs between children and adolescents with attention-deficit/hyperactivity disorder (ADHD) and depression. *Frontiers in Psychiatry*, *12:* 633880.

Berluti, K., Ploe, M., & Marsh, A. (2023). Emotion processing in youths with conduct problems: an fMRI meta-analysis. *Translational Psychiatry*, *13*(1): 105.

Berridge, K., & Robinson, T. (2016). Liking, wanting and the incentive-sensitization theory of addiction. *American Psychologist*, *71:* 670–679.

Bevilacqua, L., & Goldman, D. (2009). Genes and addictions. *Clinical Pharmacology and Therapeutics*, *85:* 359–361.

Bezdjian, S., Raine, A., Baker, L., & Lynam, D. (2011). Psychopathic personality in children: Genetic and environmental contributions. *Psychological Medicine*, *41:* 589–600.

Bierut, L., Agrawal, A., Bucholz, K., Doheny, K., Laurie, C., Pugh, E., Fisher, S., Fox, L., Howells, W., Bertelsen, S., & Hinrichs, A. (2010). A genome-wide association study of alcohol dependence. *Proceedings of the National Academy of Sciences*, *107:* 5082–5087.

Bitler, M., & Karoly, L. (2015). Intended and unintended effects of the war on poverty: What research tells us and implications for policy. *Journal of Policy Analysis and Management*, *34:* 639–696.

Blank, R., & Schoeni, R. (2003). Changes in the distribution of children's family income over the 1990's. *American Economic Review*, *93:* 304–308.

Bleidorn, W., Schwaba, T., Zheng, A., Hopwood, C., Sosa, S., Roberts, B., & Briley, D. (2022). Personality stability and change: A meta-analysis of longitudinal studies. *Psychological Bulletin*, *148:* 588–619.

Bobb, A., Castellanos, F., Addington, A., & Rapoport, J. (2006). Molecular genetic studies of ADHD: 1991 to 2004. *American Journal of Medical Genetics—Neuropsychiatric Genetics*, *132:* 109–125.

Bøg, M., Filges, T., Brännström, L., Jørgensen, A., & Fredrikksson, M. (2017). 12-step programs for reducing illicit drug use. *Campbell Systematic Reviews, 13:* 1–149.

Boisvert, D. (2021). *Biosocial factors and their influence on desistance.* Washington, DC: National Institute of Justice.

Boisvert, D., Wells, J., Armstrong, T., & Lewis, R. (2018). Serotonin and self-control: A genetically moderated stress sensitization effect. *Journal of Criminal Justice, 56:* 98–106.

Bond, R., & Saunders, P. (1999). Routes of success: Influences on the occupational attainment of young British males. *British Journal of Sociology, 50:* 217–240.

Bonham, V., Warhauer-Baker, E., & Collins, F. (2005). Race and ethnicity in the genome era. *American Psychologist, 60:* 9–15.

Bonnycastle, K., Davenport, E., & Cousin, M. (2021). Presynaptic dysfunction in neurodevelopmental disorders: Insights from the synaptic vesicle life cycle. *Journal of Neurochemistry, 157:* 179–207.

Boonstra, H. (2000). Welfare law and the drive to reduce illegitimacy. *The Guttmacher Report on Public Policy, 3:* 7–10.

Bouchard Jr, T., & McGue, M. (2003). Genetic and environmental influences on human psychological differences. *Journal of Neurobiology, 54:* 4–45.

Boyce, W., & Kobor, M. (2015). Development and the epigenome: The 'synapse' of gene–environment interplay. *Developmental Science, 18:* 1–23.

Branco, M., & Chuong, E. (2020). Crossroads between transposons and gene regulation. *Philosophical Transactions of the Royal Society B, 375*(1795): 20190330.

Brandt, L., Chao, T., Comer, S., & Levin, F. (2021). Pharmacotherapeutic strategies for treating cocaine use disorder—what do we have to offer? *Addiction, 116:* 694–710.

Brannigan, A. (1997). Self-control, social control, and evolutionary psychology: Toward an integrated perspective on crime. *Canadian Journal of Criminology, 39:* 403–431.

Bratina, M., Antonio, M., Brewster, M., & Carsello, J. (2020). Jail-to-community medication-assisted treatment: Perceptions of clients and staff. *Salus Journal, 8:* 24–54.

Brennan, P., Grekin, E., & Mednick, S. (1999). Maternal smoking during pregnancy and adult male criminal outcomes. *Archives of General Psychiatry, 56:* 215–219.

Brennan, P., Raine, A., Schulsinger, F., Kirkegaard-Sorenen, L., Knop, J., Hutchings, B., Rosenberg, R., & Mednick, S. (1997). Psychophysiological protective factors for male subjects at high risk for criminal behavior. *American Journal of Psychiatry, 154:* 853–855.

Brody, G., Beach, S., Philibert, R., Chen, Y., & Murry, V. (2009). Prevention effects moderate the association of 5-HTTLPR and youth risk behavior initiation: Gene× environment hypotheses tested via a randomized prevention design. *Child development, 80:* 645–661.

Brody, G., Chen, Y., Beach, S., Kogan, S., Yu, T., DiClemente, R., Wingood, G., Windle, M., & Philibert, R. (2014). Differential sensitivity to prevention programming: A dopaminergic polymorphism-enhanced prevention effect on protective parenting and adolescent substance use. *Health Psychology, 33:* 182–191.

Broidy, L., & Agnew, R. (1997). Gender and crime: A general strain theory perspective. *Journal of Research in Crime and Delinquency*, *34:* 275–306.

Bromberg-Martin, E, Matsumoto, M., & Hikosaka, O. (2010). Dopamine in motivational control: rewarding, aversive, and alerting. *Neuron*, *68:* 815–834.

Bronson, J., Stroop, J., Zimmer, S., & Berzofsky, M. (2017). *Drug use, dependence, and abuse among state prisoners and jail inmates, 2007–2009.* Washington, DC: United States Department of Justice, Office of Juvenile Justice and Delinquency Prevention.

Brown, J., Long-McGie, J., Wartnik, A., Oberoi, P., Wresh, J., Weinkauf, E., Falconer, G., & Kerr, A. (2014). Fetal alcohol spectrum disorders in the criminal justice system: A review. *The Journal of Law Enforcement*, *3:* 1–10.

Brownlee, K., Moore, A., & Hackney, A. (2005). Relationship between circulating cortisol and testosterone: Influences of physical exercise. *Journal of Sports Science and Medicine*, *4:* 76–83.

Brush, L. (2003). Impacts of welfare reform. *Race, Gender & Class*, *10:* 173–192.

Burgess, R., & Akers, R. (1966). A differential association-reinforcement theory of criminal behavior. *Social Problems*, *14:* 128–147.

Burt, C., & Simons, R. (2014). Pulling back the curtain on heritability studies: Biosocial criminology in the postgenomic era. *Criminology*, *52:* 223–262.

Burt, C., & Simons, R. (2015). Heritability studies in the postgenomic era: The fatal flaw is conceptual. *Criminology*, *53:* 103–112.

Burt, S. (2009). Rethinking environmental contributions to child and adolescent psychopathology: A meta-analysis of shared environmental influences. *Psychological Bulletin*, *135*: 608–637.

Butler, T., Schofield, P., Greenberg, D., Allnutt, S., Indig, D., Carr, V., D'Este, C., Mitchell, P., Knight, L., & Ellis, A. (2010). Reducing impulsivity in repeat violent offenders: An open label trial of a selective serotonin reuptake inhibitor. *Australian & New Zealand Journal of Psychiatry*, *44:* 1137–1143.

Buydens-Branchey, L., Branchey, M., & Hibbeln, J. (2008). Associations between increases in plasma n-3 polyunsaturated fatty acids following supplementation and decreases in anger and anxiety in substance abusers. *Progress in Neuropsychopharmacological Biological Psychiatry*, *32: 568–575.*

Byrd, A., & Manuck, S. (2014). MAOA, childhood maltreatment, and antisocial behavior: Meta-analysis of a gene-environment interaction. *Biological Psychiatry*, *75:* 9–17.

Byrd, A., Manuck, S., Hawes, S., Vebares, T., Nimgaonkar, V., Chowdari, K., Hipwell, A., Keenan, K., & Stepp, S. (2019). The interaction between monoamine oxidase A (MAOA) and childhood maltreatment as a predictor of personality pathology in females: Emotional reactivity as a potential mediating mechanism. *Development and Psychopathology*, *31:* 361–377.

Cao, L. (2004). *Major criminological theories: Concepts and measurements.* Belmont, CA: Wadsworth.

Cao, L., Adams, A., & Jensen, V. (1997). A test of the black subculture of violence thesis: A research note. *Criminology*, 35:367–369.

Cardinale, E., Breeden, A., Robertson, E., Lozier, L., Vanmeter, J., & Marsh, A. (2018). Externalizing behavior severity in youths with callous–unemotional traits corresponds to patterns of amygdala activity and connectivity during judgments of causing fear. *Development and Psychopathology, 30:* 191–201.

Carey, G. (2003). *Human genetics for the social sciences.* Thousand Oaks, CA: Sage.

Carey, N. (2015). *Junk DNA: A journey through the dark matter of the genome.* New York: Columbia University Press.

Carnac, T. (2022). Schizophrenia hypothesis: Autonomic nervous system dysregulation of fetal and adult immune tolerance. *Frontiers in Systems Neuroscience, 16:* 68–121.

Carrasco, X., Rothhammer, P., Moraga, M., Henríquez, H., Chakraborty, R., Aboitiz, F., & Rothhammer, F. (2006). Genotypic interaction between DRD4 and DAT1 loci is a high risk factor for attention-deficit/hyperactivity disorder in Chilean families. *American Journal of Medical genetics (Neuropsychiatric Genetics), 141B:* 51–54.

Casey, B., Somerville, L., Gotlib, I., Ayduk, O., Franklin, N., Askren, M., Jonides, J., Berman, M., Wilson, N., Teslovich, T., & Glover, G. (2011). Behavioral and neural correlates of delay of gratification 40 years later. *Proceedings of the National Academy of Sciences, 108:* 14998–15003.

Caspi, A., McClay, J., Moffitt, T., Mill, J., Martin, J., Craig, I., Taylor, A., & Poulton, R. (2002). Role of genotype in the cycle of violence in maltreated children. *Science, 297:* 851–854.

Caspi, A., Moffitt, T., Silva, P., Stouthamer-Loeber, M., Krueger, R., & Schmutte, P. (1994). Are some people crime-prone? Replications of the personality-crime relationship across countries, genders, races, and methods. *Criminology, 32:* 163–196.

Caspi, A., Williams, B., Kim-Cohen, J., Craig, I., Milne, B., Poulton, R., Schalkwyk, L., Taylor, A., Werts, H., & Moffitt, T. (2007). Moderation of breastfeeding effects on the IQ by genetic variation in fatty acid metabolism. *Proceedings of the National Academy of Sciences, 104:* 18860–18865.

Cecil, C., & Nigg, J. (2022). Epigenetics and ADHD: Reflections on current knowledge, research priorities and translational potential. *Molecular Diagnosis and Therapy, 26:* 581–606.

Cecil, K., Brubaker, C., Adler, C., Dietrich, K., Altaye, M., Egelhoff, J., ... & Lanphear, B. (2008). Decreased brain volume in adults with childhood lead exposure. *PLoS Medicine, 5*: 742–750.

Centers for Disease Control and Prevention. (2022). Percent of babies born to unmarried mothers by state. www.cdc.gov/nchs/pressroom/sosmap/unmarried/unmarried.htm.

Chabris, C., Lee, J., Cesarini, D., Benjamin, D., & Laibson, D. (2015). The fourth law of behavior genetics. *Current Directions in Psychological Science, 24*: 304–312.

Chai, Y., Nandi, A., & Heymann, J. (2018). Does extending the duration of legislated paid maternity leave improve breastfeeding practices? Evidence from 38 low-income and middle-income countries. *BMJ Global Health, 3:* e001032.

Chakraborty, B., Lee, H., Wolujewicz, M., Mallik, J., Sun, G., ... & Chakraborty, R. (2008). Low dose effect of chronic lead exposure on neuromotor response impairment in children is moderated by genetic polymorphisms. *Journal of Human Ecology, 23:* 183–194.

Chalfin, A., Hansen, B., Weisburst, E., & Williams, M., Jr. (2020). *Police force size and civilian race. Working Paper 28202.* National Bureau of Economic Research.

Chamera, K., Trojan, E., Szuster-Głuszczak, M., & Basta-Kaim, A. (2020). The potential role of dysfunctions in neuron-microglia communication in the pathogenesis of brain disorders. *Current Neuropharmacology, 18:* 408–430.

Chapman, B. (2021). New York City homicides and shootings rose dramatically in 2020. *Wall Street Journal*, January 7.

Chapple, C., & Johnson, K. (2007). Gender differences in impulsivity. *Youth Violence and Juvenile Justice, 5:* 221–234.

Chen, M., & Chan, K. (2016). Effects of parenting programs on child maltreatment prevention: A meta-analysis. *Trauma, Violence, & Abuse, 17:* 88–104.

Chen, Y., Prescott, C., Walsh, D., Patterson, D., Riley, B., Kendler, K., & Kuo, P. (2011). Different phenotypic and genotypic presentations in alcohol dependence: Age at onset matters. *Journal of Studies on Alcohol and Drugs, 72:* 752–762.

Cherkasova, M., French, L., Syer, C., Cousins, L., Galina, H., Ahmadi-Kashani, Y., & Hechtman, L. (2020). Efficacy of cognitive behavioral therapy with and without medication for adults with ADHD: A randomized clinical trial. *Journal of Attention Disorders, 24:* 889–903.

Chetty, R., Hendren, N., & Katz, L. (2016). The effects of exposure to better neighborhoods on children: New evidence from the moving to opportunity experiment. *American Economic Review, 106:* 855–902.

Cheung, R., Boise, C., Cummings, E., & Davies, P. (2018). Mothers' and fathers' roles in child adjustment: Parenting practices and mothers' emotion socialization as predictors. *Journal of Child and Family Studies, 27:* 4033–4043.

Chiao, J., & Ambady, N. (2007). Cultural neuroscience: Parsing universality and diversity across levels of analysis. In Cohen, D. (ed.), *Handbook of cultural psychology*, pp. 237–254. New York: Guilford Press.

Chiao, J., & Blizinsky, K. (2010). Culture-gene coevolution of individualism-collectivism and the serotonin transporter gene. *Proceedings of the Royal Society of London B; Biological Sciences. 277:* 529–537.

Choy, O., Farrington, D., & Raine, A. (2015). The need to incorporate autonomic arousal in developmental and life-course research and theories. *Journal of Developmental and Life-Course Criminology, 1:*189–207.

Chugani, H., Behen., M., Muzik, O., Juhasz, C., Nagy, F., & Chugani, D. (2001). Local brain functional activity following early deprivation: A study of postinstitutionalized Romanian orphans. *Neuroimage, 14:* 1290–1301.

Clay, J., & Parker, M. (2018). The role of stress-reactivity, stress-recovery and risky decision-making in psychosocial stress-induced alcohol consumption in social drinkers. *Psychopharmacology, 235:* 3243–3257.

Cloward, R., & Ohlin, L. (1960). *Delinquency and opportunity.* New York: Free Press.

Cocaine Anonymous. (ND). What is cocaine anonymous? https://ca.org/literature/what-is-ca/.

Coccaro, E., Lee, R., & Kavoussi, R. (2009). A double-blind randomized, placebo-controlled trial of fluoxetine in patients with intermittent explosive disorder. *Journal of Clinical Psychiatry, 70:* 653–662.

Coccaro, E., McCloskey, M., Fitzgerald, D., & Phan, K. (2007). Amygdala and orbitofrontal reactivity to social threat in individuals with impulsive aggression. *Biological Psychiatry, 15:* 168–178.

Cochran, C., & Malone, E. (1999). *Public policy: Perspectives and choices.* Boston, MA: McGraw-Hill.

Cochran, J., & Bjerregaard, B. (2012). Structural anomie and crime: A cross-national test. *International Journal of Offender Therapy and Comparative Criminology, 56:* 203–217.

Cohen, A. (1955). *Delinquent boys.* New York: Free Press.

Cohen, L., & Felson, M. (1979). Social change and crime rate trends: A routine activities approach. *American Sociological Review, 44:* 588–608.

Coley, R. (1998). Children's socialization experiences and functioning in single-mother households: The importance of fathers and other men. *Child Development, 69:* 219–230.

Collins, F. (2006). *The Language of God: A scientist presents evidence for belief.* New York: Free Press.

Comrie-Thomson, L., Mavhu, W., Makungu, C., Nahar, Q., Khan, R., Davis, J., Stillo, E., Hamdani, S., Luchters, S., & Vaughan, C. (2020). Male involvement interventions and improved couples' emotional relationships in Tanzania and Zimbabwe: 'When we are walking together, I feel happy'. *Culture, Health & Sexuality, 22:* 722–739.

Conley, D., Rauscher, E., Dawes, C., Magnusson, P., & Siegal, M. (2013). Heritability and the equal environments assumption: Evidence from multiple samples of misclassified twins. *Behavior Genetics, 43:* 415–426.

Connolly, E., & Beaver, K. (2014). Examining the genetic and environmental influences on self-control and delinquency: Results from a genetically informative analysis of sibling pairs. *Journal of Interpersonal Violence, 29:* 707–735.

Coolidge, F., Thede, L., & Young, S. (2000). Heritability and the comorbidity of attention deficit hyperactivity disorder with behavioral disorders and executive function deficits: A preliminary investigation. *Developmental Neuropsychology, 17:* 273–287.

Cooper, J., Walsh, A., & Ellis, L. (2010). Is criminology moving toward a paradigm shift? Evidence from a survey of the American Society of Criminology. *Journal of Criminal Justice Education, 21:* 332–347.

Cornet, L., de Kogel, C., Nijman, H., Raine, A., & van der Laan, P. (2014). Neurobiological factors as predictors of cognitive-behavioral therapy outcome in individuals with antisocial behavior: A review of the literature. *International Journal of Offender Therapy and Comparative Criminology,* 58: 1279–1296.

Cornet, L., van der Laan, P., Nijman, H., Tollenaar, N., & de Kogel, C. (2015). Neurobiological factors as predictors of prisoners' response to a cognitive skills training. *Journal of Criminal Justice, 43:* 122–132.

Cortie, C., Byrne, M., Collier, C., Parletta, N., Crawford, D., Winberg, P., Webster, D., Chapman, K., Thomas, G., Dally, J., & Batterham, M. (2020). The effect of dietary supplementation on aggressive behaviour in Australian adult male prisoners: A feasibility and pilot study for a randomised, double blind placebo controlled trial. *Nutrients, 12:* 2617.

Cosby, B., & Poussaint, A. (2007). *Come on, people: On the path from victims to victors.* Nashville, TN: Thomas Nelson.

Costa, K., & Schoenbaum, G. (2022). Dopamine. *Current Biology, 32:* R817–R824.

Crabbe, J. (2002). Alcohol and genetics: New models. *American Journal of Medical Genetics, 114: 969–974.*

Craig, M., Catani, M., Deeley, Q., Latham, R., Daly, E., Kanaan, R., Picchioni, M., McGuire, P., Fahy, T., & Murphy, D. (2009). Altered connections on the road to psychopathy. *Molecular Psychiatry, 14:* 946–953.

Craig, S., Goulter, N., & Moretti, M. (2021). A systematic review of primary and secondary callous-unemotional traits and psychopathy variants in youth. *Clinical Child and Family Psychology Review, 24*: 65–91.

Cronk, N., Slutske, W., Madden, P., Bucholz, K., Reich, W., & Heath, A. (2002). Emotional and behavioral problems among female twins: An evaluation of the equal environments assumption. *Journal of the American Academy of Child & Adolescent Psychiatry, 41:* 829–837.

Cullen, F., & Agnew, R. (2011). *Criminological theory: Past to present* (4th ed.). New York: Oxford University Press.

Cullen, F., & Gendreau, P. (2000). Assessing correctional rehabilitation: Policy, practice, and prospects. *Criminal Justice, 3:* 299–370.

Dabiri, M., Dehghani Firouzabadi, F., Yang, K., Barker, P., Lee, R., & Yousem, D. (2022). Neuroimaging in schizophrenia: A review article. *Frontiers in neuroscience, 16:* 1042814.

Dalley, J., & Roiser, J. (2012). Dopamine, serotonin and impulsivity. *Neuroscience, 215:* 42–58.

Daly, M., & Wilson, M. (1996). Violence against stepchildren. *Current Directions in Psychological Science, 5:* 77–80.

Darwin, C. (1871). *The descent of man, and selection in relation to sex.* Princeton, NJ: Princeton University Press.

Darwin, C. (1981). *The descent of man, and selection in relation to sex.* Princeton, NJ: Princeton University Press.

DaViera, A., Roy, A., Uriostegui, M., & Fiesta, D. (2020). Safe spaces embedded in dangerous contexts: How Chicago youth navigate daily life and demonstrate resilience in high-crime neighborhoods. *American Journal of Community Psychology, 66:* 65–80.

Dawes, C., & Weinschenk, A. (2020). On the genetic basis of political orientation. *Current Opinion in Behavioral Sciences, 34:* 173–178.

Dawkins, R. (2016). *The extended phenotype: The long reach of the gene.* Oxford: Oxford University Press.

Deary, I., Cox, S., & Hill, W. (2022). Genetic variation, brain, and intelligence differences. *Molecular Psychiatry, 27:* 335–353.

De la Paz, L., Mooney, M., Ryabinin, P., Neighbor, C., Antovich, D., Nigg, J., & Nikolas, M. (2023). Youth polygenic scores, youth ADHD symptoms, and parenting dimensions: An evocative gene-environment correlation study. *Research on Child and Adolescent Psychopathology, 51*(5): 665–677.

DeLisi, M. (2011). Self-control theory: The Tyrannosaurus rex of criminology is poised to devour criminal justice. *Journal of Criminal Justice, 39:* 103–105.

DeLisi, M., Beaver, K., Vaughn, M., & Wright, J. (2009). All in the family: Genex environment interaction between DRD2 and criminal father is associated with five antisocial phenotypes. *Criminal Justice and Behavior, 36:* 1187–1197.

DeLisi, M., Beaver, K., Wright, J., & Vaughn, M. (2008). The etiology of criminal onset: The enduring salience of nature and nurture. *Journal of Criminal Justice, 36:* 217–223.

DeLisi, M., Dansby, T., Peters, D., Vaughn, M., Shook, J., & Hochstetler, A. (2014). Fledgling psychopathic features and pathological delinquency: New evidence. *American Journal of Criminal Justice, 39:* 411–424.

DeLisi, M., & Vaughn, M. (2014). Foundation for a temperament-based theory of antisocial behavior and criminal justice system involvement. *Journal of Criminal Justice, 42:*10–25.

Demontis, D., Walters, R., Martin, J., Mattheisen, M., Als, T., Agerbo, E., Baldursson, G., Belliveau, R., Bybjerg-Grauholm, J., Bækvad-Hansen, M., & Cerrato, F. (2019). Discovery of the first genome-wide significant risk loci for attention deficit/hyperactivity disorder. *Nature Genetics, 51:* 63–75.

Den Heijer, A., Groen, Y., Tucha, L., Fuermaier, A., Koerts, J., Lange, K., Thome, J., & Tucha, O. (2017). Sweat it out? The effects of physical exercise on cognition and behavior in children and adults with ADHD: A systematic literature review. *Journal of Neural Transmission, 124:* 3–26.

Department of Health and Human Services (2004). Breastfeeding practices—results from the National Immunization Survey. www.cdc.gov/breastfeeding/data/NIS.2004.htm.

Depino, A. (2006). Maternal infection and offspring brain. *The Journal of Neuroscience, 26:* 7777–7778.

Depue, R., & Collins, P. (1999). Neurobiology of the structure of personality: Dopamine, facilitation of incentive motivation, and extraversion. *Behavioral and Brain Sciences, 22:* 491–569.

De Ruigh, E., Bouwmeester, S., Popma, A., Vermeiren, R., van Domburgh, L., & Jansen, L. (2021). Using the biopsychosocial model for identifying subgroups of detained juveniles at different risk of re-offending in practice: a latent class regression analysis approach. *Child and Adolescent Psychiatry and Mental Health, 15: 1–15.*

Devaney, C., Christiansen, Ø., Holzer, J., MacDonald, M., Matias, M., Piessens, A., & Salamon, E. (2021). *The onceptualization and delivery of family support in Europe: A review of academic literature* [Online]. EurofamNet.

De Vries, B., van Busschbach, J., van der Stouwe, E., Aleman, A., van Dijk, J., Lysaker, P., Arends, J., Nijman, S., & Pijnenborg, G. (2019). Prevalence rate and risk factors of victimization in adult patients with a psychotic disorder: A systematic review and meta-analysis. *Schizophrenia Bulletin*, 45: 114–126.

De Waal, F. (2008). Putting the altruism back into altruism: The evolution of empathy. *Annual Review of Psychology*, 59:279–300.

DeWeerdt, S. (2019). How to map the brain. *Nature.* doi: 10.1038/d41586-019-02208-0.

Dincheva, I., Glatt, C., & Lee, F. (2012). Impact of the BDNF Val66Met polymorphism on cognition: Implications for behavioral genetics. *The Neuroscientist, 18:* 439–451.

Ding, Y., Chi, H., Grady, D., Morishima, A., Kidd, J., Kidd, K., Flodman, P., Spence, M., Schuck, S., Swanson, J., & Zhang, Y. (2002). Evidence of positive selection acting at the human dopamine receptor D4 gene locus. *Proceedings of the National Academy of Sciences, 99:* 309–314.

Dinkler, L., Lundström, S., Gajwani, R., Lichtenstein, P., Gillberg, C., & Minnis, H. (2017). Maltreatment-associated neurodevelopmental disorders: A co-twin control analysis. *Journal of Child Psychology and Psychiatry, and Allied Disciplines, 58:* 691–701.

Dolan, K., Larney, S., & Wodak, A. (2007). The integration of harm reduction into abstinence-based therapeutic communities: A case study of we help ourselves. *Asian Journal of Counseling, 14:* 1–19.

Dolan, M., Anderson, I. & Deakin, J. (2001). Relationship between 5-HT function and impulsivity and aggression in male offenders with personality disorders. *British Journal of Psychiatry*, 178: 352–359.

D'Onofrio, B., Singh, A., Iliadou, A., Lambe, M., Hultman, C., Grann, M., Neiderhiser, J., Långström, N., & Lichtenstein, P. (2010). Familial confounding of the association between maternal smoking during pregnancy and offspring criminality: A population-based study in Sweden. *Archives of General Psychiatry, 67: 529–538.*

Dotterer, H., Burt, S., Klump, K., & Hyde, L. (2021). Associations between parental psychopathic traits, parenting, and adolescent callous-unemotional traits. *Research on Child and Adolescent Psychopathology, 49:* 1431–1445.

Doyle, M., Shakeshaft, A., Guthrie, J., Snijder, M., & Butler, T. (2019). A systematic review of evaluations of prison-based alcohol and other drug use behavioural treatment for men. *Australian and New Zealand Journal of Public Health, 43:* 120–130.

Draper, A., Stephenson, M., Jackson, G., Pépés, S., Morgan, P., Morris, P., & Jackson, S. (2014). Increased GABA contributes to enhanced control over motor excitability in Tourette syndrome. *Current Biology, 24*: 2343–2347.

Duckworth, A., Milkman, K., & Laibson, D. (2018). Beyond willpower: Strategies for reducing failures of self-control. *Psychological Science in the Public Interest, 19:* 102–129.

Dugré, J., Radua, J., Carignan-Allard, M., Dumais, A., Rubia, K., Potvin, S. (2020). Neurofunctional abnormalities in antisocial spectrum: A meta-analysis of fMRI studies on five distinct neurocognitive research domains. *Neuroscience Biobehavioral Review, 119:* 168–183.

Dunrose, M., Cooper, A., & Snyder, H. (2014). Recidivism of prisoners released in 30 states in 2003: Patterns from 2005 to 2010. Washington, DC: Bureau of Justice Statistics.

Durkheim, E. (1951). *The division of labor in society*. Glencoe, IL: Free Press.

Durkheim, E. (1982). *Rules of the sociological method.* New York: Free Press.

Eckenrode, J., Campa, M., Luckey, D., Henderson, C., Jr., Cole, R., Kitzman, H., Anson, E., Arcoleo-Sidora, K., Powers, J., & Olds, D. (2010). Long-term effects of prenatal and infancy nurse home visitation on the life course of youths

19-year follow-up of a randomized trial. *Archives of Pediatrics and Adolescent Medicine, 164:* 9–15.

Eckenrode, J., Campa, M., Morris, P., Henderson Jr, C., Bolger, K., Kitzman, H., & Olds, D. (2017). The prevention of child maltreatment through the nurse family partnership program: Mediating effects in a long-term follow-up study. *Child Maltreatment, 22:* 92–99.

Egerton, A., Modinos, G., Ferrera, D., & McGuire, P. (2017). Neuroimaging studies of GABA in schizophrenia: A systematic review with meta-analysis. *Translational Psychiatry, 7: e*1147.

Ehrie, J., Hartwell, E., Morris, P., Mark, T., & Kranzler, H. (2020). Survey of addiction specialists' use of medications to treat alcohol use disorder. *Frontiers in Psychiatry, 11:* 1–8.

Eisenberg, D., Campbell, B., MacKillop, J., Modi, M., Dang, D., Lum, J., & Wilson, D. (2007). Polymorphisms in the dopamine D4 and D2 receptor genes and reproductive and sexual behaviors. *Evolutionary Psychology, 5: 696–715.*

El-Haj, A. (2007). The genetic reinscription of race. *Annual Review of Anthropology, 36:* 283–300.

Ellis, B., Boyce, W., Belsky, J., Bakermans-Kranenburg, M., & Van Ijzendoorn, M. (2011). Differential susceptibility to the environment: An evolutionary–neurodevelopmental theory. *Development and Psychopathology, 23:* 7–28.

Ellis, L. (2005). A theory explaining biological correlates of criminality. *European Journal of Criminology, 2:* 287–315.

Ellis, L., & Walsh, A. (2000). *Criminology: A global perspective.* Boston: Allyn & Bacon.

Ellwood, D., & Crane, J. (1990). Family changes among black Americans: What do we know? *Journal of Economic Perspectives, 4: 65–84.*

Eluvathingal, T., Chugani, H., Behen, M., Juhász, C., Muzik, O., Maqbool, M., Chugani, D., & Makki, M. (2006). Abnormal brain connectivity in children after early severe socio-emotional deprivation: a diffusion tensor imaging study. *Pediatrics, 117*: 2093–2100.

Eme, R. (2012). Attention deficit hyperactivity disorder and males in the juvenile justice system. In Norvilitis, J. (ed.), *Contemporary Trends in ADHD Research*, pp. 183–196. New York: InTech.

Eme, R. (2015). Beauchaine ontogenic process model of externalizing psychopathology a biosocial theory of crime and delinquency. *Journal of Criminal Justice, 43:* 443–449.

Empey, L., & Rabow, J. (1961). The Provo experiment in delinquency rehabilitation. *American Sociological Review, 26: 679–696.*

Engelborghs, S., Vloeberghs, E., Maertens, K., Marescau, B., & De Deyn, P. (2004). Evidence for an association between the CSF HVA: 5-HIAA ratio and aggressiveness in frontotemporal dementia but not in Alzheimer's disease. *Journal of Neurology, Neurosurgery & Psychiatry, 75:* 1080–1086.

Enoch, M. (2006). Genetic and environmental influences on the development of alcoholism: Resilience vs. risk. *Annals of the New York Academy of Sciences, 1094:* 193–201.

Errol, Z., Madsen, J., & Moslehi, S. (2021). Social disorganization theory and crime in the advanced countries: Two centuries of evidence. *Journal of Economic Behavior & Organization, 191:* 519–537.

Etkin, A., Egner, T., & Kalisch, R. (2011). Emotional processing in anterior cingulate and medial prefrontal cortex. *Trends in Cognitive Sciences, 15:* 85–93.

Evans, E., Wilson, D., & Friedmann, P. (2022). Recidivism and mortality after in-jail buprenorphine treatment for opioid use disorder. *Drug and Alcohol Dependence, 231:* 109254–109254.

Evans, E., Zhu, Y., Yoo, C., Huang, D., & Hser, Y. I. (2019). Criminal justice outcomes over 5 years after randomization to buprenorphine-naloxone or methadone treatment for opioid use disorder. *Addiction, 114:* 1396–1404.

Faraone, S., Banaschewski, T., Coghill, D., Zheng, Y., Biederman, J., Bellgrove, M., … & Wang, Y. (2021). The world federation of ADHD international consensus statement: evidence-based conclusions about the disorder. *Neuroscience & Biobehavioral Reviews, 128:* 789–818.

Faraone, S., & Larsson, H. (2019). Genetics of attention deficit-hyperactivity disorder. *Molecular Psychiatry, 24:* 562–575.

Farrell, G. (2010). Situational crime prevention and its discontents: Rational choice and harm reduction versus "cultural criminology." *Social Policy and Administration, 44:* 40–66.

Fatemi, S., & Folsom, T. (2009). The neurodevelopmental hypothesis of schizophrenia revisited. *Schizophrenia Bulletin, 35:* 528–554.

Fazel, D., Gulati, G., Linsell, L., Geddes, J., & Grann, M. (2009a). Schizophrenia and violence: Systematic review and meta-analysis. *PLoS Medicine, 6:* e1000120.

Fazel, S., Långström, N., Hjern, A., Grann, M., & Lichtenstein, P. (2009b). Schizophrenia, substance abuse, and violent crime. *Jama, 301:* 2016–2023.

Federal Bureau of Investigation. (2021). *Crime in the United States: 2020.* Washington, DC: U.S. Government Printing Office.

Felson, J. (2014). What can we learn from twin studies? A comprehensive evaluation of the equal environments assumption. *Social Science Research, 43:* 184–199.

Ferguson, C. (2010). Genetic contributions to antisocial personality and behavior: A meta-analytic review from an evolutionary perspective. *The Journal of Social psychology, 150:* 160–180.

Fields, R. (2014). Myelin—more than insulation. *Science, 344*: 264–266.

Fincher, C., Thornhill, R., Murray, D., & Schaller, M. (2008). Pathogen prevalence predicts human cross-cultural variability in individualism/collectivism. *Proceedings of the Royal Society B, 275:* 1279–1285.

Firestone, L., Firestone, A., & Catlett, J. (2013). *The self under siege: A therapeutic model for differentiation.* New York: Routledge.

Fishbein, D. (2003). Neuropsychological and emotional regulatory processes in antisocial behavior. In Walsh, A., & Ellis, L. (eds.), *Biosocial criminology: Challenging environmentalism's supremacy*, pp. 185–208. Hauppauge, NY: Nova Science.

Fixsen, D., & Blase, K. (2019). The teaching-family model: The first 50 years. *Perspectives on Behavior Science, 42:* 189–211.

Fjellvang, M., Grøning, L., & Haukvik, U. (2018). Imaging violence in schizophrenia: A systematic review and critical discussion of the MRI literature. *Frontiers in Psychiatry, 9:* 333.

Fonseca, E., Ribeiro, J., Bertoni, N., & Bastos, F. (2006). Syringe exchange programs in Brazil: Preliminary assessment of 45 programs. *Cadernos de Saúde Pública, 22:* 761–770.

Forero, D., Pereira-Morales, A., & González-Giraldo, Y. (2017). Molecular genetics and human behavior. *Module in Neuroscience and Biobehavioral Psychology.* http://dx.doi.org/10.1016/B978-0-12-809324-5.06489-0.

Fox, B. (2017). It's nature and nurture: Integrating biology and genetics into the social learning theory of criminal behavior. *Journal of Criminal Justice, 49:* 22–31.

Fox, E., & Beevers C. (2016). Differential sensitivity to the environment: Contribution of cognitive biases and genes to psychological wellbeing. *Molecular Psychiatry, 12:* 1657–1662.

Fraga, M., Ballestar, E., Paz, M., Ropero, S., Setien, F., Ballestar, M., Heine-Suñer, D., Cigudosa, J., Urioste, M., Benitez, J., Boix-Chornet, M., Sanchez-Aguilera, A., Ling, C., Carlsson, E., Poulsen, P., Vaag, A., Stephan, Z., Spector, T., Wu, Y-Z., Plass, C., & Esteller, M. (2005). Epigenetic differences arise during the lifetime of monozygotic twins. *Proceedings of the National Academy of Sciences, 102:* 10604–10609.

Franklyn, N., Kesavelu, D., Joji, P., Verma, R., Wadhwa, A., & Ray, C. (2022). Impact of key nutrients on brain and executive function development in infants and toddlers: A narrative review. *Journal of Food and Nutrition Sciences, 10:* 19–26.

Friese, M., Frankenbach, J., Job V., & Loschelder, D. (2017). Does self-control training improve self-control? A meta-analysis. *Perspectives on Psychological Science, 12:* 1077–1099.

Frisell, T., Pawitan, Y., & Långström, N. (2012). Is the association between general cognitive ability and violent crime caused by family-level confounders? *PloS one, 7:* e41783.

Froehlich, T., Anixt, J., Loe, I., Chirdkiatgumchai, V., Kuan, L., & Gilman, R. (2011). Update on environmental risk factors for attention-deficit/hyperactivity disorder. *Current Psychiatry Reports, 13:* 333–344.

Fromm, E. (1995). *The art of loving.* London: Thorsons.

Gajos, J., Fagan, A., & Beaver, K. (2016). Use of genetically informed evidence-based prevention science to understand and prevent crime and related behavioral disorders. *Criminology & Public Policy, 15:* 683–701.

Gannon, T., Olver, M., Mallion, J., & James, M. (2019). Does specialized psychological treatment for offending reduce recidivism? A meta-analysis examining staff and program variables as predictors of treatment effectiveness. *Clinical Psychology Review, 73:* 101752.

Gao, W., Salzwedel, A., Carlson, A., Xia, K., Azcarate-Peril, M., Styner, M., Thompson, A., Geng, X., Goldman, B., Gilmore, J., & Knickmeyer, R. (2019). Gut microbiome and brain functional connectivity in infants: A preliminary study focusing on the amygdala. *Psychopharmacology (Berl), 236:* 1641–1651.

Gao, Y., Raine, A., Venables, P., Dawson, M., & Mednick, S. (2010). Association of poor childhood fear conditioning and adult crime. *American Journal of Psychiatry, 167:* 6–60.

Gard, A. M., Dotterer, H. L., & Hyde, L. W. (2019). Genetic influences on antisocial behavior: recent advances and future directions. *Current Opinion in Psychology,* 27, 46–55.

Gato, W., Posick, C., Williams, A., & Mays, C. (2018). Examining the link between the human microbiome and antisocial behavior: Why criminologists should care about biochemistry, too. *Deviant Behavior, 39:* 1191–1201.

Gavin, D., & Sharma, R. (2010). Histone modifications, DNA methylation, and schizophrenia. *Neuroscience and Biobehavioral Reviews, 34:* 882–888.

Geary, D. (2005). *The origin of mind: Evolution of brain, cognition, and general intelligence.* Washington, DC: American Psychological Association.

Gendreau, P., & Ross, R. (1987). Revivification of rehabilitation: Evidence from the 1980s. *Justice Quarterly, 4:* 349–407.

Gesch, C., Hammond, S., Hampson, S., Eves, A., & Crowder, M. (2002). Influence of supplementary vitamins, minerals and essential fatty acids on the antisocial behavior of young adult prisoners. *The British Journal of Psychiatry, 181:* 22–28.

Ghasemi, M., Anvari, D., Atapour, M., Stephen Wormith, J., Stockdale, K, & Spiteri, R. (2021). The application of machine learning to a general risk–need assessment instrument in the prediction of criminal recidivism. *Criminal Justice and Behavior, 48:* 518–538.

Glueck, S. (1956). Theory and fact in criminology: A criticism of differential association theory. *British Journal of Criminology, 7:* 92–109.

Goldberg, E. (2001). *The executive brain: Frontal lobes and the civilized mind.* New York: Oxford University Press.

Golenkov, A., Large, M., Nielssen, O., & Tsymbalova, A. (2022). Forty-year study of rates of homicide by people with schizophrenia and other homicides in the Chuvash Republic of the Russian Federation. *British Journal of Psychology open, 8:* e3.

Gomes, W., Devoz, P., Araújo, M., Batista, B., Barbosa, F., & Barcelos, G. (2017). Milk and dairy products intake is associated with low levels of lead (Pb) in workers highly exposed to the metal. *Biological Trace Element Research, 178:* 29–35.

Gonen, N., Futtner, C., Wood, S., Garcia-Moreno, S., Salamone, I., Samson, S., Sekido, R., Poulat, F., Maatouk, D., & Lovell-Badge, R. (2018). Sex reversal following deletion of a single distal enhancer of Sox9. *Science, 360:* 1469–1473.

Gottesman, I., & Hanson, D. (2005). Human development: Biological and genetic processes. *Annual Review of Psychology, 56:* 263–286.

Gottfredson, D., Kearley, B., & Bushway, S. (2017). Substance use, drug treatment, and crime: An examination of intra-individual variation in a drug court population. In Natarajan, M. (ed), *Drug Abuse: Prevention and Treatment*, pp. 359–388. New York: Routledge.

Gottfredson, M. (2006). The empirical status of control theory in criminology. In Cullen, F., Wright, J., & Blevins, K. (eds.), *Taking stock*, pp. 77–100. New Brunswick, NJ: Transaction.

Gottfredson, M., & Hirschi, T. (1990). *A general theory of crime.* Stanford: Stanford University Press.

Gottfredson, M., & Hirschi, T. (1997). National crime control policies. In Fisch, M. (ed.), *Criminology, 97/98*, pp. 27–33. Guilford, CT: Dushkin Publishing.

Gottfredson, M., & Hirschi, T. (2016). The criminal career perspective as an explanation of crime and a guide to crime control policy: The view from general theories of crime. *Journal of Research in Crime and Delinquency, 53:* 406–419.

Gottfredson, S., & Moriarty, L. (2006). Statistical risk assessment: Old problems and new applications. *Crime & Delinquency, 52:* 178–200.

Graefe, D., & Lichter, D. (2008). Marriage patterns among unwed mothers: Before and after PRWORA. *Journal of Policy Analysis and Management: The Journal of the Association for Public Policy Analysis and Management*, *27:* 479–497.

Grosholz, J., & Semenza, D. (2021). Health conditions and victimization among incarcerated individuals in US jails. *Journal of Criminal Justice*, *74:* 101797.

Guàrdia, A., González-Rodríguez, A., Seeman, M., Álvarez, A., Estrada, F., Acebillo, S., Labad, J., & Monreal, J. (2021). Dopamine, serotonin, and structure/function brain defects as biological bases for treatment response in delusional disorder: A systematic review of cases and cohort studies. *Behavioral. Sciences*, *11:*141.

Gudjonsson, G., Sigurddsson, J., Young, S., Newton, A., & Peersen, M. (2009). Attention deficit hyperactivity disorder (ADHD). How do ADHD symptoms relate to personality among prisoners? *Personality and Individual Differences*, *47:* 64:68.

Gunderson, E., Tsai, A., Selby, J., Caan, B., Mayer-Davis, E., & Risch, N. (2006). Twins of mistaken zygosity (TOMZ): Evidence for genetic contributions to dietary patterns and physiologic traits. *Twin Research and Human Genetics*, *9:* 540–549.

Guo, G., Cai, T., Guo, R., Wang, H., & Harris, K. (2010). The dopamine transporter gene, a spectrum of most common risky behaviors, and the legal status of the behaviors. *PLoS One*, *5*(2): e9352.

Guo, G., Roettger, M., & Shih, J. (2007). Contributions of the DAT1 and DRD2 genes to serious and violent delinquency among adolescents and young adults. *Human Genetics*, *121:* 125–136.

Guy, R., & Chomczyński, P. (2018). Bioethics and biosocial criminology: Hurdling the status quo. *Ethics, Medicine and Public Health*, *7:* 95–102.

Haidt, J. (2001). The emotional dog and its rational tail: A social intuitionalist approach to moral judgment. *Psychological Review*, *108:* 814–834.

Hall, S., & Birney, E. (2012). Journey to the genetic interior. *Scientific American*, *307:* 80–89.

Hall, S., & Winlow, S. (2004). Barbarians at the gate: Crime and violence in the breakdown of the pseudo-pacification process. In Ferrell, J., Hayward, K., Presdee, M., & Morrison, W. (eds.). *Cultural criminology unleashed*, pp. 289–300. London: The Glass House Press.

Hankin, B., E. Nederhof, E., Oppenheimer, C., Jenness, J., Young, J., Abela, J., Smolen, A. Ormel, J., & Oldehinkel, A. (2011). Differential susceptibility in youth: evidence that 5-HTTLPR x positive parenting is associated with positive affect 'for better and worse'. *Translational Psychiatry*, *10:* e44.

Hannagan, R., & Hatemi, P. (2008). The threat of genes: A comment on Evan Charney's "genes and ideologies". *Perspectives on Politics*, *6:* 329–335.

Hannon, E., Spiers, H., Viana, J., Pidsley, R., Burrage, J., Murphy, T., Troakes, C., Turecki, G., O'donovan, M., Schalkwyk, L., & Bray, N. (2016). Methylation QTLs in the developing brain and their enrichment in schizophrenia risk loci. *Nature Neuroscience*, *19:* 48–54.

Hanson, R., & Bussiere, M. (1998). Predicting relapse: A meta-analysis of sexual offender recidivism studies. *Journal of consulting and clinical psychology*, *66*(2), 348–362.

Hanson, R., & Morton-Bourgon, K. (2009). The accuracy of recidivism risk assessments for sexual offenders: A meta-analysis of 118 prediction studies. *Psychological Assessment*, 21, 1–21.

Harden, K. (2021). "Reports of my death were greatly exaggerated": Behavior genetics in the postgenomic era. *Annual Review of Psychology*, *72:* 37–60.

Harpending, H., & G. Cochran (2002). In our genes. *Proceedings of the National Academy of Science*, *99:* 10–12.

Hassan, M., Awan, F., Naz, A., deAndrés-Galiana, E., Alvarez, O., Cernea, A., Fernández-Brillet, L., Fernández-Martínez, J., & Kloczkowski, A. (2022). Innovations in genomics and big data analytics for personalized medicine and health care: A review. *International Journal of. Molecular Sciences*, *23:* 4645.

Haveman, R., Blank, R., Moffitt, R., Smeeding, T., & Wallace, G. (2014). Policy retrospectives. *Journal of Policy Analysis and Management*, *34:* 593–638.

Hawkins, A., Amato, P., & Kinghorn, A. (2013). Are government-supported healthy marriage initiatives affecting family demographics? A state-level analysis. *Family Relations*, *62:* 501–513.

Hawkins, J., Kosterman, R., Catalano, R., Hill, K., & Abbott, R. (2005). Promoting positive adult functioning through social development intervention in childhood. *Archives of Pediatric Adolescent Medicine*, *159:* 25–31.

Hawkins, J., Kosterman, R., Catalano, R., Hill, K., & Abbott, R. (2008). Effects of social development intervention in childhood 15 years later. *Archives of Pediatrics & Adolescent Medicine*, *162:* 1133–1141.

Hawley, A. (1944). Ecology and human ecology. *Social Forces*, *22:* 398–405.

Hawthorne, N. (2003). *The scarlet letter*. New York: Barnes & Noble Classics.

Haynes, B., Sempowski, G., Wells, A., & Hale, L. (2000). The human thymus during aging. *Immunologic Research*, *22:* 253–261.

Head, B. (2015). Toward more "evidence-informed" policy making? *Public Administration Review*, *76:* 472–484.

Heck, K., Braveman, P., Cubbin, C., Chávez, G., & Kiely, J. (2006). Socioeconomic status and breastfeeding initiation among California mothers. *Public Health Reports*, *121:* 51–59.

Heikkinen, M., Taipale, H., Tanskanen, A., Mittendorfer-Rutz, E., Lähteenvuo, M., & Tiihonen, J. (2021). Real-world effectiveness of pharmacological treatments of alcohol use disorders in a Swedish nation-wide cohort of 125 556 patients. *Addiction*, *116:* 1990–1998.

Hemez, P., & Washington, C. (2021). *Percentage and number of children living with two parents has dropped since 1968*. Washington, DC: U.S. Census Bureau.

Hermawan, S., & Hananto, S. (2022). Contestation of chemical castration punishment for child sex offenders: Case in Indonesia. *UUM Journal of Legal Studies*, *13:* 25–49.

Herrnstein, R., & Murray, C. (1994). *The bell curve: Intelligence and class structure in American life*. New York: Free Press.

Hewig, J., Hagemann, D., Seifert, J., Naumann, E., & Bartussek, D. (2006). The relation of cortical activity and BIS/BAS on the trait level. *Biological Psychology*, *71:* 42–53.

Hidalgo, V., Pérez-Padilla, J., Sánchez, J., Ayala-Nunes, L., Maya, J., Grimaldi, V., & Menéndez, S. (2018). An analysis of different resources and programmes supporting at-risk families in Spain. *Early Child Development and Care*, *188:* 1528–1539.

Hiller, J. (2004). Speculations on the links between feelings, emotions and sexual behaviour: Are vasopressin and oxytocin involved? *Sexual and Relationship Therapy*, *19:* 393–412.

Hindman, J., & Peters, J. (2000). Polygraph testing leads to better understanding adult and juvenile sex offenders. *Federal Probation*, *65:* 1–15.

Hipp, J. (2010). A dynamic view of neighborhoods: The reciprocal relationship between crime and neighborhood structural characteristics. *Social Problems*, *57:* 205–230.

Hirschi, T. (1969). *Causes of delinquency.* Berkeley, CA: University of California Press.

Hirschi, T. (2004). Self-control and crime. In Baumeister, R., & Vohs, K. (eds.), *Handbook of self-regulation: Research, theory, and applications*, pp. 537–552. New York: Guilford.

Hirschi, T., & Gottfredson, M. (2001). Self-control. In Paternoster, R., & Bachman, R. (eds.), *Explaining criminals and crime,* pp. 81–96. Los Angeles, CA: Roxbury.

Hodgins, S. (2017). Aggressive behavior among persons with schizophrenia and those who are developing schizophrenia: Attempting to understand the limited evidence on causality. *Schizophrenia Bulletin*, *43:* 1021–1026.

Hodkins, S., Mednick, S., Brennan, P., Schulsinger, F., & Engberg, M. (1996). Mental disorder and crime: Evidence from a Danish birth cohort. *Archives of General Psychiatry*, *53:* 489–496.

Holoyda, B., & Kellaher, D. (2016). The biological treatment of paraphilic disorders: An updated review. *Current Psychiatry Reports*, *18*: 1–7.

Holt, J. (2012). *Why does the world exist? An existential detective story.* New York: WW Norton.

Holttinen, T., Pirkola, S., & Kaltiala, R. (2023). Schizophrenia among young people first admitted to psychiatric inpatient care during early and middle adolescence. *Schizophrenia Research*, *252:* 103–109.

Holz, N., Boecker, R., Buchmann, A., Blomeyer, D., Baumeister, S., Hohmann, S., Jennen- Steinmetz, C., Wolf, I., Rietschel, M., Witt, S., & Plichta, M. (2016). Evidence for a sex-dependent MAOA× childhood stress interaction in the neural circuitry of aggression. *Cerebral Cortex*, *26:* 904–914.

Hsueh, J., Alderson, D., Lundquist, E., Michalopoulos, C., Gubits, D., Fein, D., & Knox, V. (2012). *The supporting healthy marriage evaluation: Early impacts on low-income families. OPRE Report 2012–11.* Washington, DC: Office of Planning, Research, and Evaluation, Administration.

Hunt, G., Large, M., Cleary, M., Lai, H., & Saunders J. (2018). Prevalence of comorbid substance use in schizophrenia spectrum disorders in community and clinical settings, 1990–2017: Systematic review and meta-analysis. *Drug and Alcohol Dependence*, *191:* 234–258.

Hutchinson, G., Willner, P., Rose, J., Burke, I., & Bastick, T. (2017). CBT in a Caribbean context: A controlled trial of anger management in Trinidadian prisons. *Behavioural and Cognitive Psychotherapy*, *45:* 1–15.

Hwang, H., Ku, R., & Hashimoto-Torii, K. (2019). Prenatal environment that affects neuronal migration. *Frontiers in Cell and Developmental Biology*, *7:* 138–149.

Hyde, L., & Dotterer, H. (2022). The nature and nurture of callous-unemotional traits. *Current Directions in Psychological Science*, *31*(6): 546–555.

Hyman, S. (2007). The neurobiology of addiction: Implications for voluntary control of behavior. *The American Journal of Bioethics*, *7:* 8–11.

Inciardi, J., Martin, S., & Butzin, C. (2004). Five-year outcomes of therapeutic community treatment of drug-involved offenders after release from prison. *Crime & Delinquency*, *50:* 88–107.

International Harm Reduction Association. (2010). What is harm reduction? A position statement from the International Harm Reduction Association, London, England.

Jackson, D. (2016). The link between poor quality nutrition and childhood antisocial behavior: A genetically informative analysis. *Journal of Criminal Justice*, *44:* 13–20.

Jackson, L., Langille, L., Lyons, R., Hughes, J., Martin, D., & Winstanley, V. (2009). Does moving from a high-poverty to lower-poverty neighborhood improve mental health? A realist review of 'moving to opportunity'. *Health & Place*, *15:* 961–970.

Jaffee, S., Moffitt, T., Caspi, A., & Taylor, A. (2003). Life with (or without) father: The benefits of living with two biological parents depend on the father's antisocial behavior. *Child Development*, *74:* 109–126.

Jain, M., Palacio, L., Castellanos, F., Palacio, J., Pineda, D., Restrepo, M., Muñoz, J., Lopera, F., Wallis, D., Berg, K., & Bailey-Wilson, J. (2007). Attention-deficit/hyperactivity disorder and comorbid disruptive behavior disorders: evidence of pleiotropy and new susceptibility loci. *Biological Psychiatry*, *61:* 1329–1339.

Jamieson, A., & Radick, G. (2017). Genetic determinism in the genetics curriculum: An exploratory study of the effects of Mendelian and Weldonian emphases. *Science & Education*, *26:* 1261–1290.

Javakhishvili, M., & Vazsonyi, A. (2022). Empathy, self-control, callous-unemotionality, and delinquency: Unique and shared developmental antecedents. *Child Psychiatry & Human Development*, *53:* 389–402.

Javitt, D., Spencer, K., Thaker, G., Winterer, G., & Hajós, M. (2008). Neurophysiological biomarkers for drug development in schizophrenia. *Nature Reviews Drug Discovery*, *7:* 68–83.

Jensen, A. (1998). *The g factor: The science of mental ability*. Westport, CT: Praeger.

Jin, Y., Wang, J., Bachtiar, M., Chong, S., & Lee, C. (2018). Architecture of polymorphisms in the human genome reveals functionally important and positively selected variants in immune response and drug transporter genes. *Human Genomics*, *12:* 1–13.

Johnstone, S., Dela Cruz, G., Girard, T., Rajji, T., & Castle, D. (2022). Potential explanatory models of the female preponderance in very late onset schizophrenia. *Women*, *2:* 353–370.

Jolliffe, D., & Farrington, D. (2009). *Effectiveness of interventions with adult male violent offenders*. Stockholm: Swedish Council for Crime Prevention.

Julvez, J., Guxens, M., Carsin, A., Forns, J., Mendez, M., Turner, M., & Sunyer, J. (2014). A cohort study on full breastfeeding and child neuropsychological development: The role of maternal social, psychological, and nutritional factors. *Developmental Medicine & Child Neurology*, *56:*148–156.

Kampman, K. (2019). The treatment of cocaine use disorder. *Science Advances*, *5:* 1–8.

Kasparek, T., Theiner, P., & Filova, A. (2015). Neurobiology of ADHD from childhood to adulthood: Findings of imaging methods. *Journal of Attention Disorders*, *19*: 931–943.

Kavish, N., Boisvert, D., Wells, J., Lewis, R., Cooke, E., Woeckener, M., & Armstrong, T. (2019). On the associations between indicators of resting arousal levels, physiological reactivity, sensation seeking, and psychopathic traits. *Personality and Individual Differences*, *141:* 218–225.

Kawasawa, Y., Mohammad, S., Son, A., Morizono, H., Basha, A., Salzberg, A., Torii, M., & Hashimoto-Torii, K. (2017). Genome-wide profiling of differentially spliced mRNAs in human fetal cortical tissue exposed to alcohol. *Alcohol*, *62:* 1–9.

Kearney, M., & Levine, P. (2012). *Explaining recent trends in the U.S. teen birth rate*. NBER Working Paper No. 17964.

Kelly, J. (2017). Is alcoholics anonymous religious, spiritual, neither? Findings from 25 years of mechanisms of behavior change research. *Addiction*, *112: 929–936*.

Kelly, J., Humphreys, K., & Ferri, M. (2020). Alcoholics anonymous and other 12-step programs for alcohol use disorder. *Cochrane Database of Systematic Reviews*, Issue 3. Art. No.: CD012880.

Kendler, K., Prescott, C., Myers, J., & Neale, M. (2003). The structure of genetic and environmental risk factors for common psychiatric and substance use disorders in men and women. *Archives of General Psychiatry*, *60: 929–937*.

Keshavan, M., Nasrallah, H., & Tandon, R. (2011). Schizophrenia, "just the facts" 6. Moving ahead with the schizophrenia concept; from the elephant to the mouse. *Schizophrenia Research*, *127:* 3–13.

Khan, O., Ferriter, M., Huband, N., Powney, M., Dennis, J., & Duggan, C. (2015). Pharmacological interventions for those who have sexually offended or are at risk of offending. *Cochrane Database of Systematic Reviews*.

Khehra N., Padda I., & Swift, C. (2023). *Polymerase chain reaction (PCR)*. StatPearls. Treasure Island, FL: StatPearls Publishing, PMID: 36943981.

Khodadadi, E., Fahmideh, L., Khodadadi, E., Dao, S., Yousefi, M., Taghizadeh, S., Asgharzadeh, M., Yousefi, B., & Kafil, H. (2021). Current advances in DNA methylation analysis methods. *BioMed Research International*, *2021:* 8827516.

Kiiski, H., Bennett, M., Rueda-Delgado, L., Farina, F., Knight, R., Boyle, R., Roddy, D., Grogan, K., Bramham, J., Kelly, C., & Whelan, R. (2020). EEG spectral power, but not theta/beta ratio, is a neuromarker for adult ADHD. *European Journal of Neuroscience*, *51:* 2095–2109.

Killian, B., Yuan, T., Tsai, C., Chiu, T., Chen, Y., & Chan, C. (2020). Emission-related heavy metal associated with oxidative stress in children: Effect of antioxidant intake. *International Journal of Environmental Research and Public Health*, *17: 3920*. doi: 10.3390/ijerph17113920.

Kim, B., Merlo, A. V., Park, J., & Hong, Y. (2022). A systematic review of public housing, poverty (de) concentration, and risk behaviors: What about youth? *Trauma, Violence, & Abuse*, *23:* 73–87.

Kim, B., Benekos, P., & Merlo, A. (2016). Sex offender recidivism revisited: Review of recent meta-analyses on the effects of sex offender treatment. *Trauma, Violence, & Abuse*, *17*: 105–117.

Kim-Cohen, J., Caspi, A. Taylor, B. Williams, R. Newcombe, I. Craig, I., & Moffitt, T. (2006). MAOA, maltreatment, and gene-environment interaction predicting children's mental health: New evidence and a meta-analysis. *Molecular Psychiatry*, *11: 903–913*.

Kim, J., Kim, B. N., Kim, J. W., Hong, S., Shin, M., Yoo, H., & Cho, S. (2017). Breastfeeding is associated with enhanced learning abilities in school-aged children. *Child and Adolescent Psychiatry and Mental Health*, *11:* 1–7.

Kingsley, D. (2006). The Teaching-Family Model and post-treatment recidivism: A critical review of the conventional wisdom. *International Journal of Behavioral Consultation and Therapy, 2:* 481–497.

Kinney, D., Hintz, K., Shearer, E., Barch, D., Riffin, C., Whitley, K., & Butler, R. (2010). A unifying hypothesis of schizophrenia: Abnormal immune system development may help explain roles of prenatal hazards, post-pubertal onset, stress, genes, climate, infections, and brain dysfunction. *Medical Hypotheses, 74:* 555–563.

Kirkham, K., & Ford, D. (2009). Are state marriage initiatives having an effect? An initial exploration of the impact on divorce and childhood poverty rates. *Public Administration Review, 69:* 846–853.

Kitayama, S., King, A., Hsu, M., Liberzon, I., & Yoon, C. (2016). Dopamine-system genes and cultural acquisition: The norm sensitivity hypothesis. *Current Opinion in Psychology, 8:* 167–174.

Kitzman, H., Olds, D., Knudtson, M., Cole, R., Anson, E., Smith, J., Fishbein, D., DiClemente, R., Wingood, G., Caliendo, A., & Hopfer, C. (2019). Prenatal and infancy nurse home visiting and 18-year outcomes of a randomized trial. *Pediatrics, 144:* e20183876.

Kleber, H. (2003). Pharmacologic treatments for heroin and cocaine dependence. *The American Journal on Addictions, 12:* S5–S18.

Kling, J., Liebman, J., & Katz, L. (2007). Experimental analysis of neighborhood effects. *Econometrica, 75:* 83–119.

Knafo A., & Uzefovsky F. (2013) Variation in empathy: The interplay of genetic and environmental factors. In Legerstee, M., Haley, D., & Bornstein, M. (eds.), *The infant mind: Origins of the social Brain*, pp. 97–121. New York: The Guilford Press.

Knecht, C., de Alvaro, R., Martinez-Raga, J., & Balanza-Martinez, V. (2015). Attention-deficit hyperactivity disorder (ADHD), substance use disorders, and criminality: A difficult problem with complex solutions. *International Journal of Adolescent Medicine and Health, 27:* 163–175.

Kochanska, G., & Aksan, N. (2004). Conscience in childhood: Past, present, and future. *Merrill-Palmer Quarterly, 50:* 299–310.

Kolb, B., & Gibb, R. (2011). Brain plasticity and behaviour in the developing brain. *Journal of The Canadian Academy of Child and Adolescent* Psychiatry, *20:* 265–276.

Kolla, N., & Bortolato, M. (2020). The role of monoamine oxidase A in the neurobiology of aggressive, antisocial, and violent behavior: A tale of mice and men. *Progress in Neurobiology, 194: 1–64.*

Koller, K., Brown, T., Spurfeon, A., & Levy, L. (2004). Recent developments in low-level lead exposure and intellectual impairment in children. *Environmental Health Perspectives, 112: 987–994.*

Kornhauser, R. (1978). *Social sources of delinquency: An appraisal of analytical methods*. Chicago: University of Chicago Press.

Koukkou, M., & Lehmann, D. (2006). Experience dependent brain plasticity: A key concept for studying nonconscious decisions. *International Congress Series, 1286:* 45–52.

Kramer, K. (2021). The human family—its evolutionary context and diversity. *Social Sciences, 10:* 191–208.

Kramer, M., Aboud, F., Mironova, E., Vanilovich, I., Platt, R., Matush, L., Igumnov, S., Fombonne, E., Bogdanovich, N., Ducruet, T., & Collet, J. (2008). Breastfeeding and child cognitive development: new evidence from a large randomized trial. *Archives of General Psychiatry, 65:*578–584.

Krause, D., Matz, J., Weidinger, E., Wagner, J., Wildenauer, A., Obermeier, M., Riedel, M., & Müller, N. (2010). The association of infectious agents and schizophrenia. *World Journal of Biological Psychiatry, 11:* 739–43.

Kruk, E. (2012). Arguments for an equal parental responsibility presumption in contested child custody. *The American Journal of Family Therapy, 40:*33–55.

Kuderna, L., Gao, H., Janiak, M., Kuhlwilm, M., Orkin, J., Bataillon, T., Manu, S., Valenzuela, A., Bergman, J., Rousselle, M., & Silva, F. (2023). A global catalog of whole-genome diversity from 233 primate species. *Science, 380:* 906–913.

Kuo, S., Salvatore, J., Barr, P., Aliev, F., Anokhin, A., Bucholz, K., Chan, G., Edenberg, H., Hesselbrock, V., Kamarajan, C., & Kramer, J. (2021). Mapping pathways by which genetic risk influences adolescent externalizing behavior: The interplay between externalizing polygenic risk scores, parental knowledge, and peer substance use. *Behavior Genetics, 51:* 543–558.

Labrecque, R., Campbell, C., Elliott, J., King, M., Christmann, M., Page, K., McVay, J., & Roller, K. (2018). An examination of the inter-rater reliability and rater accuracy of the level of service/case management inventory. *Corrections, 3:* 105–118.

Lacourse, E., Nagin, D., Vitaro, F., Côté, S., Arseneault, L., & Tremblay, R. (2006). Prediction of early-onset deviant peer group affiliation: A 12-year longitudinal study. *Archives of General Psychiatry, 63:* 562–568.

LaFree, G., Drass, K., & O'Day, P. (1992). Race and crime in postwar America: Determinants of African-American and white rates, 1957–1988. *Criminology, 30:* 157–188.

Lamb, H., Weinberger, L., & Gross, B. (2004). Mentally ill persons in the criminal justice system: Some perspectives. *Psychiatric Quarterly, 75:* 107–126.

Lambez, B., Harwood-Gross, A., Golumbic, E., & Rassovsky, Y. (2020). Non-pharmacological interventions for cognitive difficulties in ADHD: A systematic review and meta-analysis. *Journal of Psychiatric Research, 120:* 40–55.

Langan, P., Schmitt, E., & Durose, M. (2003). *Recidivism of sex offenders released from prison in 1994.* Washington, DC: Bureau of Justice Statistics.

Langner, I., Garbe, E., Banaschewski, T., & Mikolajczyk, R. (2013). Twin and sibling studies using health insurance data: The example of attention deficit/hyperactivity disorder (ADHD). *PloS One, 8*(4): e62177.

Lassi, D., Malbergier, A., Negrão, A., Florio, L., De Aquino, J., & Castaldelli-Maia, J. (2022). Pharmacological treatments for cocaine craving: What is the way forward? A systematic review. *Brain Sciences, 12:*1546.

Latessa, E., Cullen, F., & Gendreau, P. (2002). Beyond correctional quackery-professionalism and the possibility of effective treatment. *Federal Probation, 66:* 43–53.

Lattimore, P., Steffey, D., Gfroerer, J., Bose, J., Pemberton, M., & Penne, M. (2014). *Arrestee substance use: Comparison of estimates from the National Survey on Drug Use and Health and the Arrestee Drug Abuse Monitoring Program.* Washington, DC: Substance Abuse and Mental Health Services Administration.

Laube, C., van den Bos, W., & Fandakova, Y. (2020). The relationship between pubertal hormones and brain plasticity: Implications for cognitive training in adolescence. *Developmental Cognitive Neuroscience, 42*: 100753.

Lawrence, R.M., & Lawrence, R.A. (2011). Breastfeeding: More than just good nutrition. *Pediatrics in Review, 32:* 267–280.

Lee, J., & Cho, K. (2013). Chemical castration for sexual offenders: Physicians' views. *Journal of Korean Medical Science, 28:* 171–172.

Legge, S., Santoro, M., Periyasamy, S., Okewole, A., Arsalan, A., & Kowalec, K. (2021). Genetic architecture of schizophrenia: A review of major advancements. *Psychological Medicine, 51:* 2168–2177.

Lesch, K., Araragi, N., Waider, J., van den Hove, D., & Gutknecht, L. (2012). Targeting brain serotonin synthesis: Insights into neurodevelopmental disorders with long-term outcomes related to negative emotionality, aggression and antisocial behaviour. *Philosophical Transactions of the Royal Society B: Biological Sciences, 367:* 2426–2443.

Leung, C., & Weiss, S. (2023). The gut microbiome of youth who have behavioral and mental health problems: A scoping review. *Mental Health & Prevention, 31:* 200288.

Levenson, R. (2014). The autonomic nervous system and emotion. *Emotion Review, 6:* 1600–112.

Lewontin, R. (1970). Further remarks on race and the genetics of intelligence. *Bulletin of the Atomic Scientist, 26:* 23–25.

Li, C., Mao, X., & Wei, L. (2008). Genes and (common) pathways underlying drug addiction. *PLoS Computational Biology, 4:28–34.*

Lichtenstein, P., Halldner, L., Zetterqvist, J., Sjölander, A., Långström, M., & Larsson, H. (2012). Medication for attention deficit-hyperactivity disorder and criminality. *New England Journal of Medicine, 367:* 2006–2014.

Lichter, D., Graefe, D., & Brown, J. (2003). Is marriage a panacea? Union formation among economically disadvantaged unwed mothers. *Social Problems, 50:* 60–86.

Liebertz, S., & Bunch, J. (2018). Examining the externalities of welfare reform: TANF and crime. *Justice Quarterly, 35:* 477–504.

Liem, M., Suonpää, K., Lehti, M., Kivivuori, J., Granath, S., Walser, S., & Killias, M. (2019). Homicide clearance in Western Europe. *European journal of criminology, 16:* 81–101.

Lilly, J., Cullen, F., & Ball, R. (2007). *Criminological theory: Context and consequences* (3rd ed.). Thousand Oaks, CA: Sage.

Lilly, J., Cullen, F., & Ball, R. (2011). *Criminological theory: Context and consequences* (4th ed.). Thousand Oaks, CA: Sage.

Lindo, J., & Packham, A. (2017). How much can expanding access to long-acting reversible contraceptives reduce teen birth rates? *American Economic Journal: Economic Policy, 9:* 348–376.

Ling, S., Umbach, R., & Raine, A. (2019). Biological explanations of criminal behavior. *Psychology, Crime & Law, 25:* 626–640.

Lipsey, M., & Cullen, F. (2007). The effectiveness of correctional rehabilitation: A review of systematic reviews. *Annual Review of Law and Social Science, 3:* 297–320.

Lischke, A., Pahnke, R., Mau-Moeller, A., Behrens, M., Grabe, H., Freyberger, H., Hamm, A., & Weippert, M. (2018). Inter-individual differences in heart rate variability are associated with inter-individual differences in empathy and alexithymia. *Frontiers in Psychology, 9:* 134–142.

Lonczak, H., Abbott, R., Hawkins, J., Kosterman, R., & Catalano, R. (2002). Effects of the Seattle Social Development Project on sexual behavior, pregnancy, birth, and sexually transmitted disease outcomes by age 21 years. *Archives of Pediatrics & Adolescent Medicine, 156:* 438–447.

Long, E., Ohlsson, H., Sundquist, J., Sundquist, K., & Kendler, K. (2019). Different characteristics and heritabilities of alcohol use disorder classes: A population-based Swedish study. *Alcohol and Alcoholism, 54:* 647–655.

Lucassen, L. (2010). A brave new world: The left, social engineering, and eugenics in twentieth-century Europe. *International Review of Social History, 55:* 265–296.

Lykken, D. (1995). *The antisocial personalities*. Hillsdale, NJ: Lawrence Erlbaum.

Lynam, D. (1996). Early identification of chronic offenders: Who is the fledgling psychopath? *Psychological Bulletin, 120:* 209–234.

Lytton, H. (2013). *Parent-child interaction: The socialization process observed in twin and singleton families*. New York: Springer Science & Business Media.

Ma, I., van Holstein, M., Mies, G., Mennes, M., Buitelaar, J., Cools, R., Cillessen, A., Krebs, R., & Scheres, A. (2016). Ventral striatal hyperconnectivity during rewarded interference control in adolescents with ADHD. *Cortex, 82:* 225–236.

Mackey, W., & Immerman, R. (2007). Fatherlessness by divorce contrasted to fatherlessness by non-marital births: A distinction with a difference for the community. *Journal of Divorce & Remarriage, 47:* 111–134.

Maclean, P. (1990). *The triune brain in evolution: Role in paleocerebral functions*. New York: Plenum Press.

Magnet, M. (2008). The great African American awakening. *City Journal*. www.city-journal.org/article/the-great-african-american-awakening.

Maletzky, B., & Field, G. (2003). The biological treatment of dangerous sexual offenders: A review and preliminary report of the Oregon pilot depo-Provera program. *Aggression and Violent Behavior, 8:* 391–412.

Manning, M., & Hoyme, H. (2007). Fetal alcohol syndrome disorders: A practical clinical approach to diagnosis. *Neuroscience and Biobehavioral Review, 31:* 230–238.

Manthey, J., Hassan, S., Carr, S., Kilian, C., Kuitunen-Paul, S., & Rehm, J. (2021). What are the economic costs to society attributable to alcohol use? A systematic review and modelling study. *PharmacoEconomics, 39:* 809–822.

Manuck, S., & McCaffery, J. (2014). Gene-environment interaction. *Annual Review of Psychology, 65:* 41–70.

Marco-Sola, S., Liao, W., Asri, M., Ebler, J., Doerr, D., Haukness, M., Hickey, G., Lu, S., Lucas, J., Monlong, J., & Abel, H. (2023). A draft human pangenome reference. *Nature, 617:* 312–324.

Marsh, R., & Walsh, A. (1995). Physiological and psychosocial assessment and treatment of sex offenders: A comprehensive victim-oriented program. *Journal of Offender Rehabilitation, 22:* 77–96.

Marsman, A., Mandl, R., Klomp, D., Bohlken, M., Boer, V., Andreychenko, A., Cahn, W., Kahn, R., Luijten, P., & Pol, H. (2014). GABA and glutamate in schizophrenia: A 7 T 1 H-MRS study. *NeuroImage: Clinical, 6:* 398–407.

Martin, J., Hamilton, B., Osterman, M., & Driscoll, A. (2021). Final data for 2019. *National Vital Statistics Reports, 70:* 1–51.

Martin, S. (2004). The links between alcohol, crime and the criminal justice system: Explanations, evidence and interventions. In McCance-Katz, E., & Clark, H. (eds.), *Psychosocial Treatments*, pp. 137–164. New York: Brunner-Routledge.

Martinson, R. (1974). What works? Questions and answers about prison reform. *The Public Interest*, *35:* 22–54.

Maruschak, L., Bronson, J., & Alper, M. (2021). *Indicators of mental health problems reported by prisoners: Survey of prison inmates, 2016*. Washington, DC: Bureau of Justice Statistics.

Mason, L., Peters, E., Williams, S., & Kumari, V. (2017). Brain connectivity changes occurring following cognitive behavioural therapy for psychosis predict long-term recovery. *Translational Psychiatry*, *7:* e1001–e1001.

Massey, D. (2002). A brief history of human society: The origin and role of emotion in social life. *American Sociological Review*, 67: 1–29.

Matthews, L., & Butler, P. (2011). Novelty-seeking DRD4 polymorphisms are associated with human migration distance out-of-Africa after controlling for neutral population gene structure. *American Journal of Physical Anthropology*, *145:* 382–389.

Matthews, L., & Turkheimer, E. (2021). Across the great divide: Pluralism and the hunt for missing heritability. *Synthese*, *198:* 2297–2311.

Mawby, R. (2001). *Burglary*. Colompton, England: Willan Publishing.

May, P., & Gossage, J. (2001). Estimating the prevalence of fetal alcohol syndrome: A summary. *Alcohol Research & Health*, *25:* 159–167.

May, P., Marais, A., De Vries, M., Buckley, D., Kalberg, W., Hasken, J., Stegall, J., Hedrick, D., Robinson, L., Manning, M., & Tabachnick, B. (2021). The prevalence, child characteristics, and maternal risk factors for the continuum of fetal alcohol spectrum disorders: A sixth population-based study in the same South African community. *Drug and Alcohol Dependence*, *218:* 108408.

Mayes, L., Bornstein, M., Chawarska, K., & Granger, R. (1995). Information processing and developmental assessments in 3-month-old infants exposed prenatally to cocaine. *Pediatrics*, *95:* 539–545.

Mazur, A. (2023). Testosterone and the "honor culture" of young Black men. *Qeios*, 1–15.

McDermott, P., Alterman, A., Cacciola, J., Rutherford, M., Newman, J., & Mulholland, E. (2000). Generality of psychopathy checklist—revised factors over prisoners and substance-dependent patients. *Journal of Consulting and Clinical psychology*, *68:* 181–186.

McEwen, B., & Gianaros, P. (2010). Central role of the brain in stress and adaptation: Links to socioeconomic status, health, and disease. *Annals of the New York Academy of Sciences*, *1186:* 190–222.

McGue, M. (1999). The behavioral genetics of alcoholism. *Current Directions in Psychological Science*, *8:* 109–115.

McGuire, J., Bilby, C., Hatcher, R., Hollin, C., Hounsome, J., & Palmer, E. (2008). Evaluation of structured cognitive–behavioural treatment programmes in reducing criminal recidivism. *Journal of Experimental Criminology*, *4:* 21–40.

McKinnon, J., & K. Humes (2003). *The Black population in the United States*. Washington, DC: U.S. Census Bureau.

McLaughlin, K., Weissman, D., & Bitrán, D. (2019). Childhood adversity and neural development: A systematic review. *Annual Review of Developmental Psychology, 1:* 277–312.

McLaughlin, V., & Mackey, W. (2008). Demographics of the upward-trending murder rate in Buffalo, New York: A harbinger of societal stress. *Journal of Social, Political, and Economic Studies, 33:* 458–471.

McNeeley, S. (2015). Lifestyle-routine activities and crime events. *Journal of Contemporary Criminal Justice, 31:* 30–52.

Meaney, M. (2010). Epigenetics and the biological definition of gene× environment interactions. *Child Development, 81:* 41–79.

Mednick, S., Machon, R., & Huttunen, N. (1988). Adult schizophrenia following prenatal exposure to an influenza epidemic. *Archives of General Psychiatry, 45:* 189–192.

Mehta, P., & Beer, J. (2009). Neural mechanisms of the testosterone-aggression relation: The role of the oribitofrontal cortex. *Journal of Cognitive Neuroscience, 22:* 2357–2368.

Mehta, T., Monegro, A., Nene, Y., Fayyaz, M., & Bollu, P. (2019). Neurobiology of ADHD: A review. *Current Developmental Disorders Reports*, 6: 235–240.

Mela, M., Hanlon-Dearman, A., Ahmed, A., Rich, S., Densmore, R., Reid, D., Barr, A., Osser, D., Anderson, T., Suberu, B., & Ipsiroglu, O. (2020). Treatment algorithm for the use of psychopharmacological agents in individuals prenatally exposed to alcohol and/or with diagnosis of fetal alcohol spectrum disorder (FASD). *Journal of Population Therapeutics and Clinical Pharmacology, 27:* e1–e13.

Melchers, M., Montag, C., Reuter, M., Spinath, F., & Hahn, E. (2016). How heritable is empathy? Differential effects of measurement and subcomponents. *Motivation and Emotion*, *40:* 720–730.

Menard, S., Mihalic, S., & Huizinga, D. (2001). Drugs and crime revisited. *Justice Quarterly, 18:* 269–299.

Merton, R. (1938). Social structure and anomie. *American Sociological Review, 3:* 672–682.

Messner, S., & Rosenfeld, R. (2001). *Crime and the American dream* (3rd ed.). Belmont, CA: Wadsworth.

Messner, S., & Sampson, R. (1991). The sex ratio, family disruption, and rates of violent crime: The paradox of demographic structure. *Social Forces, 69:* 693–723.

Messner, S., Thome, H., & Rosenfeld, R. (2008). Institutions, anomie, and violent crime: Clarifying and elaborating institutional-anomie theory. *International Journal of Conflict and Violence, 2:*163–181.

Meyer-Lindenberg, A., Buckholtz, J., Kolachana, B., Hariri, A., Pezawas, L., Blasi, G., Wabnitz, A., Honea, R., Verchinski, B., Callicott, J., & Egan, M. (2006). Neural mechanisms of genetic risk for impulsivity and violence in humans. *Proceedings of the National Academy of Sciences, 103:* 6269–6274.

Miller, J., & Maloney, C. (2013). Practitioner compliance with risk/needs assessment tools: A theoretical and empirical assessment. *Criminal Justice and Behavior, 40:* 716–736.

Miller, W. (1958). Lower class culture as a generating milieu of gang delinquency. *Journal of Social Issues, 14:* 5–19.

Miller-Butterworth, C., Kaplan, J., Shaffer, J., Devlin, M., Manuck, S., & Ferrell, R. (2008). Sequence variation in the primate dopamine transporter gene and its relationship to social dominance. *Molecular Biology and Evolution*, *25*:18–28.

Moffitt, T. (1993). Adolescent-limited and life-course-persistent antisocial behavior: A developmental taxonomy. *Psychological Review*, *100:* 674–701.

Moffitt, T. (2017). A review of research on the taxonomy of life-course persistent versus adolescence-limited antisocial behavior. In Cullen, F., Wright, J., & Blevins, K. (eds.), *Taking stock: The status of criminological theory*, pp. 277–311. New York: Routledge.

Moffitt, T., Arseneault, L., Belsky, D., Dickson, N., Hancox, R., Harrington, H., Houts, R., Poulton, R., Roberts, B., Ross, S., & Sears, M. (2011). A gradient of childhood self-control predicts health, wealth, and public safety. *Proceedings of the National Academy of Science*, *108:* 2693–2698.

Moffitt, T., & Beckley, A. (2015). Abandon twin research? Embrace epigenetic research? Premature advice for criminologists. *Criminology*, *53*: 121–126.

Moffitt, T., & Walsh, A. (2003). The adolescence-limited/life-course persistent theory of antisocial behavior: What have we learned? In Walsh, A., & Ellis, L. (eds.), *Biosocial criminology: Challenging environmentalism's supremacy*, pp. 125–144, Hauppauge, NY: Nova Science.

Mohr-Jensen, C., Bisgaard, C., Boldsen, S., & Steinhausen, H. (2019). Attention-deficit/hyperactivity disorder in childhood and adolescence and the risk of crime in young adulthood in a Danish nationwide study. *Journal of the American Academy of Child & Adolescent Psychiatry*, *58:* 443–452.

Moreno-Küstner, B., Martín, C., & Pastor, L. (2018). Prevalence of psychotic disorders and its association with methodological issues. A systematic review and meta-analyses. *PloS One*, *13:* e0195687.

Morris, D. (2012). Obama kills welfare reform. Congressional Ways and Means Committee, July 18. https://waysandmeans.house.gov/2012/07/18/obama-kills-welfare-reform/.

Mourtgos, S., Adams, I., & Nix, J. (2022). Elevated police turnover following the summer of George Floyd protests: A synthetic control study. *Criminology & Public Policy*, *21:* 9–33.

Mrazek, A., Chiao, J., Blizinsky, K., Lun, J., & Gelfand, M. (2013). The role of culture–gene coevolution in morality judgment: Examining the interplay between tightness–looseness and allelic variation of the serotonin transporter gene. *Culture and Brain*, *1:* 100–117.

Mueser, K., Deavers, F., Penn, D., & Cassisi, J. (2013). Psychosocial treatments for schizophrenia. *Annual Review of Clinical Psychology*, *9:* 465–97.

Muller, N., & Schwarz, N. (2006). Schizophrenia as an inflammation-mediated dysbalance of glutamatergic neurotransmission. *Neurotoxicity Research*, *10:* 131–148.

Munafò, M., Brown, S., & Hariri, A. (2008). Serotonin transporter (5-HTTLPR) genotype and amygdala activation: a meta-analysis. *Biological Psychiatry*, *63:* 852–857.

Murray, D., Trudeau, R., & Schaller, M. (2011). On the origins of cultural differences in conformity: Four tests of the pathogen prevalence hypothesis. *Personality and Social Psychology Bulletin*, *37:* 318–329.

Myers, D., & Dewall, C. (2018). *Psychology*. New York: Worth Publishers.

National Institute on Drug Abuse. (2016). National Institute on Drug Abuse Strategic Plan 2016–2020. Accessed from www.drugabuse.gov/about-nida/2016-2020-nida-strategic-plan.

Naumova, O., Lee, M., Koposov, R., Szyf, M., Dozier, M., & Grigorenko, E. (2012). Differential patterns of whole-genome DNA methylation in institutionalized children and children raised by their biological parents. *Development and Psychopathology*, *24:* 143–155.

Nestler, E., & Lüscher, C. (2019). The molecular basis of drug addiction: Linking epigenetic to synaptic and circuit mechanisms. *Neuron*, *102:* 48–59.

Nettle, D. (2003). Intelligence and class mobility in the British population. *British Journal of Psychology*, *94:* 551–561.

Nettler, G. (1978). *Explaining crime*. New York: McGraw Hill.

Nettler, G. (1984). *Explaining crime* (3rd ed.). New York: McGraw Hill.

Newman, O. (1972). *Defensible space*. New York: Macmillan.

Newsome, J., & Cullen, F. (2017). The risk-need-responsivity model revisited: Using biosocial criminology to enhance offender rehabilitation. *Criminal Justice and Behavior*, *44:* 1030–1049.

Ngo, F., & Paternoster, R. (2014). Contemporaneous and lagged effects of life domains and substance use: A test of Agnew's general theory of crime and delinquency. *Journal of Criminology*, *2014:* 1–20.

Niederhofer, H. (2008). Effectiveness of the repetitive Transcranical Magnetic Stimulation (rTMS) of 1 Hz for attention-deficit hyperactivity disorder (ADHD). *Psychiatria Danubina*, *20:* 91–92.

Nurk, S., Koren, S., Rhie, A., Rautiainen, M., Bzikadze, A., Mikheenko, A., Vollger, M., Altemose, N., Uralsky, L., Gershman, A., & Aganezov, S. (2022). The complete sequence of a human genome. *Science*, *376:* 44–53.

Oberwittler, D. (2004). A multilevel analysis of neighbourhood contextual effects on serious juvenile offending: The role of subcultural values and social disorganization. *European Journal of Criminology*, *1:* 201–235.

O'Donnell, K., & Meaney, M. (2020). Epigenetics, development, and psychopathology. *Annual Review of Clinical Psychology*, *16:* 327–350.

Okbay, A., Wu, Y., Wang, N., Jayashankar, H., Bennett, M., Nehzati, S. M., ... & Social Science Genetic Association Consortium. (2022). Polygenic prediction of educational attainment within and between families from genome-wide association analyses in 3 million individuals. *Nature Genetics*, *54:* 437–49.

Olds, D. (2006). The nurse–family partnership: An evidence-based preventive intervention. *Infant Mental Health Journal*, *27:* 5–25.

Olds, D., Henderson, C., Jr., Cole, R., Eckenrode, J., Kitzman, H., Luckey, D., Pettitt, L., Sidora, K., Morris, P., & Powers, J. (1998). Long-term effects of nurse home visitation on children's criminal and antisocial behavior: 15-year follow-up of a randomized controlled trial. *Jama*, *280:* 1238–1244.

Olds, D., Hill, P., Mihalic, S., & O'Brien, R. (1998). *Blueprints for violence prevention, book seven: Prenatal and infancy home visitation by nurses.* Boulder, CO: Center for the Study and Prevention of Violence.

O'Neill, J., & Hill, A. (2003). Gaining ground, moving up: The change in the economic status of single mothers under welfare reform. Civic Report, Number 35. Center for Civic Innovation, New York, NY.

Ordenewitz, L., Weinmann, T., Schlüter, J., Moder, J., Jung, J., Kerber, K., Greif-Kohistani, N., Heinen, F., & Landgraf, M. (2021). Evidence-based interventions for children and adolescents with fetal alcohol spectrum disorders–A systematic review. *European Journal of Paediatric Neurology*, *33:* 50–60.

Ortiz, J., & Raine, A. (2004). Heart rate level and antisocial behavior in children and adolescents: A meta-analysis. *Journal of the American Academy of Child & Adolescent Psychiatry*, *43:* 154–162.

Osgood, D., & Chambers, J. (2003). Community correlates of rural youth violence. *Juvenile Justice Bulletin*, May. U.S. Department of Justice.

Owen, M., Sawa, A., & Mortensen, P. (2016). Schizophrenia. *The Lancet*, *25:* 2455–2467.

Panksepp, J. (1998). *Affective neuroscience*. Oxford: Oxford University Press.

Papero, D., Frost, R., Havstad, L., & Noone, R. (2018). Natural systems thinking and the human family. *Systems*, *6:* 19–29.

Parker, K., Roberson, L., Ivanov, B., Carter, R., & Riney, N. (2021). The road to recovery from addiction: A qualitative exploration of motivators and challenges to achieving sobriety in recovery housing. *International Journal of Health, Wellness & Society*, *11: 159–172.*

Passas, N. (1995). Continuities in the anomie tradition. *Advances in Criminological Theory*, *6:* 91–112.

Patrick, C. (2006). Back to the future: Cleckley as a guide to the next generation of psychopathy research. In: Patrick, C. (ed.), *Handbook of psychopathy*, pp. 605–617. New York: Guilford Press.

Patrick, C. (2022). Psychopathy: Current knowledge and future directions. *Annual Review of Clinical Psychology*, *18:* 387–415.

Paul, D. (1984). Eugenics and the left. *Journal of the History of Ideas*, *45:* 567–590.

Paus, T., Keshavan, M., & Giedd, J. (2008). Why do so many psychiatric disorders emerge during adolescence? *Nature Reviews/Neuroscience*, *9:* 947–957.

Pearson, F., Lipton, D., Cleland, C., & Yee, D. (2002). The effects of behavioral/cognitive-behavioral programs on recidivism. *Crime & Delinquency*, *48:* 476–496.

Pelsser, L., Frankena, K., Toorman, J., & Rodrigues Pereira, R. (2017). Diet and ADHD, reviewing the evidence: a systematic review of meta-analyses of double-blind placebo-controlled trials evaluating the efficacy of diet interventions on the behavior of children with ADHD. *PloS One*, *12:* e0169277.

Penn, A. (2001). Early brain wiring: Activity-dependent processes. *Schizophrenia Bulletin*, *27:* 337–348.

Perry, B., & Pollard, R. (1998). Homeostasis, stress, trauma, and adaptation: A neurodevelopmental view of childhood trauma. *Child and Adolescent Psychiatric Clinics of America*, *7:* 33–51.

Perugi, G., De Rosa, U., & Barbuti, M. (2022). What value do norepinephrine/dopamine dual reuptake inhibitors have to the current treatment of adult attention deficit hyperactivity disorder (ADHD) treatment armamentarium? *Expert Opinion on Pharmacotherapy*, *23:* 1975–1978.

Pessoa, L., Medina, L., Hof, P., & Desfilis, E. (2019). Neural architecture of the vertebrate brain: implications for the interaction between emotion and cognition. *Neuroscience & Biobehavioral Reviews*, *107:* 296–312.

Petherick, A. (2010). Development: Mother's milk: A rich opportunity. *Nature, 468:* S5–S7.

Pfattheicher, S., Sassenrath, C., & Keller, J. (2019). Compassion magnifies third-party punishment. *Journal of Personality and Social Psychology, 117:* 124–138.

Piquero, A. (2010). A general theory of crime and public policy. In Barlow, H., & Decker, S. (eds.), *Criminology and public policy: Putting theory to work*, pp. 66–83. Philadelphia, PA: Temple University Press.

Piquero, A., Jennings, W., & Farrington, D. (2010). On the malleability of self-control: Theoretical and policy implications regarding a general theory of crime. *Justice Quarterly, 27:* 803–834.

Piquero, A., Jennings, W., Farrington, D., Diamond, B., & Gonzalez, J. (2016). A meta-analysis update on the effectiveness of early self-control improvement programs to improve self-control and reduce delinquency. *Journal of Experimental Criminology, 12:* 249–264.

Plomin, R. (2011). Commentary: Why are children in the same family so different? Non-shared environment three decades later. *International Journal of Epidemiology, 40:* 582–592.

Plomin, R. (2023). Celebrating a century of research on behavioral genetics. *Behavior Genetics, 53:* 75–84.

Plomin, R., & von Stumm, S. (2018). The new genetics of intelligence. *Nature Reviews Genetics, 19:* 148. doi: 10.1038/nrg.2017.104.

Plomin, R., & von Stumm, S. (2022). Polygenic scores: Prediction versus explanation. *Molecular psychiatry, 27:* 49–52.

Polanczyk, G., Willcutt, E., Salum, G., Kieling, C., & Rohde, L. (2014). ADHD prevalence estimates across three decades: An updated systematic review and meta-regression analysis. *International Journal of Epidemiology, 43:* 434–442.

Polderman, T., Benyamin, B., De Leeuw, C., Sullivan, P., Van Bochoven, A., Visscher, P., & Posthuma, D. (2015). Meta-analysis of the heritability of human traits based on fifty years of twin studies. *Nature Genetics, 47*: 702–709.

Popescu, A., Marian, M., Drăgoi, A., & Costea, R. (2021). Understanding the genetics and neurobiological pathways behind addiction. *Experimental and Therapeutic Medicine, 21:* 1–10.

Porto, P., Oliveira, L., Mari, J., Volchan, E., Figueira, I., & Ventura, P. (2009). Does cognitive behavioral therapy change the brain? A systematic review of neuroimaging in anxiety disorders. *The Journal of Neuropsychiatry and Clinical Neurosciences, 21:*114–125.

Pourhamzeh, M., Moravej, F., Arabi, M., Shahriari, E., Mehrabi, S., Ward, R., Ahadi, R., & Joghataei, M. (2022). The roles of serotonin in neuropsychiatric disorders. *Cellular and Molecular Neurobiology, 42:*1671–1692.

Pratt, T., & Cullen, F. (2005). Assessing macro-level predictors and theories of crime: A meta-analysis. *Crime and Justice, 32:* 373–450.

Pratt, T., Gau, J., & Franklin, T. (2010). *Key ideas in criminology and criminal justice.* Thousand Oaks, CA: Sage.

Pruett, K. (1987). *The nurturing father: Journey toward the complete man.* New York: Warner Books.

Ptáček, R., Kuželová, H., & Stefano, G. (2011). Dopamine D4 receptor gene DRD4 and its association with psychiatric disorders. *Medical Science*

Monitor: International Medical Journal of Experimental and Clinical Research, 17: RA215.
Purper-Ouakil, D., Ramoz, N., Lepagnol-Bestel, A. M., Gorwood, P., & Simonneau, M. (2011). Neurobiology of attention deficit/hyperactivity disorder. *Pediatric Research, 69:* 69r–76r.
Putnam, R. (2007). E pluribus unum: Diversity and community in the twenty-first century the 2006 Johan Skytte Prize Lecture. *Scandinavian Political Studies, 30:* 137–174.
Quinlan, R., & Quinlan, M. (2007). Evolutionary ecology of human pair-bonds: Cross-cultural tests of alternative hypotheses. *Cross-Cultural Research, 41:* 149–169.
Quinn, J., & Sneed, Z. (2008). Drugs and crime: An empirically based, interdisciplinary model. *Journal of Teaching in the Addictions, 7:* 16–30.
Rahman, M., & McGowan, P. (2022). Cell-type-specific epigenetic effects of early life stress on the brain. *Translational Psychiatry, 12:* 326.
Rebellon, C. (2012). Differential association and substance use: Assessing the roles of discriminant validity, socialization, and selection in traditional empirical tests. *European Journal of Criminology, 9:* 73–96.
Retz, W., Ginsberg, Y., Turner, D., Barra, S., Retz-Junginger, P., Larsson, H., & Asherson, P. (2021). Attention-deficit/hyperactivity disorder (ADHD), antisociality and delinquent behavior over the lifespan. *Neuroscience & Biobehavioral Reviews, 120:* 236–248.
Reuben, A., Schaefer, J., Moffitt, T., Broadbent, J., Harrington, H., Houts, R., Ramrakha, S., Poulton, R., & Caspi, A. (2019). Association of childhood lead exposure with adult personality traits and lifelong mental health. *JAMA Psychiatry, 76:* 418–425.
Rhie, A., Nurk, S., Cechova, M., Hoyt, S., Taylor, D., Altemose, N., Hook, P., Koren, S., Rautiainen, M., Alexandrov, I., & Allen, J. (2023). The complete sequence of a human Y chromosome. *Nature, 621:* 344–354.
Richardson, G., De Genna, N., Goldschmidt, L., Larkby, C., & Donovan, J. (2019). Prenatal cocaine exposure: Direct and indirect associations with 21-year-old offspring substance use and behavior problems. *Drug and Alcohol Dependence, 195:* 121–131.
Ripley, A. (2006). What happened to the gangs of New Orleans? *American Renaissance*, May 14.
Roach, J., & Pease, K. (2013). *Evolution and crime*. New York: Routledge.
Robinson, M. (2004). *Why crime? An integrated systems theory of antisocial behavior*. Upper Saddle River, NJ: Prentice Hall.
Robinson, M. (2009). No longer taboo: Crime prevention implications of biosocial criminology. In Walsh, A., & Beaver, K. (eds.), *Biosocial criminology: New directions in theory and research*, pp. 243–263. New York, Routledge.
Rocque, M., Welsh, B., & Raine, A. (2012). Biosocial criminology and modern crime prevention. *Journal of Criminal Justice, 40:* 306–312.
Rodney, H., & Mupier, R. (1999). The impact of parental alcoholism on self-esteem and depression among African-American adolescents. *Journal of Child & Adolescent Substance Abuse, 8:* 55–71.
Rolls, E. (2019). The cingulate cortex and limbic systems for emotion, action, and memory. *Brain Structure and Function, 224:* 3001–3018.

Romero-Martínez, Á., Murciano-Martí, S., & Moya-Albiol, L. (2019). Is sertraline a good pharmacological strategy to control anger? Results of a systematic review. *Behavioral Sciences, 9:* 1–14.

Roozen, S., Black, D., Peters, G., Kok, G., Townend, D., Nijhuis, J., Koek, G., & Curfs, L. (2016). Fetal alcohol spectrum disorders (FASD): An approach to effective prevention. *Current Developmental Disorders Reports, 3:* 229–234.

Rosenbaum, D., Lurigio, A., & Davis, R. (1998). *The prevention of crime: Social and situational strategies.* West/Wadsworth.

Rosenfeld, R., & Lopez, E. (2021). *Pandemic, social unrest, and crime in US cities, 2020 year-end update. 2021.* Washington, DC: Council on Criminal Justice.

Rosenfeld, R., & Wallman, J. (2019). Did de-policing cause the increase in homicide rates? *Criminology & Public Policy, 18: 51–75.*

Rosenthal, S., Chang, J., Kovtun, O., McBride, J., & Tomlinson, I. (2011). Biocompatible quantum dots for biological applications. *Chemistry & Biology, 18:* 10–24.

Rösler, M., Retz, W., R6etz, Hengesch, G., Scneider, M., & Supprian, T. (2004). Prevalence of attention deficit-hyperactivity disorder and comorbid disorders in young male prison inmates. *European Archives of Psychiatry Clinical Neuroscience, 254:* 365–371.

Ross, E., Vijan, S., Miller, E., Valenstein, M., & Zivin, K. (2019). The cost-effectiveness of cognitive behavioral therapy versus second-generation antidepressants for initial treatment of major depressive disorder in the United States: A decision analytic model. *Annals of Internal Medicine, 171: 785–795.*

Rudolph, M., & Starke, P. (2020). How does the welfare state reduce crime? The effect of program characteristics and decommodification across 18 OECD-countries. *Journal of Criminal Justice, 68: 1–12.*

Ruisoto, P., & Contador, I. (2019). The role of stress in drug addiction. An integrative review. *Physiology & Behavior, 202,* 62–68.

Rutten, B., & Mill, J. (2009). Epigenetic mediation of environmental influences in major psychotic disorders. *Schizophrenia Bulletin, 35:* 1045–1056.

Salas-Wright, C., Vaughn, M., & Maynard, B. (2014). Religiosity and violence among adolescents in the United States: Findings from the National Survey on Drug Use and Health 2006–2010. *Journal of Interpersonal Violence, 29:* 1178–1200.

Sampson, R. (2000). Whither the sociological study of crime. *Annual Review of Sociology, 26:* 711–714.

Sampson, R. (2008). Moving to inequality: Neighborhood effects and experiments meet social structure. *American Journal of Sociology, 114:* 189–231.

Sampson, R., & Bean, L. (2006). Cultural mechanisms and killing fields: A revised theory of community-level racial inequality. In *The many colors of crime: Inequalities of race, ethnicity, and crime in America*, pp. 8–36. Chicago, IL: The University of Chicago Press.

Sampson R., & Winter, A. (2018) Poisoned development: Assessing childhood lead exposure as a cause of crime in a birth cohort followed through adolescence. *Criminology, 56:* 269–301.

Saunders, V. (2020). The Naked Emperor Syndrome revisited: An evaluation of schizophrenia gene studies research methods. *International Journal of Psychiatric Research, 4:* 1–7.

Sawhill, I., & Morton, J. (2007). *Economic mobility: Is the American dream alive and well?* Washington, DC: The Economic Mobility Project/Pew Charity Trusts.
Schiffer, B., Pawliczek, C., Forsting, M., Gizewski, E., Leygraf, N., & Hodgins, S. (2014). Neural mechanisms underlying cognitive control of men with lifelong antisocial behavior. *Psychiatry Research: Neuroimaging, 222:* 43–51.
Schindler, S., Querengässer, J., Bruchmann, M., Bögemann, N., Moeck, R., & Straube, T. (2021). Bayes Factors show evidence against systematic relationships between the anchoring effect and the Big Five personality traits. *Scientific Reports, 11:* 7021.
Schmalleger, F. (2004). *Criminology Today*. Upper Saddle River, NJ: Prentice Hall.
Schnell, C., Grossman, L., & Braga, A. (2019). The routine activities of violent crime places: A retrospective case-control study of crime opportunities on street segments. *Journal of Criminal Justice, 60:* 140–153.
Schury, K., & Kolassa, L. (2012). Biological memory of childhood maltreatment: Current knowledge and recommendations for future research. *Annals of the New York Academy of Sciences, 1262:* 93–100.
Schutter, D. J. L. G., De Weijer, D. A., Meuwese, J., Morgan, B., & Van Honk, J. (2008). Interrelations between motivational stance, cortical excitability, and the frontal electroencephalogram asymmetry of emotion: A transcranial magnetic stimulation study. *Human Brain Mapping, 29:* 574–580.
Schwartz, J., Savolainen, J., Aaltonen, M., Merikukka, M., Paananen, R., & Gissler, M. (2015). Intelligence and criminal behavior in a total birth cohort: An examination of functional form, dimensions of intelligence, and the nature of offending. *Intelligence, 51:* 109–118.
Sciandra, M., Sanbonmatsu, L., Duncan, G., Gennetian, L., Katz, L., Kessler, R., Kling, J., & Ludwig, J. (2013). Long-term effects of the Moving to Opportunity residential mobility experiment on crime and delinquency. *Journal of Experimental Criminology, 9:* 451–489.
Scornavacchi, M. (2015). *Superintelligence, humans, and war*. Joint Forces Staff College, Norfolk, VA.
Sedlak, A., Mettenburg, J., Basena, M., Peta, I., McPherson, K., Greene, A., & Li, S. (2010). *Fourth national incidence study of child abuse and neglect (NIS-4)*. Washington, DC: US Department of Health and Human Services, 9, 2010.
Segal, N. (2022). Unusual behavioral similarities in twins reared apart: Genetic effects, random chance or both? *Japanese Journal of Twin Studies, 1:* 1–11.
Sekar, A., Bialas, A., de Rivera, H., Davis, A., Hammond, T., Kamitaki, N., Tooley, K., Presumey, J., Baum, M., Van Doren, V., & Genovese, G. (2016). Schizophrenia risk from complex variation of complement component 4. *Nature, 530:* 177–183.
Selita, F., & Kovas, Y. (2019). Genes and Gini: What inequality means for heritability. *Journal of Biosocial Science, 51:* 18–47.
Serin, R., Gobeil, R., & Preston, D. (2009). Evaluation of the persistently violent offender treatment program. *International Journal of Offender Therapy and Comparative Criminology, 53:* 57–73.
Sesardic, N. (2003). Heritability and indirect causation. *Philosophy of Science, 70:* 1002–10014.
Sharp, B. (2006). *Changing criminal thinking: A treatment program.* Alexandria, VA: American Correctional Association.

Shaw, C, & McKay, H. (1972). *Juvenile delinquency and urban areas*. Chicago, Il: University of Chicago Press.

Shaw, J., Hunt, I., Flynn, S., Meehan, J., Robinson, J., Bickley, H., Parsons, R., McCann, K., Burns, J., Amos, T., & Kapur, N. (2006). Rates of mental disorder in people convicted of homicide: national clinical survey. *The British Journal of Psychiatry, 188:* 143–147.

Shekhar, M., & Rahnev, D. (2018). Distinguishing the roles of dorsolateral and anterior PFC in visual metacognition. *Journal of Neuroscience, 38:* 5078–5087.

Shi, S., Cheng, T., Jan, L., & Jan, Y. (2004). The immunoglobin family member dendrite arborization and synapse maturation 1 (Dasm1) controls excitatory synapse maturation. *Proceedings of the National Academy of Sciences, 101:* 13246–13351.

Shi, Z., Jagannathan, K., Wang, A., Fairchild, V., Lynch, K., Suh, J., Childress, A., & Langleben, D. (2019). Behavioral and accumbal responses during an affective go/no-go task predict adherence to injectable naltrexone treatment in opioid use disorder. *International Journal of Neuropsychopharmacology, 22:* 180–185.

Shoda, Y., Mischel, W., & Peake, P. (1990). Predicting adolescent cognitive and self-regulatory competencies from preschool delay of gratification: Identifying diagnostic conditions. *Developmental Psychology, 26:* 978–986.

Sibley, M., Pelham, W., Molina, B., Gnagy, E., Waschbusch, D., Biswas, A., MacLean, M., Babinski, D., & Karch, K. (2011). The delinquency outcomes of boys with ADHD with and without comorbidity. *Journal of Abnormal Child Psychology, 39:* 21–32.

Silfver, M., Helkama, K., Lonnqvist, J., & Verkasalo, M. (2008). The relation between value priorities and proneness to guilt, shame, and empathy. *Motivation and Emotion*, 32:69–80.

Silke, C., Brady, B., Boylan, C., & Dolan, P. (2018). Factors influencing the development of empathy and pro-social behaviour among adolescents: A systematic review. *Children and Youth Services Review, 94*, 421–436.

Silverstein, S., Del Pozzo, J., Roché, M., Boyle, D., & Miskimen, T. (2015). Schizophrenia and violence: Realities and recommendations. *Reviewing Crime Psychology, 1:* 181–202.

Simon, D., & Kreek, M. (2016). Cocaine: Usage, misuse, and addiction processes. An overview. *Neuropathology of Drug Addictions and Substance Misuse*, 5–13. doi:10.1016/b978-0-12-800212-4.00001-7

Skinner, M., Lahmek, P., Pham, H., & Aubin, H. (2014). Disulfiram efficacy in the treatment of alcohol dependence: A meta-analysis. *PloS one, 9*(2), e87366.

Skorneck, C. (1996). *Clinton says he will sign welfare overhaul; House passes it.* Associated Press, July 31.

Soderstrom, H., Blennow, K., Sjodin, A., & Forsman A. (2003). New evidence for an association between the CSF HVA:5-HIAA ratio and psychopathic traits. *Journal of Neurology Neurosurgery and Psychiatry, 74:* 918–921

Sodhi, M., & Sanders-Bush, E. (2004). Serotonin and brain development. *International Review of Neurobiology, 59:* 111–174.

Sokol, R., Delaney-Black, V., & Nordstrom, B. (2003). Fetal alcohol spectrum disorder. *JAMA, 290: 2996–2999.*

Solomon, R. (1977). The logic of emotion. *Nous, 11:* 41–49.

Sontate, K., Rahim Kamaluddin, M., Naina Mohamed, I., Mohamed, R., Shaikh, M., Kamal, H., & Kumar, J. (2021). Alcohol, aggression, and violence: From public health to neuroscience. *Frontiers in Psychology, 12:* 699726.

Sonuga-Barke, E., Becker, S., Bölte, S., Castellanos, F., Franke, B., Newcorn, J., Nigg, J., Rohde, L., & Simonoff, E. (2023). Annual research review: Perspectives on progress in ADHD science–from characterization to cause. *Journal of Child Psychology and Psychiatry, 64:* 506–532.

Sorrentino, A., & Whittaker, D. (1994). Chicago Area Project: Addressing the gang problem. FBI *Law Enforcement Bulletin, 63:* 8–12.

Spikic, S., & Mortelmans, D. (2021). A preliminary meta-analysis of the Big Five personality traits' effect on marital separation. *Journal of Divorce & Remarriage, 62:* 551–571.

Spirtes, P., Glymour, C., & Scheines, R. (2000). *Causation, prediction, and search.* Cambridge, MA: MIT Press.

Stevens, F., Hurley, R., & Taber, K. (2011). Anterior cingulate cortex: Unique role in cognition and emotion. *The Journal of Neuropsychiatry and Clinical Neurosciences, 23:* 121–125.

Stewart, J. (2019). A computational modeling approach supports negative reinforcement theories of addiction. *Biological Psychiatry: Cognitive Neuroscience and Neuroimaging, 4:* 218–219.

Stiles, J., & Jernigan, T. (2010). The basics of brain development. *Neuropsychology Review, 20:* 327–348.

Stogner, J. (2014). General strain theory and biosocial criminology: Pathways to successful theoretical integration. In Beaver, K., Barnes, J., & Boutwell, B. (eds.), *The nurture versus biosocial debate in criminology: On the origins of criminal behavior and criminality*, pp. 199–216. Thousand Oaks, CA: Sage.

Stohr, M. (2020). Therapeutic communities in correctional institutions. In Walsh, A., Wells, J., & Gann, S. (eds.), *Correctional assessment, casework, and counseling* (6th ed.), pp. 241–256. Cham, Switzerland: Springer.

Stohr, M., & Walsh, A. (2025). *Corrections: The essentials* (5th ed.). Thousand Oaks, CA: Sage.

Storey, A., & Walsh, C. (2011). How fathers evolve: A functional analysis of fathering behavior. In Booth, A., McHale, S., & Landale, N. (eds.), *Biosocial Foundations of Family Processes*, pp. 35–47. New York: Springer.

Subramoney, S., Eastman, E., Adnams, C., Stein, D., & Donald, K. (2018). The early developmental outcomes of prenatal alcohol exposure: A review. *Frontiers in Neurology, 9:* 1108.

Sullins, D. (2021). The case for mom and dad. *The Linacre Quarterly, 88:* 184–201.

Sutherland, E. (1939). *Principles of criminology.* Philadelphia, PA: J. B. Lippincott.

Sutherland, E., & Cressey, D. (1974). *Criminology* (9th ed.). Philadelphia: J.B. Lippincott.

Suwa, G., Asfaw, B., Kono, R., Kubo, D., Lovejoy, C., White, T. (2009). The *Ardipithecus ramidus skull* and its implications for hominid origins. *Science, 326:* 68e1–68e8.

Swathy, B., & Banerjee, M. (2017). Understanding epigenetics of schizophrenia in the backdrop of its antipsychotic drug therapy. *Epigenomics, 9:* 721–736.

Talbot, T., Gilligan, L., Carter, M., & Matson, S. (2002). *An overview of sex offender management.* Silver Spring, MD: Center for Sex Offender Management.

Tancredi, L. (2005). *Hardwired behavior: What neuroscience reveals about morality*. Cambridge: Cambridge University Press.
Tanner, M. (2019). *What's missing in the war on poverty?* San Francisco, CA: The Cato Institute.
Tardelli, V., Berro, L., Gerra, G., Tadonio, L., Bisaga, A., & Fidalgo, T. (2023). Prescription psychostimulants for cocaine use disorder: A review from molecular basis to clinical approach. *Addiction Biology*, *28:* e13271.
Taxman, F., & Smith, L. (2021). Risk-need-responsivity (RNR) classification models: Still evolving. *Aggression and Violent Behavior*, *59:* 101459.
Tcherni-Buzzeo, M. (2023). Dietary interventions, the gut microbiome, and aggressive behavior: Review of research evidence and potential next steps. *Aggressive Behavior*, *49:* 15–32.
TenEyck, M., & Barnes, J. (2015). Examining the impact of peer group selection on self-reported delinquency: A consideration of active gene–environment correlation. *Criminal Justice and Behavior*, *42:* 741–762.
Terburg, D., Morgan, B., & van Honk, J. (2009). The testosterone–cortisol ratio: A hormonal marker for proneness to social aggression. *International Journal of Law and Psychiatry*, *32:* 216–223.
Theiner, P., Ustohal, L., Skřont, T., Bareš, M., & Kašpárek, T. (2015). Repetitive Transcranial Magnetic stimulation in ADHD. In Norvilitis, J. (ed.), *ADHD – New Directions in Diagnosis and Treatment*, pp. 331–350. Rijeka, Croatia: InTech.
Tielbeek, J., Uffelmann, E., Williams, B., Colodro-Conde, L., Gagnon, É., Mallard, T., Levitt, B., Jansen, P., Johansson, A., Sallis, H., & Pistis, G. (2022). Uncovering the genetic architecture of broad antisocial behavior through a genome-wide association study meta-analysis. *Molecular Psychiatry*, *27:* 4453–4463.
Tinbergen, N. (1963). On aims and methods in ethology. *Zeitschrift für Tierpsychologie*, *20:* 410–433.
Toga, A., Thompson, P., & Sowell, E. (2006). Mapping brain maturation. *Trends in Neurosciences*, *29:* 148–159.
Tomasi, D., & Volkow, N. (2012). Functional connectivity of substantia nigra and ventral tegmental area: Maturation during adolescence and effects of ADHD. *Cerebral Cortex*, *24:* 935–944.
Torrey, E., & Yolken, R. (2019). Schizophrenia as a pseudogenetic disease: A call for more gene-environmental studies. *Psychiatry Research*, *278:* 146–150.
Tosato, S., Bonetto, C., Di Forti, M., Collier, D., Cristofalo, D., Bertani, M., Zanoni, M., Marrella, G., Lazzarotto, L., Lasalvia, A., & De Gironcoli, M. (2011). Effect of COMT genotype on aggressive behaviour in a community cohort of schizophrenic patients. *Neuroscience Letters*, *495:* 17–21.
Trangenstein, P., Curriero, F., Webster, D., Jennings, J., Latkin, C., Eck, R., & Jernigan, D. (2018). Outlet type, access to alcohol, and violent crime. *Alcoholism: Clinical and Experimental Research*, *42:* 2234–2245.
Tremblay, R. (2008). Understanding development and prevention of chronic physical aggression: Towards experimental epigenetic studies. *Philosophical Transactions of the Royal Society B: Biological Sciences*, *363:* 2613–2622.
Tremblay, R., & LeMarquand, D. (2001). Individual risk and protective factors. In Loeber, R., & Farrington, D. (eds.), *Child delinquents: Development, interventions and service needs*, pp. 137–164. Thousand Oaks, CA: Sage.

Trentacosta, C., Waller, R., Neiderhiser, J., Shaw, D., Natsuaki, M., Ganiban, J., Reiss, D., Leve, L., & Hyde, L. (2019). Callous-unemotional behaviors and harsh parenting: Reciprocal associations across early childhood and moderation by inherited risk. *Journal of Abnormal Child Psychology, 47:* 811–823.

Trépanier, M., Hopperton, K., Mizrahi, R., Mechawar, N., & Bazinet, R. (2016). Postmortem evidence of cerebral inflammation in schizophrenia: A systematic review. *Molecular Psychiatry, 21: 1009–1026.*

Tsai, H., Zhang, F., Adamantidis, A., Stuber, G., Bonci, A., De Lecea, L., & Deisseroth, K. (2009). Phasic firing in dopaminergic neurons is sufficient for behavioral conditioning. *Science, 324:* 1080–1084.

Tumulty, J., Morales, V., & Summers, K. (2014). The biparental care hypothesis for the evolution of monogamy: Experimental evidence in an amphibian. *Behavioral Ecology, 25:* 262–270.

Tuninger, E., Levander, A., Bernce, R., & Johansson, G. (2001). Criminality and aggression among psychotic in-patients: Frequency and clinical correlates. *Acta Psychiatrica Scandinavica, 103:* 294–300.

Turkheimer, E. (2000). Three laws of behavior genetics and what they mean. *Current Directions in Psychological Science, 9:*160–164.

Turkheimer, E., Haley, A., Waldron, M., D'Onofrio, B., & Gottesman, I. (2003). Socioeconomic status modifies heritability of IQ in young children. *Psychological Science, 14:* 623–628.

Turner, D., Basdekis-Jozsa, R., & Briken, P. (2013). Prescription of testosterone-lowering medications for sex offender treatment in German forensic-psychiatric institutions. *The Journal of Sexual Medicine, 10:* 570–578.

Tuvblad, C., Grann, M., & Lichtenstein, P. (2006). Heritability for adolescent antisocial behavior differs with socioeconomic status: gene–environment interaction. *Journal of Child Psychology and Psychiatry, 47:* 734–743.

Twardosz, S., & Lutzker, J. (2010). Child maltreatment and the developing brain: A review of neuroscience perspectives. *Aggression and Violent Behavior, 15:* 59–68.

United States Congress. (1995). *Contract with America: Hearing on welfare reform*: Vol. 4. Washington, DC: U.S. Government Printing Office.

Unnever, J., Cullen, F., & Pratt, T. (2003). Parental management, ADHD, and delinquent involvement: Reassessing Gottfredson and Hirschi's general theory. *Justice Quarterly, 20:* 471–500.

Unnever, J., & Gabbidon, S. (2011). *A theory of African American offending: Race, racism, and crime.* New York: Routledge.

U.S. Department of Health and Human Services. (2009). *Understanding the effects of maltreatment on brain development.* Washington, DC: U.S. Government Printing Office.

UvnäsMoberg, K., Ekström-Bergström, A., Buckley, S., Massarotti, C., Pajalic, Z., Luegmair, K., Kotlowska, A., Lengler, L., Olza, I., Grylka-Baeschlin, S., & Leahy-Warren, P. (2020). Maternal plasma levels of oxytocin during breastfeeding—A systematic review. *PloS One, 15:* e0235806.

van der Meer, D., Cheng, W., Rokicki, J., Fernandez-Cabello, S., Shadrin, A., Smeland, O., Ehrhart, F., Guloksuz, S., Steen, N., Djurovic, S., & Westlye, L. (2022). Clustering schizophrenia genes by their temporal expression patterns aids functional interpretation: Genetics-based evidence in favor of the two-hit hypothesis. *MedRxiv*, Preprint, 2022–08.

van der Storm, L., van Lissa, C., Lucassen, N., Helmerhorst, K., & Keizer, R. (2022). Maternal and paternal parenting and child prosocial behavior: A meta-analysis using a structural equation modeling design. *Marriage & Family Review, 58*: 1–37. doi: 10.1080/01494929.2021.1927931.

Van Honk, J., Harmon-Jones, E., Morgan, B., & Schutter, D. (2010). Socially explosive minds: The triple imbalance hypothesis of reactive aggression. *Journal of Personality, 78:* 67–94.

Van Honk, J., Hermans, E., D'Alfonso, A., Schutter, D., Van Doornen, L., & De Haan, E. (2002). A left-prefrontal lateralized, sympathetic mechanism directs attention towards social threat in humans: Evidence from repetitive transcranial magnetic stimulation. *Neuroscience Letters, 319:* 99–102.

Vaske, J. (2017). Using biosocial criminology to understand and improve treatment outcomes. *Criminal Justice and Behavior, 44:* 1050–1072.

Vaske, J., Galyean, K., & Cullen, F. (2011). Toward a biosocial theory of offender rehabilitation: Why does cognitive-behavioral therapy work? *Journal of Criminal Justice, 39:* 90–102.

Vaughn, M. (2016). Policy implications of biosocial criminology: Toward a renewed commitment to prevention science. *Criminology & Public Policy, 15:* 703–710.

Vélez, M. (2018). An elaboration and critique of "Reassessing 'Toward a theory of race, crime, and urban inequality' ". *Du Bois Review: Social Science Research on Race, 15:* 35–46.

Verhulst, B., Neale, M., & Kendler, K. (2015). The heritability of alcohol use disorders: A meta-analysis of twin and adoption studies. *Psychological Medicine, 45:*1061–1072.

Volkow, N. (2010). Important treatment advances for addiction to heroin and other opiates. Accessed from www.drugabuse.gov/about-nida/directors-page/mesages-diector/2010/.

Volpe, J. (2019). Dysmaturation of premature brain: Importance, cellular mechanisms, and potential interventions. *Pediatric Neurology, 95:* 42–66.

Vsevolozhskaya, O., & Anthony, J. (2016). Transitioning from first drug use to dependence onset: Illustration of a multiparametric approach for comparative epidemiology. *Neuropsychopharmacology, 41:* 869–876.

Wahbeh, M., & Avramopoulos, D. (2021). Gene-environment interactions in schizophrenia: A literature review. *Genes, 12:* 1850.

Wajzer, M., & Dragan, W. (2023). It is not only the environment that matters: A short introduction to research on the heritability of political attitudes. *Political Studies Review, 21:* 144–161.

Wakschlag, L., Pickett, K., Cook, E., Jr., Benowitz, N., & Leventhal, B. (2002). Maternal smoking during pregnancy and severe antisocial behavior in offspring: A review. *American Journal of Public Health, 92:* 966–974.

Wallenborn, J., Levine, G., dos Santos, A., Grisi, S., & Brentani, A. (2021). Breastfeeding, physical growth, and cognitive development. *Development, 147:* e2020008029.

Waller, R., & Hyde, L. (2018). Callous-unemotional behaviors in early childhood: The development of empathy and prosociality gone awry. *Current Opinion in Psychology, 20:* 11–16.

Waller, R., Wagner, N., Barstead, M., Subar, A., Petersen, J., Hyde, J., & Hyde, L. (2020). A meta-analysis of the associations between callous-unemotional traits and empathy, prosociality, and guilt. *Clinical Psychology Review, 75:* 101809.

Walsh, A. (2000). Behavior genetics and anomie/strain theory. *Criminology*, *38:* 1075–1107.

Walsh, A. (2009). *Biology and criminology: The biosocial synthesis.* New York: Routledge.

Walsh, A. (2014). *Biosociology: Bridging the biology-sociology divide.* New Brunswick, NJ: Transaction Publishers.

Walsh, A. (2017). *Love: The biology behind the heart.* New Brunswick, NJ: Transaction Publishers.

Walsh, A. (2019). *Reinforcement sensitivity theory: A metatheory for biosocial criminology.* New York: Routledge.

Walsh, A., & Ellis, L. (2004). Ideology: Criminology's Achilles' Heel? *Quarterly Journal of Ideology. 27:* 1–25.

Walsh, A., & Ellis, L. (2006). *Criminology: An interdisciplinary approach.* Thousand Oaks, CA: Sage.

Walsh, A., Johnson, H., & Bolen, J. (2012). Drugs, crime, and the epigenetics of hedonic allostasis. *Journal of Contemporary Criminal Justice. 28:* 314–328.

Walsh, A., & Jorgensen, C. (2020). *Criminology: The essentials* (4th ed.). Thousand Oaks, CA: Sage.

Walsh, A., & Jorgensen, C. (2025). *Criminology: The essentials* (5th ed.). Thousand Oaks, CA: Sage.

Walsh, A., & Vaske, J. (2015). *Feminist criminology through a biosocial lens* (2nd ed.). Durham, NC: Carolina Academic Press.

Walsh, A., Wells, J., & Gann, S. (2020). *Correctional assessment, casework, and counseling* (6th ed.). Cham, Switzerland: Springer.

Walsh, A., & Wright, J. (2015). Biosocial criminology and its discontents: A critical realist philosophical analysis. *Criminal Justice Studies*, *28:* 124–140.

Walsh, A., & Yun, I. (2013). Schizophrenia: Causes, crime, and implications for criminology and criminal justice. *International Journal of Law, Crime and Justice*, *41:* 188–202.

Wand, G. (2008). The influence of stress on the transition from drug use to addiction. *Alcohol Research & Health*, *31:* 119.

Warr, M. (2002). *Companions in crime: The social aspects of criminal conduct.* New York: Cambridge University Press.

Waschbusch, D., Pelham, W., Jennings, J., Greiner, A., Tarter, R., & Moss, H. (2002). Reactive aggression in boys with disruptive behavior disorders: Behavior, physiology, and affect. *Journal of Abnormal Child Psychology*, *30:* 641–656.

Waszak, M., Cieślik, K., Skrzypczak-Zielińska, M., Szalata, M., Wielgus, K., Zakerska-Banaszak, O., Bręborowicz, G., & Słomski, R. (2017). Effects of intrauterine environment on the magnitude of differences within the pairs of monozygotic and dizygotic twins. *Twin Research and Human Genetics*, *20*: 72–83.

Weaver, I., Cervoni, N., Champagne, F., D'Alessio, A., Sharma, S., Seckl, J., Dymov, S., Szyf, M., & Meaney, M. (2004). Epigenetic programming by maternal behavior. *Nature Neuroscience*, *7:* 847–854.

Weinhold, B. (2006). Epigenetics: The science of change. *Environmental Health Perspectives*, *114:* 161–167.

Weitoft, G., Hjern, A., Haglund, B., & Rosén, M. (2003). Mortality, severe morbidity, and injury in children living with single parents in Sweden: A population-based study. *The Lancet*, *361:* 289–295.

Welsh, B., & Pfeffer, R. (2013). Reclaiming crime prevention in an age of punishment: An American history. *Punishment & Society, 15: 534–553.*

West, S. (1991). *Correctional training, industries and education.* Frankfort, KY: Correctional Education Association Correctional Industries Association.

Whiten, A., McGuigan, N., Marshall-Pescini, S., & Hopper, L. (2009). Emulation, imitation, over-imitation and the scope of culture for child and chimpanzee. *Philosophical Transactions of the Royal Society B: Biological Sciences, 364:* 2417–2428.

Whiting, D., Gulati, G., Geddes, J., & Fazel, S. (2022). Association of schizophrenia spectrum disorders and violence perpetration in adults and adolescents from 15 countries: A systematic review and meta-analysis. *JAMA Psychiatry,* 79: 120–132.

Widiss, D. (2021). Equalizing parental leave. *Minnesota Law Review, 105: 2175–2257.*

Widom, C., & Brzustowicz, L. (2006). MAOA and the "cycle of violence:" Childhood abuse and neglect: MAOA genotype and the risk for violent and antisocial behavior. *Biological Psychiatry, 60: 684–689.*

Wikstrom, P., & Loeber, R. (2000). Do disadvantaged neighborhoods cause well-adjusted children to become adolescent delinquents? A study of male juvenile serious offending, individual risk and protective factors and neighborhood context. *Criminology, 38:* 1109–1142.

Willems, Y., Boesen, N., Li, J., Finkenauer, C., & Bartels, M. (2019). The heritability of self-control: A meta-analysis. *Neuroscience & Biobehavioral Reviews, 100:* 324–334.

Williams, E., & Robinson, M. (2004). Ideology and criminal justice: Suggestions for a pedagogical model. *Journal of Criminal Justice Education, 15:* 373–392.

Williams, W. (2011). *Race & economics: How much can be blamed on discrimination?* Stanford, CA: Hoover Press.

Wilson, A., Koller, K., Ramaboli, M., Nesengani, L., Ocvirk, S., Chen, C., Flanagan, C., Sapp, F., Merritt, Z., Bhatti, F. & Thomas, T. (2020). Diet and the human gut microbiome: An international review. *Digestive Diseases and Sciences, 65:* 723–740.

Wilson, J. (1975). *Thinking about crime.* New York: Vintage.

Wilson, J. (2000). *The marriage problem: How our culture has weakened families.* New York: HarperCollins.

Wilson, V. (2020). Racial disparities in income and poverty remain largely unchanged amid strong income growth in 2019. Economic Policy Institute.

Winder, B., Fedoroff, J., Grubin, D., Klapilová, K., Kamenskov, M., Tucker, D., Basinskaya, I., & Vvedensky, G. (2019). The pharmacologic treatment of problematic sexual interests, paraphilic disorders, and sexual preoccupation in adult men who have committed a sexual offence. *International Review of Psychiatry, 31:* 159–168.

Wismer-Fries, A. Ziegler, T., Kurian, J., Jacoris, S., & Pollak, S. (2005). Early experience in humans is associated with changes in neuropeptides critical for regulating social behavior. *Proceedings of the National Academy of Sciences, 102:* 17237–17240.

Wodak, A. (2007). Ethics and drug policy. *Psychiatry, 6: 59–62.*

Wolf, R., Pujara, M., Motzkin, J., Newman, J., Kiehl, K., Decety, J., Kosson, D., & Koenigs, M. (2015). Interpersonal traits of psychopathy linked to reduced integrity of the uncinate fasciculus. *Human Brain Mapping*, *36:* 4202–4209.

Wolfgang, M., & Ferracuti, F. (1967). *The subculture of violence: Towards an integrated theory in criminology*. London: Tavistock.

Wong, A., & Landes, S. (2022). Expanding understanding of racial-ethnic differences in ADHD prevalence rates among children to include Asians and Alaskan Natives/American Indians. *Journal of Attention Disorders*, *26:* 747–754.

Wood, R., Goesling, B., & Avellar, S. (2007). *The effects of marriage on health: A synthesis of recent research evidence*. Princeton, NJ: Mathematica Policy Research Inc.

World Health Organization. (2020). Genomics. www.who.int/news-room/questions-and-answers/item/genomics.

Wright, J. (2009). Inconvenient truths: Science, race and crime. In Walsh, A. & Beaver, K (eds.), *Biosocial criminology: New directions in theory and research*, pp. 137–153. New York: Routledge.

Wright, J., Barnes, J., Boutwell, B., Schwartz, J., Connolly, E., Nedelec, J., & Beaver, K. (2015). Mathematical proof is not minutiae and irreducible complexity is not a theory: A final response to Burt and Simons and a call to criminologists. *Criminology*, *53*, 113–120.

Wright, J., & Beaver, K. (2012). The behavioral genetics of predatory criminal behavior. In Delisi, M., & Conis, P. (eds.), *Violent offenders: Theory, research, policy, and practice*, pp. 109–123. Burlington, MA: Jones and Bartlett.

Wright, J., Boisvert, D., Dietrich, K., & Ris, M. (2009). The ghost in the machine and criminal behavior: Criminology for the 21st century. In Walsh, A., & Beaver, K. *Biosocial criminology: New directions in theory and research*, pp. 73–89. New York: Routledge.

Wright, J., & Cullen, F. (2012). The future of biosocial criminology: Beyond scholars' professional ideology. *Journal of Contemporary Criminal Justice*, *28:* 237–253.

Wright, J., Dietrich, K., Ris, M., Hornung, R., Wessel, S., & Lanphear, B. (2008). Association of prenatal and childhood blood lead concentrations with criminal arrests in early childhood. *PLoS Medicine*, *5:* 732–740.

Wright, R. (1994). *The moral animal: Evolutionary psychology and everyday life*. New York: Pantheon Books.

Wu, H.-H., & Walsh, A. (2007). Teaching statistical interaction in ANOVA and OLS regression in the context of criminal justice ideology. *Free Inquiry in Creative Sociology*, *34:* 1–7.

Xia, J., Merinder, L., & Belgamwar, M. (2011). Psychoeducation for schizophrenia. *Cochrane Database of Systematic Reviews*, *6:* 1–136.

Yacubian, J., Sommer, T., Schroeder, K., Glascher, J., Kalisch, R., Leuenberger, B., Braus, D. F., & Buchel, C. (2007). Gene-gene interaction associated with neural reward sensitivity. *Proceedings of the National Academy of Sciences*, *104:* 8125–8130.

Yang, A., & Tsai, S. (2017). New targets for schizophrenia treatment beyond the dopamine hypothesis. *International Journal of Molecular Sciences*, *18:* 1689.

Yang, J., Bakshi, A., Zhu, Z., Hemani, G., Vinkhuyzen, A., Lee, S., Robinson, M., Perry, J., Nolte, I., van Vliet-Ostaptchouk, J., & Snieder, H. (2015). Genetic variance estimation with imputed variants finds negligible missing heritability for human height and body mass index. *Nature Genetics*, *47:* 1114–1120.

Young, J. (2003). Searching for a new criminology of everyday life: A review of "the culture of control. *The British Journal of Criminology*, *43:* 228–243.

Young, S., Gudjonsson, G., Wells, J., Asherson, P., Theobald, D., Oliver, B., Scott, C., & Mooney, A. (2009). Attention deficit hyperactivity disorder and critical incidents in a Scottish prison population. *Personality and Individual Differences*, *46:* 265–269.

Young, S., Sedgwick, O., Fridman, M., Gudjonsson, G., Hodgkins, P., Lantigua, M., & González, R. (2015). Co-morbid psychiatric disorders among incarcerated ADHD populations: A meta-analysis. *Psychological Medicine*, *45:* 2499–2510.

Zaalberg, A., Nijman, H., Bulten, E., Stroosma, L., & Van Der Staak, C. (2010). Effects of nutritional supplements on aggression, rule-breaking, and psychopathology among young adult prisoners. *Aggressive Behavior: Official Journal of the International Society for Research on Aggression*, *36:* 117–126.

Zetterberg, H. (1962). *Social theory and social practice*. New York: Bedminster Press.

Zhang, Y., Li, Q., Liu, X., Zhu, H., Song, A., & Jiao, J. (2013). Antioxidant and micronutrient-rich milk formula reduces lead poisoning and related oxidative damage in lead-exposed mice. *Food and Chemical Toxicology*, *57:* 201–208.

Zimring, R. (2013). What New York City teaches about police and prisons. *ACJS Today*, *38*: 12–13.

INDEX

Note: Page locators in bold and italics represents tables and figures, respectively.

FSC
www.fsc.org
MIX
Papier | Fördert
gute Waldnutzung
FSC® C083411

Kolibri 360 GmbH
Ferdinand-Jühlke-Straße 7
99095 Erfurt, Deutschland
produktsicherheit@kolibri360.de